Machine Learning Paradigm for Internet of Things Applications

Scrivener Publishing
100 Cummings Center, Suite 541J
Beverly, MA 01915-6106

Next-Generation Computing and Communication Engineering

Series Editors: Dr. G. R. Kanagachidambaresan and Dr. Kolla Bhanu Prakash

Developments in artificial intelligence are made more challenging because the involvement of multi-domain technology creates new problems for researchers. Therefore, in order to help meet the challenge, this book series concentrates on next generation computing and communication methodologies involving smart and ambient environment design. It is an effective publishing platform for monographs, handbooks, and edited volumes on Industry 4.0, agriculture, smart city development, new computing and communication paradigms. Although the series mainly focuses on design, it also addresses analytics and investigation of industry-related real-time problems.

Publishers at Scrivener
Martin Scrivener (martin@scrivenerpublishing.com)
Phillip Carmical (pcarmical@scrivenerpublishing.com)

Machine Learning Paradigm for Internet of Things Applications

Edited by

Shalli Rani, R. Maheswar
G. R. Kanagachidambaresan
Sachin Ahuja

and

Deepali Gupta

Scrivener
Publishing

This edition first published 2022 by John Wiley & Sons, Inc., 111 River Street, Hoboken, NJ 07030, USA and Scrivener Publishing LLC, 100 Cummings Center, Suite 541J, Beverly, MA 01915, USA
© 2022 Scrivener Publishing LLC
For more information about Scrivener publications please visit www.scrivenerpublishing.com.

Wiley Global Headquarters
111 River Street, Hoboken, NJ 07030, USA

For details of our global editorial offices, customer services, and more information about Wiley products visit us at www.wiley.com.

Limit of Liability/Disclaimer of Warranty
While the publisher and authors have used their best efforts in preparing this work, they make no representations or warranties with respect to the accuracy or completeness of the contents of this work and specifically disclaim all warranties, including without limitation any implied warranties of merchantability or fitness for a particular purpose. No warranty may be created or extended by sales representatives, written sales materials, or promotional statements for this work. The fact that an organization, website, or product is referred to in this work as a citation and/or potential source of further information does not mean that the publisher and authors endorse the information or services the organization, website, or product may provide or recommendations it may make. This work is sold with the understanding that the publisher is not engaged in rendering professional services. The advice and strategies contained herein may not be suitable for your situation. You should consult with a specialist where appropriate. Neither the publisher nor authors shall be liable for any loss of profit or any other commercial damages, including but not limited to special, incidental, consequential, or other damages. Further, readers should be aware that websites listed in this work may have changed or disappeared between when this work was written and when it is read.

Library of Congress Cataloging-in-Publication Data

ISBN 978-1-119-76047-4

Cover image: Pixabay.Com
Cover design by Russell Richardson

MIX
Paper from responsible sources
FSC
www.fsc.org
FSC® C013604

Contents

Preface

Machine learning (ML) is the key tool for fast processing and decision-making applied to smart city applications and next-generation IoT devices, which require ML to satisfy their working objective. Machine learning has become a common subject to all people like engineers, doctors, pharmacy companies and business people. The book addresses the problem and new algorithms, their accuracy and fitness ratio for existing real-time problems. Tapping into that data to extract useful information is a challenge that's starting to be met using the pattern-matching abilities of ML, which is a subset of the field of artificial intelligence (AI). In order to provide a smarter environment, there needs to be implemented IoT devices with machine learning. Machine learning will allow these smart devices to be smarter in a literal sense. They can analyze the data generated by the connected devices and get an insight into human behavioral patterns. Hence, it would not be wrong to say that if the IoT is the digital nervous system, then ML acts as its medulla oblongata. Without implementing ML, it would really be difficult for smart devices and the IoT to make smart decisions in real-time, severely limiting their capabilities. This book provides the challenges and the solution in these areas.

This book provides the state-of-the-art applications of Machine Learning in IoT environment. The most common use cases for machine learning and IoT data are predictive maintenance, followed by analyzing CCTV surveillance, smart home applications, smart-healthcare, in-store 'contextualized marketing' and intelligent transportation systems. Readers will gain an insight into the integration of Machine Learning with IoT in various application domains.

Lastly, we would like to thanks all the authors who contributed whole heartedly in bringing their ideas and research in the form of chapters.

Shalli Rani
R. Maheswar
G. R. Kanagachidambaresan
Sachin Ahuja
Deepali Gupta
January 2022

Machine Learning Concept–Based IoT Platforms for Smart Cities' Implementation and Requirements

M. Saravanan[1]*, J. Ajayan[2], R. Maheswar[3], Eswaran Parthasarathy[4] and K. Sumathi[5]

[1]Sri Eshwar College of Engineering, Coimbatore, Tamilnadu, India
[2]SR University Warangal, Telangana, India
[3]School of EEE, VIT Bhopal University, Bhopal, India
[4]SRM Institute of Science and Technology, Chennai, India
[5]Sri Krishna College of Technology, Coimbatore, India

Abstract

In developing countries, smart cities are a challenge due to the exponential rise in population. With the rise in demand and availability for goods and facilities, it is now one of the world's most dynamic networks. Intelligent machines are crucial in the construction of critical infrastructure and smart cities in this new age. The increase in population has created new opportunities for smart city management and administration. In the smart city model, information and communication technology (ICT) plays a vital role in policy formulation, decision-making, implementation, and, finally, effective resource allocation. The study's key objective is to explore the role of artificial intelligence, machine learning, and deep reinforcement learning in the evolution of cities. Rapid advancements in computing and hardware, as well as high-speed internet connectivity, have enabled large amounts of data to be transmitted into the physical world.

Keywords: Smart city, process management, sewage treatment plan (STP), neural networks, control centers, cloud storage

Corresponding author: saranecedgl@gmail.com

Shalli Rani, R. Maheswar, G. R. Kanagachidambaresan, Sachin Ahuja and Deepali Gupta (eds.) Machine Learning Paradigm for Internet of Things Applications, (1–26) © 2022 Scrivener Publishing LLC

1.1   Introduction

The idea of smart cities is the concept applied to the programs that uses the digital and the ICT-based innovation to increase the urban infrastructure quality and create the new economic and the prospect in the cities, and more is focused in the need of gaining the cost of the smart cities that are the distributed through all sectors with in the society emergence of the smart city projects around the world, such as analyzing the distributional impact of the individuals of the earth and the locations. The concept of smart city in the technical manner which will lead to debate the smart city varies across the countries according to the geopolitics; it implies more advanced and the necessary need to develop the city to both economically stable and more pollution-free concept. Initiatives that use the digital innovation with properly document are commitment of smart cities to enhancing the people's lives while providing the sectoral and the multi-sectoral solutions to some of the most common urban challenges; stack-holders' involvement in the local government and the strategic collaborations to improve the public engagement is maximized in private sectors positions in decision-making, and other benefits of the public access experimentation on open data with the interstate connectivity combined with the public and private people collaboration. Different regions of the world managed to establish their own smart city architecture in different manners also with approach of same belief [1]. The operable concept is complex for new setup process of the related to the increase in population to contribute in the development of technology with the social and political and the economy growth. The data that generated smart city concept are included in the networking application to monitor the application of various constrains like water monitoring and environment monitoring. Urban local bodies in particular for management service providers would be a crucial factor in evaluating the progress of smart cities mainly in India. Implementation approach will be consulted with pervious established architecture already present in various region of the globe. The well-developed cities like Singapore and Dubai UAE have the well-integrated business models, and the creative local collaborations will resolve the problems to get faced in India in nearly future [1]. In order to manage the data intelligently, IoT requires data to either represent improved customer services or optimize the effectiveness of the IoT system. In this way, applications should be able to access raw data across the network from different resources and evaluate this data to extract information.

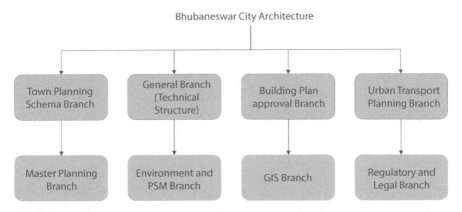

Figure 1.1 Bhubaneswar smart city structure.

1.2 Smart City Structure in India

1.2.1 Bhubaneswar City

In India, Bhubaneswar has the best infrastructural setup of smart city project. It is the city where center of economic and having more religious importance in Eastern part of India. Consistently, this city has proved its efficiency in assessment among top smart city around the globe. It plays vital role in digital communication with advanced technologies. Figure 1.1 shows the Bhubaneswar smart city structure. This project included with construction engineering and green and park areas with road and development accessibility and slum accommodation.

1.2.1.1 Specifications

For government entities smart city specifications are, technology for the traffic, parking, emergency response, and emergency control, digitalized payment services via command payment methods schema capital of business planning and e-governance in this smart project [2].

1.2.1.2 Healthcare and Mobility Services

The smart city's primary focus is more on the child and elderly friendly option. Most of the homeless camp, however, defecate in the open. In an integrated safe urban transport scheme, several positive measures have been taken, including low carbon mobility program, and the e-rickshaws are introduced to reduce the carbon emission in environment and also to control the pollution-free society [2]. It is still in the planning stage, and a variety of commuters are debating that it is continuous to have the poor transport facilities.

1.2.1.3   Productivity

Few centers for the skill development and the microbusiness incubators have also been developed. Most of these projects are small. Despite of that nearly 85 lakhs are unemployed in the year 2018, the rate of unemployment has soared to 6.77 from the past year percent of 4.7. In the first quarter of 2018, this state has ranked as the 7th among the state in India. In Bhubaneswar, there are 565 buses are linking the 67 wards with the help of the IT-backend support options the e-mobility attempt to update and develop the service under the Atal mission.

1.2.2   Smart City in Pune

Vision of smart city in Pune is to redesign its streets and roads and its equal for all people. Pune Smart City overview is shown in Figure 1.2. Design of the city is based upon the universal accessibility for the elderly and physically challenged and increased focus on the pedestrians, modern

Figure 1.2 Pune smart city overview.

world infrastructure through the creation of appropriate arrangements for underground utilities [3]. Allocation is mainly to motorized traffic, continuous excavation of roads, and weak pedestrian crossing for layout facilities.

1.2.2.1   Specifications

This city has been developed to create an overall master plan based on a patented econometric model that will make Pune fit for the future up to 2030 comprehensive infrastructure specifications that have been completed for the next 5 years. It aims at a comprehensive range of urban options, including job opportunities creation, socio-economic growth, and beyond infrastructure and habitability [4].

1.2.2.2   Transport and Mobility

Real monitoring system of the live ongoing buses in the city is to track the location of different locations. Smart bus stops with the public information systems. This live tracking of the buses is availed through the mobile app by the people in this eco system. Around 319 signals are present in the city where the pedestrian right get the way for the emergency response system [4]. Also, advanced traffic management system by using the CCTV and the mobile GPS-based traffic system analysis is similar to Google live traffic system and intelligent road asset management system to help all.

1.2.2.3   Water and Sewage Management

New advanced technologies for water management are introduced in the smart bulk meters with the SCADA, for the commercial establishment; it used for the domestic households through the campaign along with a revised telescopic traffic.

1.3   Status of Smart Cities in India

According to the report the government of India has planned to launch 100 smart city missions (SCMs). These cities are able to provide decent roads, to build housing for everyone in the city, and also to create green spaces. Five years back, a substantial portion of the capital earmarked was no spent. A single network is yet to be completed by many smart cities. Actually, the project initial proposed for smart city was around 5,151 projects but only 3,629 have been actively pursued. In those number, only 25%

of the projects are only have been completed [6]. But in the terms of value, the proportion of work done is just 11% of the total.

1.3.1   Funding Process by Government

Over 5 years, the central government has allocated Rs 48,000 crore to the mission. That amounts to an average of Rs 96 crore per city per year, maybe enough in many cities to create a sewage drain. An equivalent amount would have to be contributed by the states and urban local bodies of amount 96 crore. The city administration had to raise the remainder of the necessary financing through a host of sources-public-private partnerships, grants, resource monetization, and the likes. While renowned planners have created the smart city ideas, with the financial arrangements planned out in advance, most urban local authorities are struggling to raise the funds needed. While several bodies have raised concerns that the financing of the central government is insufficient, the government itself is not sympathetic [5, 6] and funds raised by government of India as shown in Figure 1.3. That any of the 30 cities will have no trouble collecting funds because they have A++ credit scores.

Pune is an smart example that has successfully launched a municipal bond, documenting its own process and replicating the success of the other cities.

The source of funds may vary in different countries; the sources of the smart city projects are provided by government and the private organizations; they are state government and the urban local bodies and central

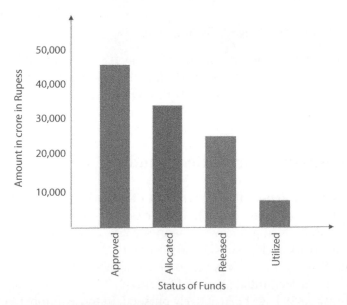

Figure 1.3 Funds raised by government of India.

government. Public-private partnership organizations, convergence with the other government mission resources, and also load providers are all contributing in this mission progress. Analysts think that national transformative projects such as the Smart Cities Mission will take time to implement in a vast country like India. The mission is also suffering from the lack of urban planners.

1.4   Analysis of Smart City Setup

The vision of a community and the priorities of people form an important aspect of the planning of smart cities. Since each city has distinct strength and the disadvantages, it is possible that their respective approaches to creating a smart city will vary. Here are some attempt to analyze the possible variation of the city setup by economical-based setup architecture [6]. Cities can be turned smart with any mixture of different smart components. A city does not need to be branded as smart for all the components. The number of smart components depends on the cost and available technologies.

1.4.1   Physical Infrastructure-Based

Digital innovations, in terms of physical technology, a smart city, transform into improved public facilities for people and better resource use while reducing environmental impacts. A city that integrates physical infrastructure, IT infrastructure, social infrastructure, and business infrastructure with a view to exploiting the city's collective intellect. Technologies for embedded sensing allow data collection and analysis in real time [7]. This data is then presented to infrastructure companies as meaningful and accurate information, allowing them to make more sophisticated decisions [8]. AI learning is introduced in the infrastructure-based architectural-based systems which have more result in the accuracy and the beneficial purposes. For a deeper understanding of the usage of resources, AI may use accurate, robust, and practical knowledge obtained and processed by smart infrastructure. A change in urban planning and development leads to a more efficient and secure infrastructure that is better tailored to the needs of people. The data collection are carried through the process by the collecting the individual responses.

1.4.2   Social Infrastructure-Based

The standardization position involves many facets of the smart city's architecture, organization, and functioning. Indian national smart city has principles that govern the unified criteria for radically new possibilities of centralized

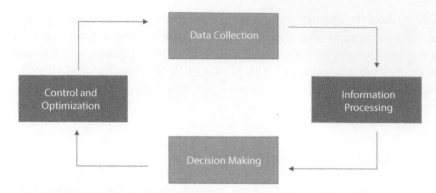

Figure 1.4 Physical infrastructure workflow.

urban process management. The article describes the social infrastructure roles and tasks of single-industry cities, which should be taken into account in the introduction of the smart city framework. The Figure 1.4 shows the physical infrastructure workflow. The selected fields of operation set out in the smart city concept are closely linked to the growth of single-industry social infrastructure [8–10]. The dynamic system of social engineering that lead to enhancement of quality of life through the use of innovative decision-making technology through the economic and the eco-friendly of the life systems.

This entire infrastructure aims system of objects essential for the promotion of human activity, communications, as well as businesses, organizations, and organizations, delivering social and household services to the community, management bodies, and workers whose operations are structured to meet the social needs of people in conjunction with the quality of life indicators created [11]. Certain areas should be covered in the social engineering process like the electricity supply with the higher energy and sustainable solid waste management robust connectivity and digitalization.

1.4.3 Urban Mobility

Mobility system encompasses a variety of operating technology used for the purpose of transportation system and also in management system, including the payment facilities, monitoring remote display devices which are used to track and maintain the traffic conditions along transport routes [12].

1.4.4 Solid Waste Management System

This scheme allows for the systematic storage of sewage in well-designed sewers that are delivered to the Sewage Treatment Plant (STP) to be handled there in such a manner that the effluent follows the parameters specified by India's Central Pollution Control Board. For horticulture, road-side drainage, road sweeping, and irrigation, the treated water can be recycled.

1.4.5 Economical-Based Infrastructure

Innovation-driven and university-supported economy focuses on cutting-edge innovation, not just for technology, industry, and business but also for architecture, planning, growth, and the cultural heritage. Cities are a prosperous location, but their prosperity depends on their population size and other factors. In the last two decades, urban India has developed at an exponential pace [14]. An optimistic estimation of India's population growth indicates that the total population is projected to hit around 1.5 billion by 2031, with an increased urban population of about 600 million, or about 40%, by 2031.

India has the large economic growth development in the world. Unfortunately, economic data is not calculated for urban agglomerations, but rather for the district administrative unit, which has no association with the border of urban agglomerations. In India, the extent of urbanization of the different states and union territories varies widely. The increased population base of cities resulted in higher demand for manufacturing goods and commodities. This was the case of cities and towns which grew in Europe in the 19th century in the industrial belts and regions. More often, a polycentric, nature-based and people-friendly urban structure was invented when center city regions became congested with growing population and increasing industrial emissions [14, 15].

1.4.6 Infrastructure-Based Development

Spending on infrastructure is crucial not only for the development of India and for sustaining the region's fight against poverty but also for laying the foundation for stronger future economic growth. The 11th Plan emphasized the importance of investment in infrastructure to achieve a sustainable and inclusive increase in GDP of 9% to 10% over the next decade. The growth of infrastructure is a core focus of the 11th Five Year Plan of the Government of India (2007–2012). In 2010, the nation initiated 94 new projects and saw an investment of US$71.9 billion in 2010, a rise of 85% from 2009. The investment is the highest amount witnessed by any developed nation in the entire 1990–2010 period in any given year [16]. In 2010, India alone accounted for 43% of the overall expenditure in private ventures in developing countries.

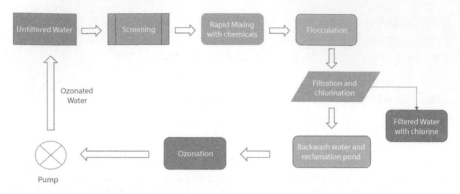

Figure 1.5 Water supply chain in city structure.

1.4.7   Water Supply System

The consistency of the groups of organic surface and groundwater, known as raw water, will also not fulfil the quality requirements of domestic and industrial consumers. In such cases, water treatment is required prior to its use. Water, typically via a network of storage tanks and drains, can be collected and circulated throughout the metropolitan environment until handled. Figure 1.5 shows the water supply chain in city structure.

1.4.8   Sewage Networking

The concentrations of municipal sewers and their amounts of pollutants differ over a typical day of a typical week and over the course of a year. The conditions of flow may differ from free surface to supercharged flow, from constant to turbulent flow [18], and from static to non-uniform flow that varies rapidly or gradually.

1.5   Ideal Planning for the Sewage Networking Systems

1.5.1   Availability and Ideal Consumption of Resources

An equal and responsible distribution of services, including water and power, will be a smart city is most prominent feature one, which often requires access to proper sanitation and the disposal of solid waste. In order to ensure availability for future generations, smart cities must ensure proximity to services while placing a focus on the conscientious consumption of natural resources.

1.5.2   Anticipating Future Demand

India has becoming the most populated country around the world in the near decade. So, urbanization is expected to grow to 50% by 2030. Therefore, urban planning agencies need to consider potential demands to control and track the use of energy in today's society. In industry and workplaces, we witness routine sanitization campaigns, daily sweeping in households, and intensified handwashing. It is estimated that a family of five needs 100 to 200 liters of water per day just to wash their hands. This would result in the development of about 200 liters of wastewater each day that would raise water demand and waste water generation from human habitation by 20% to 25%.

The aim of the architecture is to provide numerous APIs as well as visual web services with public smart city information via data [13]. In this particular instance, the system design can make it easy to transmit sensor data to a back-end system and be incorporated into the "standard" city monitoring system.

1.5.3   Transporting Networks to Facilitate

Multiple major companies, such as OLA, Uber, and the car manufacturers, are increasingly developing autonomous vehicles. For self-parking vehicles, the Indian Department of Transportation has just paved the way. This are projected to be on the market and generally available as early as 2020, likely with significant market shares. More users in the city nowadays are using the private transport more than the public transportation such that it has some effects in the public transportation and lead to more pollution around the economical city [16]. They should encourage the public mode of transportation to others and to help the environment.

It is possible that traffic control in a smart city would be drastically different. Future methods would be collaborative, unlike the individual driver-focused current solution, where the aim is to maximize flow in a road system. This could include a drop in waiting times for traffic lights and average delay, a decrease in mean cumulative travel time, or an increase in overall highway productivity. Traffic management now also uses traffic light networks that track road traffic with timers and sensors [17]. Efforts are being made to develop software that can forecast traffic flows, a smart trip simulation system built on the neural network that can simulate speed profile conditions with a high degree of accuracy at various sensor locations.

1.5.4   Control Centers for Governing the City

Recognizing these threats and prospects, the government of India initiated the 100 Smart Cities Mission in June 2015. Almost 100 smart cities have been established since the mission was launched and cities have begun to implement public infrastructure and ICT initiatives according to mission guidelines. Cities have conceptualized projects that enable them to do more, increase their organizational effectiveness, and provide residents with timely and reliable services.

1.5.5   Integrated Command and Control Center

The Integrated Command and Control Center (ICCC) serves as the "Nerve Center" for Operations Administration, Day-to-Day Exception, and Crisis Management. It also provides insights through the analysis of diverse aggregated data sets to produce information for better planning and policy making. The ICCC is intended to aggregate information through various applications and sensors distributed across the region and then provide actionable information with sufficient representation for decision-making. Although few cities have begun implementing ICCC with necessary software, networks, and sensors under the Smart Cities Mission, they are at different stages of maturity as far as informed decision-making is concerned [19]. As these ICCCs are introduced, it is imperative to assess the sophistication of productivity using a common methodology across the world ensuring that improvements made by cities can provide sufficient benefits for cities and people in the future.

While few cities have begun to deploy ICCCs with the necessary software, networks, and sensors under the Smart Cities Mission, they are at different stages when it comes to informed decision-making. As these ICCCs are introduced, it is imperative to assess the sophistication of productivity using a common methodology across the world ensuring that improvements made by cities can provide sufficient benefits for cities and people in the future. The purpose of this evaluation system is to provide communities with a do-it-yourself toolkit to measure the maturity and efficacy of the Centralized Command and Control Center in municipal operations management, day-to-day emergency management, crisis management, preparation, and policy-making.

It is envisaged that the ICCCs would be the brain of metropolitan service, exception handling, and crisis management [19, 20]. Figure 1.6 shows the smart city control flow for command and control centers. Sensors and edge devices can collect and produce real-time data from different services such as water, waste management, electricity, accessibility, the urban environment, education, health, and safety.

Figure 1.6 Smart city control flow for command and control centers.

The ICCC used to the following:

1. Enhanced understanding of circumstances by providing information through sensor deployment across the city for civic officials through urban functions.
2. Standardizing urban response protocol by developing modern protocols for repeated incidents, complaints, and requirement scenarios.
3. Strengthen cooperation inside and beyond various agencies local urban bodies and municipal authorities.
4. Institutionalization of daily activities decision-making guided by evidence and in the case of a crises around the city level—from the owners to the city managers.
5. Engaging on-site service workers in dealing with social concerns and residents' complaints.

1.6   Heritage of Culture Based on Modern Advancement

India's growth mechanism has been affected, in part, by the transnationalization of capital within the global economy, which has enabled the deployment of capital and labor within India by both foreign financing institutions (e.g., the World Bank) and private multinational companies (e.g., Union Carbide). In order to sustain capital-intensive modes of industrial and agricultural production, the Indian economy depends on foreign technology and finance [23]. As a result, the Indian state has accrued a huge foreign debt with both the US and the USSR and has encouraged a phase of growth that has a significant effect on the relationship within its borders between the state and the different indigenous cultures.

The state is not an individual fact, of course. It is composed of organizations tied, in turn, to the international economy. Therefore, amid some external financial and technical dependency, the dominant classes of India's state capitalist system, namely, the bureaucratic elite and the governing alliance of the national bourgeoisie (large private enterprise), the army, wealthy peasant farmers, small traders, and money lenders, are steering indigenous production in India.

Western models of production, growth, and transformation, which in part view rural development as an issue of sectoral development based on an industrial urban economy, have profoundly shaped the ideological paradigm of development embraced by the state. India has been subject to a modernization phase that has already evolved in the West due to its reliance on international technologies and finance and its acceptance of western growth models.

An unjust cultural exchange that emphasizes Western traditions and devalues indigenous forms of knowledge has preceded the unequal economic exchange that occurs between industrialized capitalist states and developing nations. In the emphasis put on modernity within the development phase in India, this Western bias is evident [24]; it equates modern scientific rationality and technology with an effective process of development and devalues non-modern societies and their conventional information structures.

1.7   Funding and Business Models to Leverage

The business model is a very new term, and even though it is commonly debated, there is a lack of a common description. A business model defines the reasoning for creating, providing, and capturing value (economic, social, cultural, and other sources of value) through an entity. A business model concerns "the design of goods, facilities, and knowledge flows", one of the most commonly known concepts derives from. This definition considers players, functions, market potential, and revenue streams. Four elements and positions, the meaning proposal, are in the middle of the business model structure or "canvas". While multiple value ideas could be put forward, business models can be ranked in five different trends according to the following:

- Business models unbundling, which could be used by organizations carrying out these three basic business types: customer relations; product innovation and infrastructure enterprises (e.g., private banking).

- The long tail business model where an organization is seeking to sell less for more. This paradigm can be solved by selling a diverse variety of specialty items, each of which sells relatively infrequently (i.e., LEGO).
- Multi-sided networks, which put together two or more separate but interdependent classes of consumers (i.e., video console manufacturers).
- Free market model consistently rewards at least one large consumer group from a free-of-charge deal (i.e., mobile phone operators).

1.7.1   Fundings

Web-based market models match the trends described above. These findings suggest that the open pattern "conquers" web-based models, though there are still unbundling instances. Except in web-based situations, contemporary business models remain and the city acts as a direct information and service provider to its residents and businesses, on the other side, published on different smart city market models. While market models are not to be followed in public institutions (i.e., Masdar and Gdansk) [24], even in these ways the municipality uses smart cities to draw tourists, inhabitants, and investment. These studies also named members to two contemporary business model classes:

1. E-Service market model.
2. Openness in ownership of the private enterprise and the ICT network.

A specific provider (or stakeholder groups) was treated as provided in each service category. The network owner creates value for people and businesses. A significant result of this assignment process is the appointment of business model trends in cases that have no relevant network-related business models. This is fair because all of these municipal types need different resources (networks and grids, sensors, etc.). The unbundled trend is still in effect even though these facilities are leased for service provision. When the IoT is used as the main resource that results in the IoT market models involved, circumstances change [24, 25]. In the above-mentioned situations, though, cities have still not capitalized IoT, which helps start-ups and other vendors to build value.

1.8   Community-Based Development

1.8.1   Smart Medical Care

This approach aim, however, is focused on the individual experiences of professionals and/or neighborhood associations, to recognize the health concerns of the whole community. The value of such an approach is both cheap and constant, but it lacks the rigors of more rigorous quantitative methods and less likely to detect latent challenges within the group. In comparison, the practice of formal group consensus methods will address this role more thoroughly and rigorously in order to create consensus strategies so as to avoid narrowing the number of possible problems to consider, as is the tendency of various quantitative approaches.

Using data, however, the data must be extrapolitanized from wide region information in order to recognize urban health issues. The validity of the method ultimately relies on the amount of burden the wide region has taken on the society [21]. By using secondary data, such as vital statistics and census data, more comprehensive research is difficult for the practice as general problems are established.

Tendency, though to rely on some health conditions, may miss a significant issue merely because it was not part of the dataset. For example, an epidemiological analysis of diastolic blood pressure within the population may produce advanced data on distribution, correlates, and hypertension determinants. At the cost of a larger data collection, though, the information in the hypertension set is collected. The use of these data to classify the health issues of the population may also make it easier for the profession to ignore some (maybe more critical) problems of health.

1.8.2   Smart Safety for The IT

A smart public safety infrastructure is being built to provide the public with a better atmosphere for ordinary people. This system is complicated, distributed over all campuses of the University. It consists of a smart cameras tracking system, a backroom system with workflow engine and a smartphone device within the context of a collaboration concept. The intelligent cameras are deployed and this last year the smartphone device and the back-office device with acceptable results are used. The smartphone app is the user entry point for documenting many problems pertaining to security and campus management which are instantly forwarded to the responsibilities team when they are taken directly in the event of security or join an integrated working flow engine when running the campus [21].

This paper reveals the framework for achieving a more intelligent climate for public protection, specifics of operation, and statistical evidence obtained by the system.

1.8.3   IoT Communication Interface With ML

The preparation and preparing of information for such interactions is a critical activity. To respond to this issue, various types of data processing, such as edge analytics, stream analysis, and database IoT analysis, must be applied [22]. Computing frameworks play an vital role in connecting the server with neighboring computer structures and frameworks that depend on the location and the processing server where the data is processed. Architecture is basically classified into several categories for the networking and filter data for data centers.

Edge Computing: This approach to computation allows data to initially be stored on edge computers. Edge devices cannot be linked continuously to the network, so a backup of the master data/reference data is required for offline processing.

Cloud Computing: This approach and the design has high latency and high load balance, which means that this architecture is not ideal for the processing of IoT data since it can work for other processing at high speeds.

There are several other type of cloud computing services like Iaas, Paas, and Saas. These are equipped with the data transmission via API or several other SDK kit for the user interface.

1.8.4   Machine Learning Algorithms

ML allows a computer to automatically learn and grow (without directly being programmed). Overall, ML algorithms can be classified as being (i) managed, (ii) unmonitored, and (iii) evolutionary computation. In reinforcement methods, a description is associated with each input value, while input values remain unlabeled in unsupervised learning. Learning algorithm implements a reinforcement-based mechanism in which the goal is to choose the set of environmental activities that optimize the overall benefit. There are some several types of machine learning algorithms, namely, SVM (Support Vector Machine). For both classification and regression queries [33], SVMs are valid, but they are widely used for the former. A binary SVM performs a binary division, generating a hyperplane such that it is possible to classify input values into two groups.

For applications with a restricted number of stakeholders, SVMs are highly important. The system relies on numerous voice recording sensors to track the voices of patients such as handheld computers, voice recorders, and smartphones. To differentiate between the characteristics of good and unsafe consumers at a higher accuracy rate, SVM is then added to the data (on a cloud-based server). Storage processing method in the machine learning branched into cloud storage and processing and edge storage and processing.

1.8.5   Smart Community

The entire SCM program is supervised by an Apex governance system which consists of many national committees at state and city level. The SCM is a three-level governance structure. A special purpose vehicle (SPV) is used for executing the mission on a city scale. The SPV manages the funding, executes the programs, and administers and reviews them. The company is headed by a full-time CEO and has nominated on the board by the Federal Government, the State Government and ULB (Urban Development Ministry, 2015) [26]. The SC schemes are carried out by joint ventures, subsidiaries, PPP, etc. In addition, the cities have used a convergence process to support the SC initiative. These structures of convergence allow the cities to receive funds from other successful missions such as Digital India, Housing for everyone, production of national patrimony skills, and the Missions of Swachh Bharat, for the creation and development of a number of intelligent cities initiatives.

Countries and clever communities are regarded as a catalyst to boost city citizens' quality of life. However, due to insufficient evidence, in particular from developed countries, current awareness of the risks that could hamper the progress of smart city projects remains minimal. A rare incentive is the new SCM in India.

Examine the risk type, possibility, and consequences on adoption of smart city projects, including risk definition data in the submitted smart city proposals for the Area Projects (ABD) (small scale) and Pancake Projects (large scale) [24]. We have used (quantitative and qualitative) theme modeling for risk classification, followed by risk effect analysis for priority assessment and a keyword co-occurrence network.

1.9   Revolutionary Impact With Other Locations

IoT applications can lead to maximizing, innovating, and transforming customer and business process items.

- **Optimization:** IoT aims to minimize costs while maximizing effective utilization of assets during business processes.
- **Innovation:** IoT applications help to create diversified products/services, improve operations, and ultimately better service for customers.
- **Transformation:** By allowing disruptive business models, IoT is blurring industry boundaries; telematics, for example, covers both the transportation industry and the insurance sector.

In particular, IoT is supposed to add value to enterprise processes and to push value eneration to the next level for industrial applications.

- IoT is potentially Industry 4.0's most critical element in terms of Digital automation of industrial processes and structures.
- Diverse technologies related to this are evolving, including quality sensors, more stable, efficient networks, high performance computing, robots, artificial intelligence, and computational technologies and increased reality.
- In the manufacturing and automotor sectors, IoT demand growth will be powered mainly by linked units with transport and logistics as the major part of the industry-specific IoT sales. The largest volume of IoT adoption is anticipated in industrial and automotive sectors. Built linking units are projected to be around 0.7 billion in both sectors by 2020.
- While the number of industrial facilities projected to rise by over 2× between 0.32 and 0.68 billion in 2014, 37× will increase from 0.02 billion in 2014 to 0.74 trillion in 2020 for the automobile market.
- The car industry is expected to see the highest level of revenue growth up to 303 billion dollars by 2020. Transportation and logistics, on the other hand, are expected to increase IoT revenue for the industry.

The Indian IoT ecosystem has a selection of around 120 participants, including hardware vendors, device vendors, network operators, and device integrators.

- IoT provides players with prospects across the supply chain with application vendors aiming to capture 50% of the IoT market in India.

- Technology providers concentrate on both vertical and horizontal applications, including commercial and industrial IoT solutions. In addition to appealing to a broad portion of customers, they seek to deliver tailored solutions to the niche consumer community.

1.10   Finding Balanced City Development

The first step is to identify and deploy a secure networking system that, in most situations, is enabled by wireless networks. Networks as they allow knowledge sharing with a more scalable and low-cost implementation than wired networks. However, owing to the complexities of sustainable smart city environments, in most situations, heterogeneous connectivity systems and diverse network architectures can be introduced, based on the requirements of particular networks that need to be incorporated [27] (e.g., the appropriate low or high data bit rate) or technical limitations (e.g., the availability of a power source), the area to be covered.

A town that wants to be an educated and prosperous town must generally become more desirable, resilient, egalitarian, and equilibrate with its inhabitants, work, and tourists.

- Exchange expertise, knowledge, and programmers, as well as responsibility for decisions affecting people's lives in coming years between residents, stakeholders, and other institutions.
- Improve the city's identity as capital town for popular features (e.g., healthy food, culture, and music) and enhance the city's appeal for city residents, businesses, and tourists.
- Focus on the legal, social, and services values of both workers and businesses.

1.11   E-Industry With Enhanced Resources

They noted that IoT has actually been applied to support the technologies and people in relatively few implementations. IoT's spectrum is very broad and almost all application areas will be captured by IoT in the near future. They found out that energy efficiency is one of the main facets of society, and IoT will help create a smart energy management system that saves energy and money [28]. In terms of the smart city definition, you mentioned an IoT architecture. The writers have addressed the immaturity of IoT hardware and software as one of the difficulties in doing this. They proposed addressing these problems to ensure a secure, effective, and user-friendly IoT device.

The transition from rural to urban environment leads to a growing urban population. Intelligent mobility, electricity, healthcare, and infrastructure solutions are also required. Smart city is one of the big IoT developer apps. It discusses several topics, including traffic control, air pollution management, public security solutions, intelligent parking, intelligent lightning, and intelligent waste disposal. You said IoT works tirelessly to solve these tough problems. In the domain of Smart Cities Technology pioneers is able to access the need for better intelligent urban infrastructure with accelerated urbanization. The authors have concluded that technology allowed by IoT is very relevant for sustainable growth in smart cities.

A weekly visit is often needed to gather information from the sensors mounted at the site under investigation. Often, some details remained lacking, which may not contribute to a very reliable review. The IoT-based system is thus able to address this issue and can provide high precision in analysis and forecasting. Later, concern is expressed for the handling of domestic wastewater. They addressed many shortcomings in the wastewater treatment process and complex control method and recommended effective alternatives based on IoT [29, 30]. They claimed that IoT can be very efficient in the treatment and control of wastewater.

The main design challenges for a successful IoT architecture in a heterogeneous setting are scalability, modularity, interoperability, and transparency. The IoT architecture must be configured to satisfy the criteria of cross-domain communications, convergence of various structures with the ability for easy and flexible control functions, analytics and storage of big data, and user-friendly applications. The design should also be able to scale up the functionality of the IoT devices in the system and incorporate some intelligence and automation.

1.12   Strategy for Development of Smart Cities

1.12.1   Stakeholder Benefits

A policy with consistent advantages assigned to particular stakeholders is a success indicator that can be visible in the ongoing input obtained from stakeholders, showing the smart city components' level of fulfilment or dissatisfaction. For strategies which are formed on the basis of specific needs, a observable effect is more probable. For ordinary people and for senior leadership who need to be on board with the strategy, particular plans can be very complicated. It is necessary to spend the extra time putting in the strategies that both political officials and people can clearly grasp in detail.

1.12.2   Urban Integration

In most cities worldwide, the incorporation of technology within the public sphere is an evolving theme. It is important to enhance the quality of life for residents to have an urban planning aspect within the Smart City Strategy.

We have also seen examples of the accelerated introduction of technologies in our cities and no concern about the effect on customer care or the experience of people [30]. There are also innovations which have not been prepared for or have not been integrated with other agencies. This may look "cool" for some of the more technically focused persons; it will reflect and depict for others.

The community's picture of chaos: As part of policy growth, attention should be given to implementation guidance. The implementation of the Smart City Strategy as an organized initiative within the urban master plan phase is one solution. This strategy means that, at the highest level, the discussion about technology and the built environment takes place. Strategies seek to describe a wide range of programmers and projects with longer horizons in time for distribution. Some are more fundamental; others are beyond some. With the pace of technological transition, by the time they are finished, even short-term programmers that fund efforts will look different. Spending too much time on the strategy's technological specifics can just make it seem obsolete in a limited timeframe [30]. The strongest implementations of technologies are those that offer societal advantages, are not physically distracting in the public domain, and are applied with a long-term view.

1.12.3   Future Scope of City Innovations

In our modern world, many cities are facing big obstacles, such as a rising population, a shortage of physical and social resources, environmental, and regulatory standards, diminishing tax bases and budgets, and higher prices. They need to learn how to recognize innovative and intelligent ways of handling urban life's complexities and challenges ranging from congestion, overcrowding, and urban sprawl to insufficient infrastructure, high unemployment, resource utilization, conservation of the environment, and increasing crime rates.

Cost efficiencies, resilient networks, and an increased local environment result from the use of smart city technology [31]. When it comes to designing the cities of the future, "smart cities" is the new term. To bring a new brand and distinctive appeal to the lifestyle, smart cities are supposed to be the cornerstone to balancing a prosperous future with sustained economic development and job production.

Cloud-based output and storage face common obstacles to smart city applications. For example, the complexities of cloud-based smart grids include cost-effective provisioning without replacing ageing infrastructure and stable integration of modern capabilities with existing networks [33]. Although the ML has both added advantage and disadvantages, it leads to the deep learning process which enhances development in the technologies like the data visualization in real-time modern world.

Development accomplished by cities is tied to their desire to holistically solve urbanization-based problems and related social, environmental, and economic issues, while at the same time making the most of potential opportunities [30]. It is possible to interpret the smart city idea as a paradigm for incorporating this vision of advanced and modern urbanization. In future, vision is the urban center of the future, making sustainable, safe, eco-friendly, and competitive as all buildings are designed, built, and controlled using new, manufactured materials, sensors, electronics, and networks integrated with computerized systems consisting of databases, surveillance, and de-connected networks.

1.12.4   Conclusion

To make civic processes more cost-effective and environmentally competitive, smart cities make use of digital technologies. By turning streetlights on only when a road is in service, sensors installed in buildings and grid networks will help communities embrace green technologies and conserve electricity [32]. Sensors, smart cards, and digital cameras feed real-time data into advanced control systems, and better infrastructure and analytical technologies will enable decision-making. Rapid urbanization has contributed to extreme road jams as large numbers of citizens choose to enter cities by vehicle. As a result, air pollution has been a major challenge for cities. Development in smart cities has led to the introduction of creative integrated transport networks designed to satisfy the needs of residents. For starters, able to implement real-time mobility systems, smart travel passes, shared car trips, smart vehicles (driverless cars), and personal rapid transit.

One of the largest smart city projects currently taking place is the India Smart Cities Competition, a contest where 100 cities can receive funds from the Ministry of Urban Development and Bloomberg Philanthropies. Competition is meant to promote more innovation from municipal officers and their partners, as well as more involvement from people, in the development of smart city plans [31, 32]. As several critics find out that critical needs such as drinking water and sanitation need to be resolved, this problem has been scrutinized.

Using technologies and data improves resistance to urban problems, through greater efficiencies, and using creativity and industry introduces these fantastic opportunities for our communities. Those with good leadership and productive public-private collaborations working with community participation are the cities positioned to build on these possibilities.

References

1. Su, K., Li, J., Fu, H., Smart city and the applications. *International Conference on Electronics*, Communications and Control (ICECC), Ningbo, China, 2011.
2. Fan, L., Boshnakov, K., Lv, J., Integrated control for the urban wastewater treatment. BHUBANESWAR SMART CITY PROPOSAL, 2015, smartcities. gov.in.
3. Lavalle, A.G., Serafim, L., de Oliveira, O.P., Hordijk, M., Takano, G., Sridharan, N., Participatory Governance, Inclusive Development and Decentralization in the Global South, Literature Review, pmc.gov.in, 2011.
4. Janawani, Paritcipatory Governance in Pune and berlin, Janwani, 2013. www. janwani.org
5. Keruwala, N., Participatory Budgeting in India: The Pune experiment, OWSA, 2016. developmentcentral.wordpress.com
6. Smart Cities Mission Ministry of Urban Development Government of India hosted, 2015, http://mohua.gov.in/cms/smart-cities.php
7. Anthopoulos, L., Janssen, M., Weerakkody, V., Comparing Smart Cities with Different Modelling Approaches. *International World Wide Web Conference Committee (IW3C2)*, 2015.
8. Harekrishna, M., How Relevant is E-Governance Measurement? Experiences in Indian Scenario EGOSE, Conference on Electronic Governance and Open Society: Challenges in Eurasia(EGOSE'14), DOI:10.13140/RG.2.1.4930.9282 2014.
9. Desa, U., United nations department of economic and social affairs population division: World urbanization prospects, 2014, https://population. un.org/wup/

10. Neirotti, P., De Marco, A., Cagliano, A.C., Mangano, G., Scorrano, F., *Current trends in smart city initiatives: Some stylised facts*, Cities, vol. 38, pp. 25–36, Elsevier, 2014.

11. Shapiro, J.M., Smart cities: quality of life productivity and the growth effects of human capital. *Rev. Econ. Stat.*, 88, 2, 324–335, 2006.

12. Torres, Pina, V., Acerete, B., E-government developments on delivering public services among eu cities. *Gov. Inf. Q.*, 22, 2, 217–238, 2005.

13. Yovanof, G.S. and Hazapis, G.N., An architectural framework and enabling wireless technologies for digital cities & intelligent urban environments. *Wirel. Pers. Commun.*, 49, 3, 445–463, 2009.

14. Brännström, R. and Granlund, D., Sensor monitoring of bridge movement: a system architecture. *Proceedings of Local Computer Networks, IEEE Communications Society*, pp. 797–800, 2011.

15. Zhang, P., Yan, M., Wang, H., Yu, G., Integration Automation System of Wastewater Treatment Plant. *6th World Congress on Intelligent Control and Automation Dalian*, pp. 6626–6630, 2006.

16. Humoreanu, B. and Nascu, I., Wastewater treatment plant SCADA application. *IEEE International Conference on Automation Quality and Testing Robotics*, pp. 575–580, 2012.

17. Grieu, S., Traore, A., Polit, M., Fault detection in a wastewater treatment plant. *8th International Conference on Emerging Technologies and Factory Automation*, vol. 1, pp. 399–402, 2001.

18. Stephens, J.C., Wilson, E.J., Peterson, T.R., *Smart Grid Evolution*, Cambridge University Press, Smart Grid and Renewable Energy, Vol. 6 No. 8, August 31, 2015.

19. Paul, A., Cleverley, M., Kerr, W., Marzolini, F., Reade, M., Russo, S., *Smarter Cities Series: understanding the IBM approach to public safety*, IBM Corporation, www.aeiciberseguridad.es/descargas/categoria6/6193257.pdf, 2011.

20. Achaerandio, R., Gallotti, G., Curto, J., Bigliani, R., Maldonado, F., *Smart cities analysis in Spain*, White paper, IDC, 2011.

21. Bria, F., Gascó, M., Halpin, H., Baeck, P., Almirall, E., Kresin, F., *Growing a digital social innovation ecosystem for Europe*, DSI final report, European Union, 2015. https://media.nesta.org.uk/documents/dsireport.pdf

22. Hernández-Munoz, J.M. *et al.*, Smart Cities at the Forefront of the Future Internet, in: *The Future Internet, Lecture Notes in Computer Science*, vol. 6656, pp. 447–462, 2011.

23. Fan, L., Boshnakov, K., Lv, J., System Based on Multivariable Regulator. *29th Chinese Control Conference*, pp. 4975–4980, 2010.

24. Kumar, A., Maurya, B., Chandra, D., Dimension reduction and controller design for a waste water treatment plant. *International Conference on Power and Advanced Control Engineering (ICPACE)*, pp. 413–417, 2015.

25. Gil-García, J.R. and Pardo, T.A., E-government success factors: Mapping practical tools to theoretical foundations. *Gov. Inf. Q.*, 22, 2, 187–216, 2005.

26. Giffinger, R., Fertner, C., Kramar, H., Kalasek, R., Pichler-Milanoviü, N., Meijers, E., *Smart Cities: Ranking of European Medium-Sized Cities*, Centre of Regional Science (SRF), Vienna University of Technology, Vienna, Austria, 2007.

27. Eek, R.T.P., Sahlan, S., Wahab, N.A., Modeling of Waste Water Treatment Plant via system ID & model reduction technique. *IEEE Conference on Control Systems & Industrial Informatics*, pp. 131–136, 2012.

28. Chintalacheruvu, N. and Muthukumar, V., Video based vehicle detection and its application in intelligent transportation systems. *J. Transp. Technol.*, 2, 4, 305–314, 2012.

29. Sandhu, S.S., Jain, N., Gaurav, A., Iyengar, N. Ch. S. N., Agent based intelligent traffic management system for smart cities. *Int. J. Smart Home*, 9, 12, 307–316, 2015.

30. Borja, J., Counterpoint: Intelligent cities and innovative cities. *UOC Papers: E-Journal on the Knowledge Society*, 2007.

31. Mitchell, W., Designing the Digital City, in: *Digital Cities: Technologies, Experiences, and Future Perspectives*, T. Ishida and K. Isbister, (Eds.), pp. 1–6, Springer, Berlin/Heidelberg, 2000.

32. Odendaal, N., Information and communication technology and local governance: Understanding the difference between cities in developed and emerging economies. *Comput. Environ. Urban Syst.*, 27, 6, 585–607, 2003.

33. Nfuka, E.N. and Rusu, L., Critical success factors for effective IT governance in the public sector organizations in a developing country: The case of Tanzania. *18th European Conference on Information Systems (ECIS)*, Pretoria, South Africa, 2010.

2

An Empirical Study on Paddy Harvest and Rice Demand Prediction for an Optimal Distribution Plan

W. H. Rankothge

Sri Lanka Institute of Information Technology, Colombo, Sri Lanka

Abstract

Rice is one of the main types of nutrient supplying foods in Asian communities and has a direct impact on the socioeconomic development of the communities. Generally, paddy harvest, price, and demand for rice depend on several factors: rainfall, humidity, paddy cultivation area, temperature, etc. Therefore, precisely predicting the future harvest of paddy and consumption demand of rice is complicated. It creates a necessary requirement of a management platform to predict future paddy harvest and rice demands considering important parameters. Such platform will help the countries in the processes of national strategy development, to maintain a sustainable approach between paddy cultivation and rice demand.

We have proposed a centralized management platform, where we would analyze numerous factors affecting on the amount of crop yield on the next harvesting season and the factors affecting on future demand for rice. The proposed platform follows the smart agri/farm approach for paddy related processes, with three functional features: (1) paddy harvest prediction module, (2) rice demand prediction module, and (3) an optimal planning module for crop distribution. Two popular machine learning algorithms, Recurrent Neural Network (RNN) and Long Short-Term Memory (LSTM), are used to develop the prediction modules. The optimal planning module was developed using a heuristic-based approach: Genetic Algorithms (GAs). The algorithm performances were evaluated for Sri Lankan context, using real data sets.

Keywords: Recurrent Neural Networks (RNN), Long Short-Term Memory (LSTM), prediction, planning, and scheduling, genetic algorithms

Email: windhya.r@sliit.lk

Shalli Rani, R. Maheswar, G. R. Kanagachidambaresan, Sachin Ahuja and Deepali Gupta (eds.) Machine Learning Paradigm for Internet of Things Applications, (27–52) © 2022 Scrivener Publishing LLC

2.1   Introduction

Rice is considered to be one of the most popular crop grains in Southeast Asia [1]. In the context of Sri Lanka, socioeconomic development of the country is directly affected by rice consumption, as it is one of the major items in any Sri Lankan's diet. An accurate understanding, with a prediction mechanism for paddy harvest and rice consuming demand, is crucial, as the fluctuations of paddy crops and rice demand directly affect Sri Lanka's economy, its food security, and citizen's sustainable lifestyle.

In Sri Lanka, rice is cultivated during "Yala" (September to March) and "Maha" (May to August) cropping seasons, but currently, there is no any systematic approach to predict the paddy harvest or demand of the next season [2]. With the help of machine learning approaches, development of such systematic approach is a timely requirement, as it will be useful for many stakeholders of the process: farmers, traders, consumers, and Paddy Marketing Board of Sri Lanka. A single platform with modules: (1) to predict the harvest on next Yala/maha cropping season, (2) to estimate the demand for rice, and (3) to develop an optimized distribution schedule for rice crop yields, will help to keep the sustainability between supply and demand and ensure food security and enhance farmers as well as consumers standards of living [3].

Therefore, this research aims to find most suitable prediction models using suitable machine learning approaches, that describe trends in past paddy harvest and rice consumption data and then implement an optimized crop distribution schedule. We have implemented a centralized online platform: "isRice: Intelligent and Sustainable Approach for Paddy Harvest and Rice Demand", with three main components: (1) predict paddy harvest, (2) predict rice demand, and (3) plan crop distribution considering the end users: farmers, traders, consumers, and Paddy Marketing Board of Sri Lanka.

The annual paddy yields and rice consumption can be seen as a sequence of time series, and therefore, when predicting the seasonal paddy harvest and rice demand, many methods applied in prediction of time series can be considered. Recurrent Neural Network (RNN) is one of these methods and it is used with tasks that have sequential data to capture their time dependencies [4]. RNNs have hidden units (state vector) to keep the history of all past elements sequentially and process input sequence accordingly, one element at a time. RNNs are considered to be powerful models for sequence modeling; however, training process of RNNs is very challenging. Therefore, RNNs are further strengthened by LSTM (Long Short-Term

Memory) cells: a set of repeated neurons that have been designed to perform well in sequence modeling applications [5]. LSTM cells use a special unit (memory cell) for remembering inputs for a long time and for preventing the problem of vanishing gradient. Therefore, two prediction modules of "isRice" platform are developed using RNN and LSTM.

Traditionally, achieving an optimal plan or an optimal schedule is modeled as an optimization of Integer Linear Programming (ILP), but the process suffers from the inherent characteristic as a NP-complete problem. As such, obtaining solutions for limited, small scenarios might take long time [6]. Hence, for dynamic natured optimization problems, the ILP calculation is considered to be unfeasible, although we can expect an exact solution though an ILP formalization of the problem. With the dynamic nature of rice distribution process, use of an approximation approach (heuristic-based approach) would be better, when planning the rice distribution. Therefore, the distribution panning module is developed a heuristic-based optimization approaches: Genetic Programming (GP) [6, 7].

The front-end of the system is implemented in a user-friendly manner, as a combination of an android platform and a web platform. The android application is for consumers, farmers, and rice mill owners. The web platform is for Paddy Market Board and Rice Research and Development Center.

2.2   Background

Rice is one of the major essential food in Asian communities, and therefore, multiple researches have been carried out on paddy harvest as well as rice demand prediction, as well as planning an optimal distribution for rice crop using well-known approaches. Most of these empirical studies are carried out in the Asian context, as rice is most sought-after crop grains in Asian countries.

2.2.1   Prediction of Future Paddy Harvest and Rice Consumption Demand

To maintain a sustainable balance between rice production and demand of a country, it is necessary to implement proper forecasting models to support decision-making processes. Currently, the Government of Sri Lanka is conducting the "the crop cutting survey" to estimate the average yield of paddy in Sri Lanka at the district level, by calculating the means of a sample survey [8]. A sample of 3,000 villagers for the main season "Maha" and 2,000 villagers for the second season "Yala" are considered for this study. This process requires a considerable amount of manpower, resources, and it is time-consuming [8]. Therefore, it is essential to introduce a systematic approach to gather required data and forecast the paddy harvest and rice consumption, so that the supply and demand is well-known in advance.

Several studies have used a machine learning approach to build models to identify these trends on paddy harvest as well as rice demand. The review work of [9] uses machine learning approaches to predict rice crop of India. Their approach used sequential minimal optimization (SMO) as the classifier, adopting the "WEKA" framework for a data set that covers 27 districts in Maharashtra state (India). They have explored a set of parameters: precipitation, min/max/average temperature, crop evaporation, cultivation area, final production, and yield (Kharif season: mid-June to mid-November) from year 1998 to 2002. The authors of [10] have analyzed the trends of paddy harvest of Sri Lanka for past, present, and future and developed a time series model to predict long-term trends (for 3 years). Following their results, the ARIMA (2, 1, 0), was observed as the as the best fitted model to the used data set, with minimum Akaike Information Criterion (AIC) and Bayesian Information Criterion (BIC). The authors of [11] have identified one of the main reasons for paddy industry problems; that is, dissatisfaction of farmers, even with the self-sufficiency because of the increase in average yield and extent of cultivation. They have explored several variables which are important for paddy production: extent sown with distinct water suppliers, percentage of crop failure, crop production, min/max/average harvest, etc., to investigate the causes for major problems in paddy industry and used statistical techniques as well as time series analysis.

As observed over past few years, paddy price fluctuation is a huge problem for socioeconomic development, and therefore, it is very crucial to have an accurate approach for rice demand forecast. This will create a sustainable balance in the rice industry and avoid unexpected price raises, especially during rice scarcities and manage the surpluses effectively. The authors of [12] present a platform for information gathering/management and a decision-making process for paddy production targeting decision-making authorities as well as farmers. They considered parameters that control the rice demand and predicted the price that is to be expected for rice in well advance using a systematic approach: a decision tree following classification model. The authors of [13] have studied rice production and consumption from the viewpoint of supply and demand in each region and used population of each region to approximate the rice consumption using simple and multiple regression curves. A study on [14] analyzed of food consumption patterns in Sri Lanka. They have examined the variation of food consumption patterns and economic parameters determining the demand for the period. The analysis has done using ADIS model. They have relieved that food consumption patterns are moving from starch-foods to non-starched foods and that Sri Lanka consumers are more responsive for price changes in rice.

2.2.2   Rice Distribution

The Genetic Algorithm (GA) approach is a well-established algorithmic approach for planning and scheduling [15–23]. However, there are only a limited set of research works related to harvest distribution that have used GAs. The study [24] uses a GA-based approach to identify cost-effective cropping pattern that maximizes profits for an Indian irrigation development project. They have considered a set of constraints: continuity, land/water requirements, crop diversification, and storage restrictions. Their results show that GA approach provides reasonable solutions fast, compared to traditional linear programming approach. The authors of paper [25] discuss a novel approach for the logistics facilities for rice distribution, which is a problem that can be categorized as a Vehicles Routing Problem. They have implemented a Taboo Search–based algorithm and optimize the process of distribution centers based on GA. They have mainly focused on sugar production industry and milled rice distribution centers of Thailand, specially targeting export. They propose a framework to minimize the cost of sugar and milled rice transports from the mills to a seaport. The research work on [26] has used Linear Programming method for the optimization of rice allocation for the poor in Bandung. Their work shows that the proposed model plans the rice distribution with minimum transportation and warehouse cost. The work on [27] explores the design of logistics network, including rice supplier, onsite warehouse, and customer distribution centers in Indonesia: the province of Sulawesi. A mixed ILP model has been used to adopt the problem, to minimize the procurement, inventory, and transportation costs.

2.3   Methodology

We have implemented a centralized online platform: "isRice: Intelligent and Sustainable Approach for Paddy Harvest and Rice Demand", with three main components: (1) predict future harvest of paddy, (2) predict

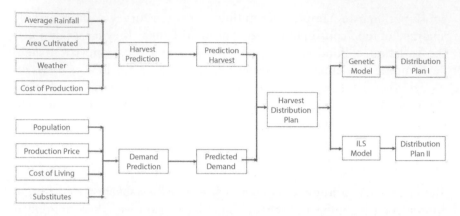

Figure 2.1 System diagram of "isRice".

future demand for rice, and (3) plan crop distribution to maintain a sustainable balance between paddy harvest and demand for rice. Two popular machine learning algorithms: RNN and LSTM have been used to develop the prediction modules. The distribution panning module is developed using a heuristic-based optimization approach, adopting GP. The system diagram of "isRice" is shown in Figure 2.1.

2.3.1   Requirements of the Proposed Platform

As the initial stage of developing "isRice" platform, we decided to study the existing paddy harvest as well as rice related processes/methodologies in the world. We initiated the process for the Sri Lankan context and carried out interviews (physical and over the phone) and questionnaires to gather information. We have used a data set that includes 80 farmers and 30 rice mill owners covering three districts of Sri Lanka (Anuradhapura, Kurunegala, and Matara).

During our study, we focused on identifying the feasibility and requirements of a management platform for paddy harvest and rice related processes. We expected three responses: (1) a system is highly required (required), (2) a system is required but tends to rely on traditional methods for predictions and planning (not critical), and (3) a system is not required (not required). The results are summarized at the Table 2.1.

Summarized statistics shows that 56.7% of farmers agreed that a proper system is required; 32.5% of farmers agreed for the system but did not see it as a crucial requirement; 17.5% farmers disagreed with the system; nearly, 50.0% of the rice millers' owners agreed with the requirement of a system;

Table 2.1 Feasibility study summary.

District	Farmers			Rice mill owners		
	Required	Not crucial	Not required	Required	Not crucial	Not required
Anuradapura	80%	20%	0%	50%	50%	0%
Kurunegala	50%	37.5%	12.5%	66.67%	33.3%	0%
Matara	40%	40%	40%	33.3%	33.3%	33.3%
Total	56.7%	32.5%	17.5%	50%	38.9%	11.1%

and 38.9% did not see it as a crucial requirement and only 11.1% has disagreed with the system.

The statistics proved that the management platform for rice related processes is a timely requirement for both farmers as well as for rice mill owners to keep the sustainability between supply and demand and ensure food security and enhance farmers as well as consumers standards of living.

2.3.2   Data to Evaluate the 'isRice" Platform

For the training as well as evaluation of the platform, we required historical data about paddy and rice related processes, specifically data on paddy harvest and demands. Since it is a challenging task to gather data from entire country, we decided to select few districts in Sri Lanka that represents the paddy harvesting communities of Sri Lanka.

As observed through our survey, "rainfall" was identified as the major parameter that affects the rice production in Sri Lanka. Sri Lanka can be divided into three climate zones: DZ-Dry Zone, IZ-Intermediate Zone, and WZ-Wet Zone, based on the average annual rainfall. Therefore, we conducted the study for three districts: Kurunegala (covering IZ), Anuradhapura (covering DZ), and Matara (covering WZ).

We gathered paddy harvest and demands statistics for the Anuradhapura, Kurunegala, and Matara districts for year 1990 to 2017, from different sources as follows:

- Paddy cultivation statistics (Yala and Maha seasons): Agriculture Department
- Paddy harvest purchasing statistics: Paddy Marketing Board (PMB) and Department of Census and Statistics.
- Producer's prices for paddy: Sri Lanka Central Bank.
- Factors affecting annual paddy harvest: Rice Research and Development Institute.
- Factors actors affecting paddy harvesting practices and purchasing prices in different regions: Regional farming centers.
- Consumer behavior factors affecting distribution and transportation: Rice mills owners.

2.3.3   Implementation of Prediction Modules

The two main prediction modules of "isRice" management platform were developed using RNN and LSTM models.

2.3.3.1 Recurrent Neural Network

The RNN is a widely used field of artificial neural networks. In a RNN, connections between each network unit are established sequentially following directed graphs [4]. RNNs have hidden units (state vector) to keep the history of all past elements sequentially and process input sequence accordingly, one element at a time. Therefore, RNNs have the capability to identify the dynamic temporal behaviors of time sequences. With RNN, each element of the sequence will be allocated to the same task, and each node's output is directly affected by the previous nodes computational value. As RNN utilizes the memory (internal state) to handle the input sequences that are connected, during the training itself, RNN keeps records on relationship of these sequences. Therefore, with the help of these relationship records of all previous inputs, RNN predicts an accurate output. Handwriting recognition, speech recognition, etc., are among the applications that use RNNs to achieve better results.

The structure of RNN is shown in Figure 2.2.

S (a neural network block) takes I_t (the input) and outputs O_t (the output). A loop is used to pass the information passed from step x to step $(x + 1)$. A RNN can be thought as a collection of n copies of the network a, and each network forwards an output to network $a + 1$ which is the successor (as output feedback).

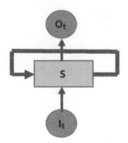

Figure 2.2 Structure of RNN.

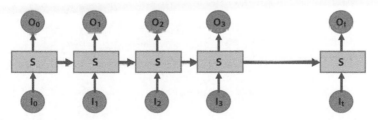

Figure 2.3 Output feedback for RNN.

An unfolded RNN loop is shown in Figure 2.3, where the chain structure detones that RNNs are generally applied as sequences (and lists).

2.3.3.2   Long Short-Term Memory

The LSTM concept was introduced in 1997 by research Hochreiter and Schidhuber, and they are a special class of RNNs which have the capacity to learn long-term dependencies [5]. Generally, RNNs have a chain of neural network modules, which are repeated, and each repeated module has one tanh layer (as shown by Figure 2.4).

Following the same, LSTMs follow the structure of a chain, with a different structure for repeating modules. As for the LSTM network, a module generally comprises of four neural network layers and three gates (as shown in Figure 2.5).

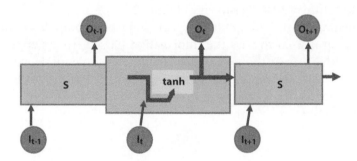

Figure 2.4 Structure of a standard RNN cell.

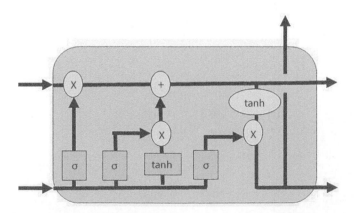

Figure 2.5 Structure of a standard LSTM cell.

The first gate (forget gate) decides on information that should be removed from the cell state. Considering prior cell output (O_{t-1}) and present cell input (I_t), the sigmoid activation layer (σ) is applied for each hidden unit, to get a value between 0 and 1. If the output is a "1", then network will keep the information whicle if the output is "1", network will discard the information.

The next gate (update gate) passes O_{t-1} and I_t (the same input), to two activation layers: sigmoid (σ) and tanh (tanh). An element-wise multiplication is performed to two outputs of the respective layers and the result r is obtained. Finally, an elment wise addition is performed to output of "forget gate" and result r. The new indformation is used to update the state.

The third gate (output gate) has the responsible of deciding on the information that will be forwarded to the following state. The layer n's output, works as the filter that decides the output O_p that is to be passed to the next LSTM cell.

2.3.3.3   Paddy Harvest Prediction Function

The paddy harvest prediction function was developed with an objective to generate the fittest model for the paddy harvest prediction, with high accuracy. The process was initiated be collecting data, including statistics of paddy harvest for two main seasons (yala and maha) for past 12 years, for three main Sri Lankan districts (Anuradhapura, Kurunegala, and Matara).

The collected statistics comprised of year, annual paddy harvest, and parameters effecting paddy harvest (area of the harvest and annual rainfall). We have selected above parameters considering each parameter's co-efficient values, especially considering the scale of changes in the paddy production, when changing the input parameters (every 1 unit).

Table 2.2 summarizes the raw data fields used for the study.

For the initial process of organizing the data set, the year was treated as the index of Pandas which is the most widely used python library in data analysis tasks. "Null" values of the data set were substituted with "0". Next, the fields which are considered to be negligible for the process of prediction (based on the coefficient values) were dropped. The prepared data set is shown in Table 2.3.

The finalized data was used for forecast problem modeling: when the area of paddy cultivation and historical rainfall was given, the system forecasts the future paddy harvest.

Once the data set was finalized, the LSTM was fit to formulate the problem. The data set was prepared for supervised learning approach data set, while input variables were normalized. The harvest prediction was

Table 2.2 Harvest prediction: Raw data fields.

ID	Row number
district	Kurunegala/Anuradhapura/Matara
season	Yala/Maha
year	Corresponding year for data
harvest	Seasonal paddy harvest
cultivation area	Paddy yield area (per district per season)
rainfall	Average rainfall (per crop season)

Table 2.3 Paddy harvest prediction - Data set.

Year	Paddy harvest (Mt)	Cultivated area (ha)	Annual rainfall (mm)
2006	77,260	16,940	60
2007	56,500	11,760	60
2008	170,500	38,790	60
2009	63,280	14,300	50
2010	89,630	18,340	40

formulated into a supervised learning model; when the area of paddy cultivation and historical rainfall was given, the system forecasted the harvest of the current year (t).

The organized data set was split into two: train data component and test data component, to fit a LSTM on to the multi-variate inputs. The train data component and test data component were further split into vectors: "x" input and "y" output. Finally, inputs were reformed as to a 3D format, expected by LSTM, with three dimensions: samples, time steps, and features.

The LSTM was defined as first hidden layer with 50 neurons and output layer with a single neuron for prediction of paddy harvest. The MSE (Mean Absolute Error) was used as the parameter to evaluate the model. The model was fit for 250 training epochs with a batch size of 75. We set the "validation data" argument of the fitness function to observe training as well as test losses during the phase of training. Finally, a combination of the forecast and the test data set was inverted for the scaling. The model's error score was calculated using Root Mean Squared Error (RMSE), using the original scale of forecasts and actual values. Note that the RMSE shows the error value in the similar units of variable.

2.3.3.4   Rice Demand Prediction Function

The rice demand prediction function was developed with an objective to discover the fittest model for the rice demand prediction with high accuracy. The rice demand prediction followed the similar approach (methods and evaluation matrices) as of harvest prediction function.

Table 2.4 summarizes the raw data fields used for the study.

The process of data formatting was same as the paddy harvest predicting function. A final data set sample is given in Table 2.5.

The data set was processed using feature normalization process as input component X and output component Y. The input component X includes annual income, substitute consumptions, and district population, while the output component, Y is the rice consumption. The data set was split into train component (75%) and test component (25%), so that it can be fit

Table 2.4 Demand predict: Raw data fields.

ID	Row number
Year	Corresponding year for data
Annual income	District basis, average per person income
Annual population	Population for each district
Consumption	District basis consumption rates

Table 2.5 Rice demand prediction: Data set.

Year	Population of each district	Income (per person) (Rs)	Substitution consumption (Mt)	Rice consumption (Mt)
1990	14,846	3,549	2.6	95.2
1991	18,728	3,549	2.6	117.5
1992	19,500	3,800	2.2	118.6
1993	19,600	3,540	2.5	119.9

to an LSTM for the multi-variate inputs. The data set was fed into LSTM network using Keras, which was built with 100 initial neurons and a single output node. The batch processing ran for 100 epochs with the batch size of 10.

2.3.4 Implementation of Rice Distribution Planning Module

The main objective of rice distribution planning module was to optimize the paddy harvest distribution considering facts such as supply, demand, transportation cost, and storage cost. We have selected four districts of Sri Lanka (Anuradhapura, Polonnaruwa, Kurunegala, and Mathara) as the main rice supplying districts and Colombo, Gampaha, and Kalutara as three main consuming districts.

Traditionally, achieving an optimal plan or an optimal schedule is modeled as an optimization of ILP, but the process suffers from the inherent characteristic as a NP-complete problem. As such, obtaining solutions for limited, small scenarios might take long time [6]. Hence, for dynamic natured optimization problems, the ILP calculation is considered to be unfeasible, although we can expect an exact solution though an ILP formalization of the problem. With the dynamic nature of rice distribution process, use of an approximation approach (heuristic-based approach) would be better, when planning the rice distribution. Therefore, the distribution panning module is developed a heuristic-based optimization approaches: GP [6, 7].

The rice distribution planning module was formulated as a minimization problem, which tries to minimize profit loss due to surplus, profit loss due to deficit, transportation cost, storage cost, etc. Also, we have utilized constraints considering supply availabilities, storage capacities, preferences of consumer for different rice varieties, etc.

Optimum distribution plan can be derived as the optimization problem given in Equation (2.1):

Minimize:

$$\sum_{i=1}^{N} (S_i + D_i + T_i) \qquad (2.1)$$

Where,

N	Number of consumer districts
S_i	Profit loss due to surplus in district i

D$_i$	Profit loss due to deficit in district i
T$_i$	Total transport cost to deliver rice to district i from supply districts

2.3.4.1   Genetic Algorithm–Based Rice Distribution Planning

GAs are a subset of evolutionary computing algorithms, which were intro-duced as a computational analogy of adaptive systems [6, 7]. They are loosely modeled according to natural evolution principles via selection, while having a population of individuals that face the selection process in the presence of different variations, provoking genetic operators: mutation and crossover. Each individual is evaluated using a fitness function, and reproductive success depends on the fitness.

GAs follows five key steps [6, 7]:

1. Generation of the initial population P(0) with x solutions.
2. Computation of fitness g(p) for every individual solution p in the present population P(t).
3. Generation of the following population P(t+1), by selecting y fittest solutions from P(t).
4. Application of the genetic operators such as mutation/cross-over to population P(t + 1) to produce of offspring.
5. Repetition from Step 2 until a termination condition is satisfied.

As shown in Figure 2.6, a solution (optimal rice distribution plan), which is also known as the chromosome is encoded. The *n* number of chromo-somes: CA1, CA2, CA3, and CA4, constructs the solution pool: population.

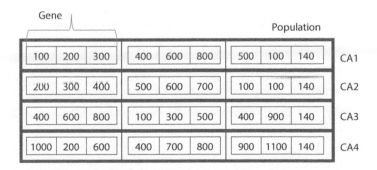

Figure 2.6 Chromosome structure.

In a chromosome, each gene denotes two main informations: (i) gene index number represents the consumer district and (ii) value in the gene indicates the allocated rice harvest from each supply district. The value of the first gene in first chromosome (CA1) is {100, 200, 300}, demonstrating rice units 100, 200, and 300 have been allocated to first consumer district from first, second, and third supply districts, respectively.

Each of the chromosome in the population is assessed according to a derived fitness function: Equation (2.2).

$$Fitness = \sum_{i=1}^{N} (S_i + D_i + T_i) \tag{2.2}$$

We have executed mutation and crossover: two genetic operators that produce offspring. The crossover operator is expected to bring in the population to a local min/max and considered as a convergence operation. The mutation operator is expected to pull off one (or multiple) solutions of a population from a local min/max occasionally and explore an improved space. Therefore, the mutation is considered as a divergence operation. Each ith generation of GA approach follows mutations/crossovers.

In the crossover process, as demonstrated in Figure 2.2, we employed the single-point crossover technique to generate an offspring. Initially, we have selected a random point from two chromosomes (CA1 and CA2) and divide each chromosome into two parts. The offspring (CA3) is then created by copying the first part from chromosome 1, and second part from chromosome 2. As demonstrated in Figure 2.7, gene 7 (100, 200, 300) and 2 (400, 600,800) are copied from chromosome 1 (CA1). The gene 3 (400,

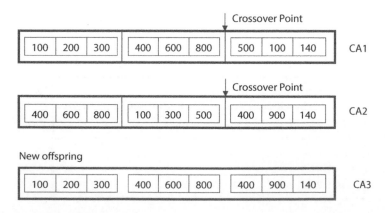

Figure 2.7 One-point crossover.

900, 140) is copied from chromosome 2 (CA2) to generate the offspring (CA3).

As the mutation technique, we have used is the swap method, and it shown in the Figure 2.8. Initially, we have selected two genes from a randomly selected chromosome (CA1). The offspring (CA4) is then created by swapping the values of these two genes. The newly generated offspring (CA4) consists of the swapped genes values.

The freshly generated solutions are assessed according to the derived fitness function. The generation-wise process is repeated until a condition is satisfied: either n generations are executed, or the optimal solution (with the minimum fitness value) is found.

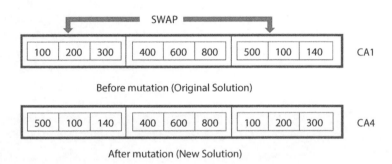

Figure 2.8 Mutation: swap operator.

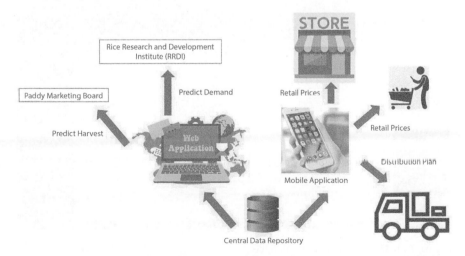

Figure 2.9 Business model of "isRice".

2.3.5   Front-End Implementation

As shown in Figure 2.9, the front-end of the "isRice" system is implemented in a user-friendly manner, as a combination of an android platform and a web platform. The android application is for farmers, rice mill owners and consumers. The web platform is for Paddy Market Board and Rice Research and Development Center.

Figures 2.10 to 2.12 show main interfaces of the "isRice" system.

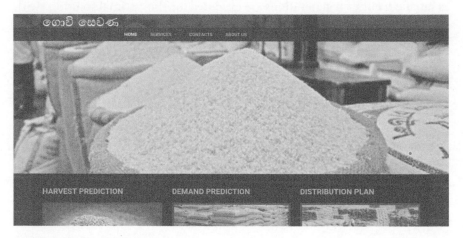

Figure 2.10 "isRice" main interface.

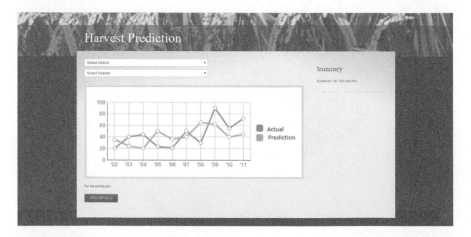

Figure 2.11 Harvest prediction interface.

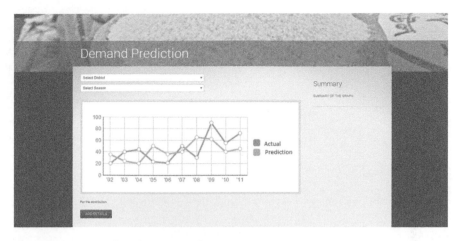

Figure 2.12 Demand prediction interface.

2.4   Results and Discussion

This section will discuss the experiments results that measure the performances of "isRice" platform with three main modules: (1) predict paddy harvest, (2) predict rice demand, and (3) plan crop distribution. The prediction functions were implemented using machine learning approaches: RNNs and LSTM. The optimal planning module was developed using a heuristic-based approach: GAs. The proposed algorithms were assessed with real data sets of Sri Lankan context.

2.4.1   Paddy Harvest Prediction Function

The summary for the paddy harvest predicting function is as follows:

- Harvest prediction LSTM network: 200 iterations.
- Performance evaluation: Mean Squared Error (MSE) and RMSE for both training score as well as test score of the models.
- 78% for train score with MSE = 0.04.
- 75% test score with MSE = 0.11.

The MAE for train set as well as test set for paddy harvest prediction function is shown in Figure 2.13.

Mean Absolute Error

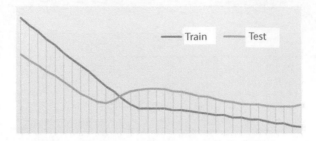

Figure 2.13 MAE for train set and test set: Paddy harvest prediction.

2.4.2   Rice Demand Prediction Function

The summary for rice demand predicting results is as follows:

- Harvest prediction LSTM network: 90 iterations.
- Performance evaluation: MSE and RMSE for both training score as well as test score of the models.
- 79% for train score with MSE = 0.17.
- 74% test score with MSE = 0.37.

The MAE for train set as well as test set for harvest prediction module is shown in Figure 2.14.

2.4.3   Rice Distribution Planning Module

As the evaluation of rice distribution planning module, we are summarizing the GA approach results, which was used to generate an optimal plan

Mean Absolute Error

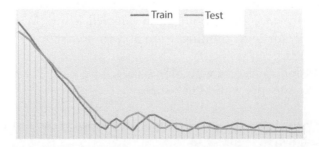

Figure 2.14 MAE for train set and test set: Rice demand prediction.

for rice distribution process. As the genetic operators, single-point cross-over with two-points swapping mutation were used.

The key terms used for our experiments are as follows: *g* (number of generations), **Fbest** (best fitness value calculated over *g* generations), *AVG* (average *Fbest*), *MIN* (minimum *Fbest*), and *STD* (standard deviation of *Fbest*), *Pm* (mutation rate), and *P* (population size).

As explained in previous sections, the genetic operators: mutation and crossover are utilized to enhance the given initial solution, over *n* generations. To observe the improvements granted by genetic operators, we performed 30 experiment rounds, where we started with a set of initial solutions, then enhance them by applying GA steps. Since we formulated our problem as a minimization problem, the fitness value needed to be decreased for the solution to be improved. As demonstrated in Figure 2.15, the majority of the enhancements in the fitness function (decrease of the fitness value) were observed during first 200 generations: very early stages of the process.

To identify how the proposed algorithm scales with the increase in number of consumer districts, experiment rounds were performed. We increased the number of consumer districts, to simulate different scenarios and executed the GA with a population with the size of 20 over 200 of generations. Figure 2.16 demonstrates the computational time for different scenarios, as number of consumer districts increases.

We have evaluated our proposed GA to explore an effective mutation rate, to obtain the optimal solutions fast. We have assumed a population with the size of 20 and number of consumer districts are 3. The algorithm was executed for 200 generations. Mutation probability was kept as 0.15

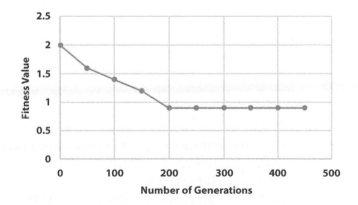

Figure 2.15 Number of generations vs. fitness value.

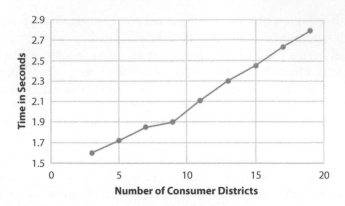

Figure 2.16 Time vs. number of consumer districts.

Table 2.6 Mutation rate effect.

Mutation probability	Mutation rate	Average fitness	Best fitness
0.15	0.002	0.9	0.9
0.15	0.012	0.95	0.9
0.15	0.025	1.15	1
0.15	0.125	1.2	1.1

Table 2.7 Mutation probability effect.

Mutation probability	Mutation rate	Average fitness	Best fitness
0	0.002	1.2	1
0.01	0.002	1.24	1.2
0.1	0.002	0.9	0.9
0.15	0.002	1	0.9
0.25	0.002	1.15	0.9
0.5	0.002	1.22	1

(constant) while the mutation rate was varied. As summarized in Table 2.6, improved solutions are obtained when the mutation rate is low: 0.002: the lowest mutation rate, produced the best fitness value, within a shorter time.

Next, we have evaluated our proposed GA to explore an effective mutation probability, to obtain the optimal solutions fast. We have assumed a population with the size of 20 and 3 consumer districts. The GA is executed for 200 generations. Mutation rate was kept as 0.002 (constant) while the mutation probability was varied. As summarized in Table 2.7, 0.1 mutation probability produced the best average fitness value.

2.5   Conclusion

We have implemented a centralized online platform: "isRice: Intelligent and Sustainable Approach for Paddy Harvest and Rice Demand", with three main components: (1) predict paddy harvest, (2) predict rice demand, and (3) plan crop distribution considering the end users: farmers, traders, consumers, and Paddy Marketing Board of Sri Lanka. We have analyzed numerous factors affecting the crop yield of the next harvesting season and the factors affecting the future demand for rice. Two popular machine learning algorithms: RNN and LSTM have been used to develop the prediction modules. The distribution panning module is developed using a heuristic-based optimization approach, adopting GP. The algorithm performances were evaluated for Sri Lankan context, using real data sets.

According to our observations, the proposed prediction models can produce precise results in a short period of time. Also, the distribution planning module, which was implemented using GA-based approach, is providing optimal distribution plan within few seconds.

As the future work, we are planning to extend our data set and test our system to have more accuracy and fast performances.

References

1. Dhanapala, M., The Wet Zone Rice Culture in Sri Lanka: A Rational Look. *J. Natl. Sci. Found. Sri Lanka*, 33, 4, 277, 2005.
2. Crop forecast, Doa.gov.lk, 2018, Colombo, Sri Lanka, [Online]. Available: https://doa.gov.lk/index.php/en/18-english-news/307-crop-forecast-4. [Accessed: 14- Aug- 2018].
3. Pivoto, D., Waquil, P.D. *et al.*, Scientific development of smart farming technologies and their application in Brazil. *Inf. Process. Agric.*, 5, 1, 31, 2018.
4. Hammer, B., Learning with Recurrent Neural Networks, in: *Lecture Notes in Control and Information Sciences*, Springer, Springer-Verlag London, 2000.
5. Hochreiter, S. and Schmidhuber, J., Long Short-Term Memory. *Neural Comput.*, 9, 8, 1735–1780, 1997.

6. Hartmann, S., A competitive genetic algorithm for resource-constrained project scheduling. *Nav. Res. Logist.*, 45, 7, 733–750, 1998.

7. Mitchell, M., *An Introduction to Genetic Algorithms*, MIT Press, Cambridge, MA, USA, 1998.

8. Crop forecast, Doa.gov.lk, Colombo, Sri Lanka, 2019, [Online]. Available: https://doa.gov.lk/index.php/en/18-english-news/307-crop-forecast-4. [Accessed: 15- September- 2020].

9. Gandhi, N., Armstrong, L. *et al.*, Rice Crop Yield Prediction in India using Support Vector Machines, in: *International Joint Conference on Computer Science and Software Engineering*, Khon Kaen, Thailand, July 2016, pp. 1–5.

10. Sivapathasundaram, V. and Bogahawatte, C., Forecasting of Paddy Production in Sri Lanka: A Time Series Analysis using ARIMA Model. *Trop. Agric. Res.*, 24, 1, 21, 2015.

11. Razmy Mohamed, A. and Ahmed Naseer, A., Trends in paddy production in Sri Lanka, Ir.lib.seu.ac.lk. *J. Manage.*, 3, 1, 20–26, 2005, [Online]. Available: http://ir.lib.seu.ac.lk/123456789/47. [Accessed: 30- Oct- 2018].

12. Ponweera, P. and Premaratne, S., Information and decision support system to enrich paddy cultivation in Sri Lanka, Information Technology Research Unit (ITRU) conference, 2018, [online] Dl.lib.mrt.ac.lk. Available at: http://dl.lib.mrt.ac.lk/handle/123/8438.

13. Kubo, M. and Purevdorj, M., The future of rice production and consumption. *J. Food Distrib. Res.*, 35, 1, 15, 2004.

14. Hearath, R.M., Warnakulasuriya, H.W., Thilakarathne, K.G., Gunawardhana, J.A.T.P., Analysis of food consumption patterns in Sri Lanka with special reference to energy intake. Annual Symposium of Department of Agriculture, Sri Lanka, 2013.

15. Rankothge, W., Ma, J., Le, F., Towards making network function virtualization a cloud computing service. *Proc. IEEE IM*, pp. 89–97, 2015.

16. Rankothge, W., Le, F., Russo, A., Lobo, J., Optimizing Resource Allocation for Virtualized Network Functions in a Cloud Center Using Genetic Algorithms. *Proc. IEEE IM*, pp. 89–97, 2015.

17. Rankothge, W., Le, F., Russo, A., Lobo, J., Experimental results on the use of genetic algorithms for scaling virtualized network functions. *Proc. IEEE SDN/NFV*, pp. 47–53, 2015.

18. Muthusinghe, M.R.S., Palliyaguru, S.T., Weerakkody, W.A.N.D., Hashini Saranga, A.M., Rankothge, W.H., Towards Smart Farming: Accurate Prediction of Paddy Harvest and Rice Demand. *R10-HTC*, 2018.

19. Perera, D., Rathnayaka, C., Dilan, S., Siriweera, L., Rankothge, W.H., Sustainable Tourism: Application of Optimization Algorithms to Schedule Tour Plans. *R10-HTC*, 2018.

20. Jayasuriya, M.C., Galappaththi, K.T., Sampath, D., Experimental Study on an Efficient Dengue Disease Management System: Planning and Optimizing Hospital Staff Allocation. *Int. J. Adv. Comput. Sci. Appl.*, 9, 11, 50–54, 2018.

21. Fernando, W.D.I. and Rankothge, W.H., Optimization of Customer-Friendly Manual Load Shedding System. *ICAC*, 2019.
22. Senarath, S.M.M.M. and Perera, M.T.K., Smart Platform for Film Shooting Management. *CICT*, 2019.
23. Thiranjaya, C., Rushan, R., Udayanga, P., Towards a Smart City: Application of Optimization for a Smart Transportation Management System. *ICIAfS*, 2018.
24. Komaragiri, S.R. and Nagesh Kumar, D., Irrigation Planning using Genetic Algorithms. *Water Resour. Manage.*, 18, 2, 163–176, April 2004.
25. Ekasingh, B. *et al.*, The Development of Competitive Commercial Agriculture in Northeast Thailand. Multiple Cropping Center, Multiple Cropping Center, Faculty of Agriculture, Chiang Mai University, January 2008.
26. Sutarman, and Hidayat, E., Rice distribution planning for "the poor people" in Bandung, in: *Conference Series Materials Science and Engineering*, December 2017.
27. Hanafi, R. *et al.*, Logistics Network Design for Rice Distribution in Sulawesi, Indonesia, in: *Environmental Sustainability in Asian Logistics and Supply Chains*, pp. 45–63, January 2019.

3

A Collaborative Data Publishing Model with Privacy Preservation Using Group-Based Classification and Anonymity

Carmel Mary Belinda M. J.*, K. Antonykumar, S. Ravikumar
and Yogesh R. Kulkarni

*Dept. of Computer Science and Engineering, Vel Tech Rangarajan Dr. Sagunthala
R & D Institute of Science and Technology, Avadi, India*

Abstract

The security of privacy is currently a field of critical importance in data mining. Organizations and corporations in this dynamic environment are constantly trying to somehow get the database of their competitors. A detailed review of such databases can be done to retrieve a variety of confidential and sensitive information, links, connections, inferences, and findings. It can implicitly or explicitly cause a major loss to the database owner. The owners of the database sell their data to third parties for money. If a database is not held until it is revealed to a third party, then the data owner can suffer disasters. We consider the issue of collective publication of data to anonymize horizontally separated data on multiple data providers. The proposed work discusses and contributes to this new challenge of data publishing. First, we introduce the notion of group-based classification, which guarantees that the anonymized data satisfies a given privacy constraint against any group of data providers. We present a collaborative data publishing model with privacy preservation for efficiently checking in a group of records. Privacy preservation can be used to identify abnormal behavior in data sharing. Many privacy-preserving data publishing techniques were developed but failed to consider the data set because of its complexity and domain specific nature. Various organizations release information about persons in public for resource sharing. But maintaining the confidentiality of individual information is a difficult task with various data releases from multiple organizations where coordinating before

Corresponding author: Kulkarni.yr@gmail.com

Shalli Rani, R. Maheswar, G. R. Kanagachidambaresan, Sachin Ahuja and Deepali Gupta (eds.) Machine Learning Paradigm for Internet of Things Applications, (53–66) © 2022 Scrivener Publishing LLC

data publication. The proposed model is compared with traditional models and the results depicts that proposed model exhibits better performance.

Keywords: Data publishing, privacy preservation, classification, anonymity, optimization, data mining

3.1   Introduction

The data publisher is a person in charge of applying PPDM techniques to privacy databases. It should be a trusted individual to publish data. Data publisher must be familiar with sensitive knowledge and rules in advance [2]. It is evaluated at the publisher's end from all angles before it opens a database for mining purposes to various data users/miners. Data publisher is responsible for the publication of data to allow others to use it easily [11]. Data publishers change their databases to keep confidential information unrevealed to miners. Publisher must spend considerable time building or restructuring the database before sending it to miners/users [17]. The database is not revealed in the original database. All preventive measures should be taken to avoid the leakage of sensitive information prior to publishing the miner's database. Publisher analyzes the whole database and tries to hide from the database all of the sensitive information, patterns, and inferences. Two types of privacy, personal privacy and collective privacy, are of major concern [13].

Individuals or the organizations may produce data which is collected through various sources for analysis in repository [19]. Data owner may release the collected data to public for analysis or research purposes with good intention. If some intruders access this data, then it may be combined with some external data which is available publicly to get the personal information. To solve this, the data owner releases masked data in such a way to maintain the confidentiality of individuals and data utility [16]. Even this masked data may be linked with external data to disclose confidential information about the individual [18]. The data collection and publishing model is depicted in Figure 3.1.

On the off chance that authority needs to distribute gathered information either freely or to the diggers for information investigation reason without revealing the private subtleties of the delicate information [24]. In such cases, conservation of security might be achieved by anonymizing the records prior to delivering [21]. Security preserving data mining at information distributing is named as privacy preserving data publishing (PPDP). It has been seen that straightforwardly eliminating ascribes that expressly perceive clients is not ordered as compelling measure [12]. Miners can actually

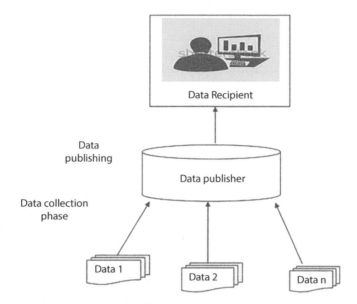

Figure 3.1 Data collection and publishing model.

perceive by utilizing and delicate traits and semi-identifiers (QIDs). QID is a non-touchy property or a bunch of traits that do not straightforwardly recognize a client, however when it contrasted or joined and information from different sources to unveil the mystery of a record, distinguished as linkage assaults. In an information base, anonymization of records can be carried out by utilizing diverse security models [20]. These models are useful to make secret the character of record's proprietor by apply one, or a combination of information disinfecting strategies is utilized.

Data containing personal data from distributed databases are increasingly needed for sharing. In the healthcare field, for example, there is also a national agenda in developing the National Health Information Network (NHIN) 1 for the sharing of health information with hospitals and other providers [29]. Data analysis protection and publication have, in recent years, received considerable attention as promising approaches to data sharing while safeguarding the personal privacy [10]. The data provider, for example, in a hospital, publishes in a non-interactive model a sanitized "version of the data", at the time, providing data users with usefulness (for example, researchers) and the protection of data privacy (for example, patients) for individuals represented in the data [23].

Huge information is a moving exploration documented these days because of the advancement of web and computerized climate [28]. Zeroing-in on issues identified with enormous information, treatment of the huge data set has been simplified by distributed computing [25]. The cloud climate helps 1,000,000 clients everywhere on the world to store, oversee, and recover data. One of the significant difficulties engaged with information distributing is protection. Applications, like clinics, bank, government records, and interpersonal interaction destinations do not wish to unveil the data content [30]. Consequently, these applications utilize the choice emotionally supportive network and, in this way, dealt with large information productively. For building the choice help, enormous information should be gathered from the Information Providers (IPs) [22]. Since the information associated with preparing is high, getting the security of every information is troublesome. Prior to pronouncing the information to be public, it is important to conceal the delicate data substance, and this can be alluded to as PPDP. A few works have contributed toward the PPDP, despite the fact that the harmony among security and utility is not accomplished [26].

Information proprietor should utilize great security model and encryption procedures for keeping unique data set secure. In any case, there are a few cases wherein information proprietors need to offer their data sets to others for bringing in cash through it [6]. All things considered they should recruit an information distributer to make changes in the current data set, with the goal that private data in the first data set remaining parts concealed to the information client/excavator. Information publisher ought to be a trustable individual in light of the fact that toward the finish of examination measure information distributer has a deep understanding of the subtleties of the data set, essential data, and productive outcomes broke down from the data set. Digger/client gets some information about data set to the information proprietor or distributer for examination reason, then, at that point, distributer ought to be sufficiently shrewd to take choices in this matter. Prior to trading, data set to the excavator delicate data ought to be ensured. Distributer needs to invest abundant measure of energy to plan or remake the data set prior to sending it to excavator/client. So, most delicate data and deductions drawn from unique data set remaining parts protected after conveyance of data sets to different diggers. Measure of protection conservation relies upon the sort of data sets and level of affectability of the data contained in the first information base [14]. PPDM techniques ought to guarantee a guaranteed level of protection while amplifying the utility of the data set to take into account proficient information mining.

3.2   Literature Survey

Yang, K *et al.* [1] examined about information order in which information is partitioned into delicate and non-touchy items. Non-sensitive items are those which are prepared to move to the beneficiary with no security saving. Delicate items are those which require protection safeguarding. Different procedures like ordinary mode and touchy mode are talked about. In critical cases assuming delicate data is required, access system and the mode are changed from typical to touchy in which touchy data is likewise accessible.

Jyothi, M et al. [3] explored different spaces of security safeguarding information mining information mining and calculations. Techniques are talked about for conveyed security safeguarding digging and for on a level plane and in an upward direction parceled information. Issue of debasing the viability of the procedures identified with information mining is likewise examined. The paper likewise discusses number of various applications in which protection safeguarding information mining could assume a significant part. An introductory part on the techniques to preserve privacy such as suppression, randomization, summarization, and cryptography is focused. It also discusses the maintenance of data quality while using techniques for protecting privacy. Application fields for privacy protection are also discussed. A case in which two parties had confidential databases was discussed by Ilavarasi, A.K. et al. [4]. If the both parties decide to run a data mining algorithm on their databases, then the database of both parties will be merged, with no secret information disclosed. The work is to safeguard and distribute confidential information for mining purposes on both sides. For secure multi-party calculation, the requirement for a more efficient protocol was necessary.

J. Zhang et al. [5] addressed data mining related privacy issues in broad way. Author also pointed out different approaches that can facilitate to protect sensitive information. It also introduced about four different types of users concerned to area of data mining applications. These are data provider, data collector, data miner, and decision maker. Privacy concerns related to each type of user and the methods that can be used to protect sensitive information at each user level are also discussed. Liabilities of different users are assigned with respect to security of sensitive information.

Huang Xuezhen et al. [8] studied several techniques available for PPDP. An algorithm has been proposed in this paper which focuses on the privacy preservation of anonymous database. This algorithm after preserving the individual privacy does the classification of the data into some prespecified categories and also checks the classification efficiency. Purpose of the proposed algorithm is to preserve the privacy in such a way after doing reconstruction of the anonymous database, it will not lost its fruitfulness and can be used by the receiver to draw conclusions from it and do classifications on that database.

A new collaborative framework is designed by Lei Xu *et al.* [9] using vertically partitioned cooccurrence matrices in fuzzy co-cluster structure estimation. In collaborative framework, the cooccurrence information between the objects and the items are stored in many sites. For the distributed data sets, exclusive of information leaks, a privacy preserving procedure is designed in fuzzy clustering for categorical multivariate data (FCCM). A large integer data set shared vertically with two parties [7]. The secured computing divides kth and (k + 1)th while collecting the additional information.

3.3   Proposed Model

Hiding of the sensitive items and rules provides the data publishing in private manner without any restrictions and loss of accuracy. But, algorithm takes large amount of time for optimal hiding. Optimization techniques used to hide the sensitive item sets and for minimizing the side effects while publishing the sensitive items and rules. Optimization preserves the high confidential privacy rules for enhancing the privacy rate of sensitive rules. Optimization technique determines the maximum number of transactions deleted for hiding the sensitive item sets. Though, the privacy preserving accuracy remained unaddressed. Data perturbation–based techniques are used to provide the higher privacy accuracy when hiding the sensitive items and rules. The ensuring of sensitive information and rules for data publishing was not considered. The general problem is that the data publishing complexity arises on hiding the highly confidential data.

The data privacy preservation uses the significant interests in data mining techniques. Data publishing in PPDM suggests a new threats and challenges to the individual privacy and organizational confidentiality. Security is a serious problem while hiding the sensitive rules in data publishing. Several protocols are designed to provide the secure rule hiding for improving the privacy preservation accuracy. Secure mining is a key technique for hiding sensitive rules in order to realize the privacy protection in the data publishing environment. Though, the mining technique provides higher computational costs and logarithmic communication overhead when encryption takes place [27]. Efficient encryption approach is designed to support the sensitive data hiding process. The resultant hiding data is unclear in the encryption model.

Let T = {t1, t2, ...} be a set of records with the same attributes gathered from n data providers P = {P1, P2, ..., Pn}, such that Ti ⊆ T are records provided by Pi. Let AS be a sensitive attribute with a domain DS. If the records contain multiple sensitive attributes then, we treat each of them as the sole sensitive attribute, while remaining ones we include to the quasi-identifier. However, for our scenarios, we use an approach, which preserves more utility without sacrificing privacy [15]. Let D be the micro data table to be published, which contains n number of attributes, the attributes are represented as follows:

A tuple t $\in$ D that is represented as t = (t[a1], t[a2], ..., t[an]) where t[ai] is the ai value of t.

$$A = \{a1, a2, ..., an\} \tag{3.1}$$

The value of each attribute is considered for correlation measurement. A tuple is represented as where is the value of t. Initially, a number of attributes are extracted from the micro data table D. The value of each attribute is selected for correlation measurement. Pearson's correlation coefficient is broadly used for evaluating correlation between two continuous attributes.

The formula for Pearson's correlation coefficient (r) is mathematically expressed as follows:

$$r(x, y) = \frac{\sum_{i=1}^{n}(x_i - \bar{x})(y_i - \bar{y})}{\sqrt{\sum_{i=1}^{n}(x_i - \bar{x})^2}\sqrt{\sum_{i=1}^{n}(y_i - \bar{y})^2}} \tag{3.2}$$

The privacy fitness score is defined as the minimum fitness score of privacy constraints. In our example, $score_{FC}$ is defined as follows:

$$score_{FC}(T^*) = \min\left\{\frac{|T^*|}{k}, \frac{|\{t[A_S]: t \in T^*\}|}{l}\right\} \tag{3.3}$$

Minimum distance between s_i points and s_j centroids is not always same as the distance between s_j points and s_i centroids. Thus, distance between s_i and s_j is computed using mean of these two values:

$$d_{ij} = d_{ji} - \frac{1}{2}\left[\frac{min(D_i.j)}{j} + \frac{min(D_j.i)}{i}\right] \tag{3.4}$$

where $D_{i:j}$ is the jth column of D_i and $D_{j:i}$ is ith column of D_j.

Calculate the weight function of every data owner based on the resources allotted and the task to be completed. The weights are calculated as follows:

$$W(CU_i) = \frac{\sum_{U=1}^{N} K + DO(D,i) + E(Do) + L(Do)}{S(CU) + L} \qquad (3.5)$$

The data transferred by every node is calculated as follows:

$$DT = \frac{\sum_{u=1}^{N} Tot(DP) - Tr(DP)}{\sigma n} * 100 \qquad (3.6)$$

Here, Tot is the total data packets, and Tr is the transmitted data packets. σn is the total data packets count transferred by the neighboring nodes in an organization.

The logarithmic functions are calculated for reducing the iterations done on the record set of a data set for providing security before publishing. It is calculated as follows:

$$log_r(Ni) \approx log\ \lambda\left(Ri + (DT)\right) + \sum_{i=1}^{k} Wi - N\,\lambda(Ri) \qquad (3.7)$$

The similar records are identified and grouped as a cluster with minimum iterations and is calculated as follows:

$$sim(Ri, Ri+1) = \frac{Ri.N}{||W|| * ||R||} \qquad (3.8)$$

In an iterative setting, the "output" of the algorithm is not merely necessary but includes all intermediate results generated and exchanged during the optimization process. Check the data transmitted and data received levels and perform the calculations based on trust factor Tf as

if $(T_F < \beta)$ where β is the Threshold Trust factor.

Data loss is calculated as follows:

$$DL(N) = log\left(\frac{\lambda n + T(i)}{\sum_{u=1}^{N} \lambda i * Tot(DP)}\right) \qquad (3.9)$$

The similarity of the data that is gathered and published is calculated as follows:

$$sim(D, D', S) = sin(\theta) = \frac{DP.sim(Ri, Ri+1)}{||DL|| * ||Tf||} \qquad (3.10)$$

The data publishing rate is calculated as follows:

$$\lambda_{n(x,y)} = T_n \times \sqrt{\frac{\sigma\left(NT_{n'(x,y)}^1\right)}{\sigma\left(I_{n(x,y)}^1\right)}} \times T_{n(x,y)} \qquad (3.11)$$

$$\mu_n = \max\left(\frac{\sigma\left(NT_n^1\right)}{\sigma(I^1)}, \frac{\sigma(I^1)}{\sigma\left(NT_n^1\right)}\right), \qquad (3.12)$$

3.4   Results

The proposed model is implemented in python using ANACONDA. The training and testing data sets are merged from the adult data set considered. Records with missing values have been removed. All remaining 45,222 records have been randomly distributed among n providers. As a sensitive attribute AS, we chose occupation with 14 distinct values. The comparison of classification accuracy of proposed model over dLink model and other methods is depicted in Table 3.1.

The classification accuracy of the proposed model is depicted with the traditional models and the accuracy of the proposed model is high when compared to traditional models. Figure 3.2 depicts the accuracy levels of the proposed and traditional models.

The comparison of the privacy preservation rate is depicted in Figure 3.3. The privacy preservation rate of the proposed model is high when compared to traditional methods.

The data publishing security level of the proposed model is depicted in Figure 3.4. The security level for the data publishing is more in the proposed model when compared to traditional models.

Although the data publishing methods eliminate the discovering information like name, disease, and salary but other attributes like gender, age, and zip code are associated to recognize the individual and confidential information. The large amount of data is obtainable, and it is possible to determine more information about individuals from public data.

Table 3.1 Classification accuracy.

| Data set record size | Classification accuracy levels (%) | | | | | | | |
| | Adult data set | | | Spain census data set | | | |
	Proposed model	Dlink model	t-closeness		Proposed model	Dlink model	t-closeness
10,000	89	78	67		86	75	65
20,000	91	79	69		86	76	66
30,000	91.5	82	73		88	78	67.5
40,000	93	81	75		89.5	79.5	69
50,000	95	84	79		91	82	71.5

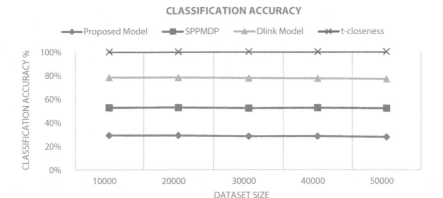

Figure 3.2 Classification accuracy.

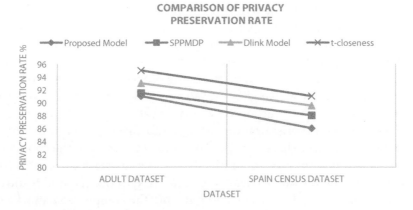

Figure 3.3 Comparison of privacy preservation rate.

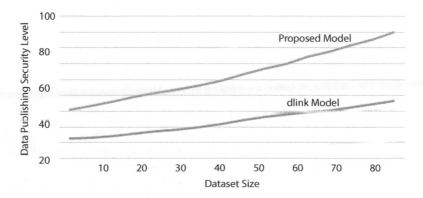

Figure 3.4 Data publishing security level.

Hence, people are aware of the privacy interruptions on their personal data and are very reluctant to distribute their sensitive information. In addition, various organizations release the information about persons in public for resource sharing. But the confidential information of an individual may be compromising with the various data releases.

3.5 Conclusion

Privacy-preserving data publishing is a method for preserving the privacy and utility and preventing the attack during data transmission and publication. The objective of the privacy is discussed as sharing of information in a controlled way. It is an efficient method to distribute anonymous data and ensure privacy against identity disclosure rate of an individual. Securing the privacy of the data in an organization by developing the optimization-driven anonymization is developed in this work. The proposed model introduces a group-based classification for performing classification and also for privacy preservation. The proposed anonymization scheme developed the anonymization database by choosing the optimal values for the anonymization. Based on the fitness, the proposed model develops the anonymized database with high utility and privacy. Experimentation of the proposed model with the group-based classification is done by evaluating the database. Several organizations release information about individuals in public for resource sharing as per law of the country. But the confidential information of an individual may be affected by several composition attacks through the various releases of data. An effective method is introduced for improving the privacy and reducing the composition attacks in data sharing. The sensitive attributes are sorted to measure the distance between the sensitive values for reducing the information loss.

References

1. Yang, K., Zhang, K., Jia, X., Hasan, M.A., Shen, X.S., Privacy Preserving Attribute-Keyword Based Data Publish-Subscribe Service on Cloud Platforms. *Inf. Sci.*, 387, 116–131, 2017.
2. Hua, J., Tang, A., Pan, Q., Choo, K.K.R., Ding, H., Ren, Y., Practical–Anonymization for Collaborative Data Publishing Without Trusted Third Party. *Secur. Commun. Netw.*, 2017, 9532163, 10, 2017.
3. Jyothi, M. and Rao, M.C.S., Preserving the Privacy of Sensitive Data Using Data Anonymization. *Int. J. Appl. Eng. Res.*, 12, 8, 1639–1663, 2017.

4. Ilavarasi, A.K. and Sathiyabhama, B., An Evolutionary Feature Set Decomposition Based Anonymization for Classification Workloads: Privacy Preserving Data Mining. *Cluster Comput.*, 20, 4, 3515–3525, 2017.

5. Zhang, J. *et al.*, On Efficient and Robust Anonymization for Privacy Protection on Massive Streaming Categorical Information. *IEEE Trans. Dependable Secure Comput.*, 14, 5, 507–520, Sept.-Oct. 1, 2017.

6. Wu, X., Zhu, X., Wu, G.Q., Ding, W., Data Mining With Big Data. *IEEE Trans. Knowl. Data Eng.*, 26, 1, 97–107, 2014.

7. Yang, J., Liu, Z., Jia, C., Lin, K., Cheng, Z., New Data Publishing Framework in the Big Data Environments, in: *Proceedings of IEEE International Conference on P2P, Parallel, Grid, Cloud, and Internet Computing*, pp. 363–366, 2014.

8. Xuezhen, H., Jiqiang, L., Zhen, H., Jun, Y., A New Anonymity Model for Privacy-Preserving Data Publishing, in: *Communications System Design*, pp. 47–59, 2014.

9. Xu, L., Jiang, C., Wang, J., Yuan, J., Ren, Y., Information Security in Big Data: Privacy and Data Mining. *IEEE Access*, 2, 1149–1176, 2014.

10. Xu, Y., Ma, T., Tang, M., Tian, W., A Survey of Privacy Preserving Data Publishing Using Generalization and Suppression. *Int. J. Appl. Math. Inf. Sci.*, 8, 3, 1103–1116, 2014.

11. Fung, B., Wang, K., Chen, R., Yu, P., Privacy-Preserving Data Publishing: A Survey of Recent Developments. *ACM Comput. Surv.*, 42, 1–53, 2010.

12. Liu, P. and Li, X., An Improved Privacy Preserving Algorithm for Publishing Social Network Data, in: *Proceedings of International Conference on High-Performance Computing and Communications & Embedded and Ubiquitous Computing*, IEEE Computer Society, pp. 888–895, 2013.

13. Tang, J., Cui, Y., Li, Q., Ren, K., Liu, J., Buyya, R., Ensuring Security and Privacy Preservation for Cloud Data Services. *ACM Comput. Surv.*, 49, 1, 13.1–13.39, 2016.

14. Zakerzadeh, H., Aggarwal, C.C., Barker, K., Privacy-Preserving Big Data Publishing, in: *Proceedings of the 27th International Conference on Scientific and Statistical Database Management*, ACM, p. 26, 2015.

15. Martin, K., Wang, W., Agyemang, B., Efran: Efficient Scalar Homomorphic Scheme on MapReduce for Data Privacy Preserving, in: *Proceedings of IEEE International Conference on Cyber Security and Cloud Computing*, ACM, pp. 66–74, 2016.

16. Fung, B.C.M., Wang, K., Yu, P.S., Anonymizing Classification Data for Privacy Preservation. *IEEE Trans. Knowl. Data Eng.*, 19, 5, 711–725, May 2007.

17. Xiao, X. and Tao, Y., Anatomy: Simple and Effective Privacy Preservation, in: *Proc. of 32nd Int'l Conf. Very Large Data Bases (VLDB '06)*, pp. 139–150, 2006.

18. Goswami, P. and Madan, S., Privacy Preserving Data Publishing and Data Anonymization Techniques: A Review, in: *Proceedings of IEEE International*

Conference on Computing, communication and Automation, pp. 139–142, 2017.

19. Allard, T., Nguyen, B., Pucheral, P., METAP: Revisiting Privacy Preserving data Publishing Using Secure Devices. *Distrib. Parallel Database*, 32, 2, 191–244, 2014.

20. Jaina, I., Jain, V.K., Jain, R., Correlation Feature Selection Based Improved-Binary Particle Swarm Optimization for Gene Selection and Cancer Classification. *Appl. Soft Comput.*, 62, 203–215, 2018.

21. Sabin Begum, R. and Sugumar, R., Novel Entropy-Based Approach for Cost-Effective Privacy Preservation of Intermediate Datasets in Cloud. *Clust. Comput.*, 22, 9581–9588, 2017, https://doi.org/10.1007/s10586- 017-1238-0.

22. Komninos, N. and Junejo, A.K., Privacy Preserving Attribute-Based Encryption for Multiple Cloud Collaborative Environment, in: *Proceedings of IEEE/ACM 8th International Conference on Utility and Cloud Computing*, pp. 595–600, 2015.

23. Fahad, A., Tari, Z., Almalawi, A., Goscinski, A., PPFSCADA: Privacy Pre-Serving Framework for SCADA Data Publishing. *Future Gener. Comput. Syst.*, 37, 496–511, 2014.

24. Wang, H., Privacy-Preserving Data Sharing in Cloud Computing. *J. Comput. Sci. Technol.*, 25, 3, 401–414, 2010.

25. Dwork, C., Differential Privacy: A Survey of Results, in: *Proc. of the 5th Intl. Conf. on Theory and Applications of Models of Computation*, pp. 1–19, 2008.

26. Fung, B.C.M., Wang, K., Chen, R., Yu, P.S., Privacy-Preserving Data Publishing: A Survey of Recent Developments. *ACM Comput. Surv.*, 42, 14:1–14:53, June 2010.

27. Dwork, C., A Firm Foundation for Private Data Analysis. *Commun. ACM*, 54, 86–95, January 2011.

28. Mohammed, N., Fung, B.C.M., Hung, P.C.K., Lee, C., Centralized and Distributed Anonymization for High-Dimensional Healthcare Data. *ACM Trans. Knowl. Discovery Data*, 4, 4, 18:1–18:33, October 2010.

29. Jiang, W. and Clifton, C., Privacy-Preserving Distributed k-anonymity, in: *DBSec*, vol. 3654, pp. 924–924, 2005.

30. Jiang, W. and Clifton, C., A Secure Distributed Framework for Achieving k-anonymity. *VLDB J.*, 15, 4, 316–333, 2006.

4

Production Monitoring and Dashboard Design for Industry 4.0 Using Single-Board Computer (SBC)

Dineshbabu V.[1]*, Arul Kumar V. P.[1]† and Gowtham M. S.[2]‡

[1]Department of Information Technology, Karpagam Institute of Technology, Coimbatore, India
[2]Department of Electronics and Communication Engineering, Karpagam Institute of Technology, Coimbatore, India

Abstract

Industry 4.0 standard is presently enabled in all industrial sectors to enhance its production activity and to understand the nature of the machine health and to take better prognostics. The transformation of Industry 3.0 to 4.0 is critical due to old aged machinery and other security issues in the transformation. The single-board computers (SBCs) in the present market are capable to deliver the requested content from industrial machines and capable to satisfy the client requirement to switch over to Industry 4.0. This chapter envisages the dashboard design and monitoring of industry production activity with SBCs. This also discusses on architecture and role of machine intelligence in monitoring such events. A Raspberry Pi–based production monitoring system is designed with ultrasonic sensors, camera to catch up the event, and RFID to monitor the production activity. The artificial intelligence–based algorithm is incorporated to identify the faulty production orders in the lane. The computational complexity of the same is analyzed in this paper.

Keywords: Industry 4.0, single-board computers, image processing, system complexity

*Corresponding author: dineshbabukit@gmail.com
†Corresponding author: arulkumarssk@gmail.com
‡Corresponding author: msgowtham05@gmail.com

Shalli Rani, R. Maheswar, G. R. Kanagachidambaresan, Sachin Ahuja and Deepali Gupta (eds.) *Machine Learning Paradigm for Internet of Things Applications,* (67–74) © 2022 Scrivener Publishing LLC

4.1   Introduction

Digital twin design and technology is the most important strategic trends in the modern Industry 4.0 standards. This methodology helps in better understanding the machinery and meeting industrial expectation. The digital twin technology provides better prognostics and care to the machines [1–4]. The virtual/digital representation of the physical industrial machines and process makes the engineers and researchers to easily predict the performance efficiency and characteristics. This methodology of monitoring, i.e., digital representations, is represented throughout the product lifecycle for simulation purposes. This approach capable to demonstrate and mimic the design changes, scenario on usage, and other environmental conditions. This also reduces the approach on reducing the development time and aids in increasing the quality of finalized products. Important developments in Internet of Things (IoT), data science, and artificial intelligence have made the possibility to propose new standards in manufacturing strategies [5–9]. The common objective of this Industry 4.0 digital twin modeling is to increase the productivity and enhance the lifetime of the machine with high production quality. The reach of smart

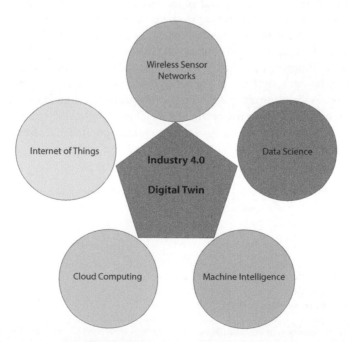

Figure 4.1 Domain technologies aiding Industry 4.0.

interconnection and operability in physical and digital space creates more challenges in interfacing monitoring. Figure 4.1 illustrates the technologies aiding Industry 4.0 modeling opportunities.

Security, reliability, and fault tolerant are the most expected features in Industry 4.0 for better operation and production [10–13].

4.2   Related Works

Numerous researches on digital twin and smart factories manufacturing have come in recent days. The existing IDS are well suited in real time, and deployment in virtual domain creates more complexities. The challenges in security of IDS are defined in [6], in which light weight cryptography algorithms are mainly focused. The state machine replication through stochastic mathematical approach is described in detail in [14–16]. The assumption on fault-based state machine realization in many approaches. The article explains the important objective of digital design as health analysis and lifetime monitoring of equipment. Penetration-based testing is also done in [17–19] through Industry 4.0 which is more challenging in nature. The approach on state synchronization with IoT security was suggested in article [15]. This mainly covers only modeling and does not address the complete digital twin security frameworks. An autonomous ML and PLC middle attack was deeply discussed in article [17]. The input physical parameters are considered in passive replication problem modeling and purely based on physical world parameters.

4.3   Industry 4.0 Production and Dashboard Design

Remote production monitoring is the request from many of the production companies to the IoT engineers. The industrial expectation on IoT is really high and expects remote monitoring through intranet and secure data communication. This design is done through economical single-board computer (SBC) along with the node java scripting. The sensors used for monitoring is ultrasonic or laser-based light-depended resistors. The sensors used in the industries are normally 12 or 24 volts. A voltage divider circuit is designed to convert the sensor value as per the SBC power constraint. The AMS1117 IC in the board avoids increasing voltage and spikes due to industrial actions and safeguards the SBC. The SBCs are interfaced with the wireless network or existing wired infrastructure throughout the industries, so that the workers can able to see the production outcome

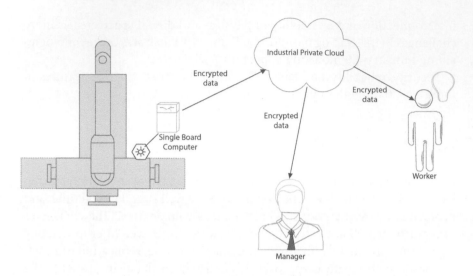

Figure 4.2 Industrial production monitoring system through IIoT.

anywhere within the industries. This happens with the secret key sharing and authentication mechanism. The data is secured through encryption algorithm. Figure 4.2 illustrates the proposed system architecture; key sharing is done through authenticated channel.

Algorithm

Begin Process
Input from PLC controller is recorded in single-board computer;
Share data to the industrial Cloud;
Once authentication is received share data to the concerned worker
Data security through elliptic curve cryptography
End Process

4.4 Results and Discussion

The digital twin creation setup for a battery production monitoring system is created through the proposed architecture. Raspberry Pi–based SBC is used for monitoring the production process and the same is interfaced with the industrial internet. Figure 4.3 illustrates the battery production unit with anode-cathode plate's assembly. The anode and cathode plates are assembled and moved for welding zones.

Figure 4.3 Production unit in industries.

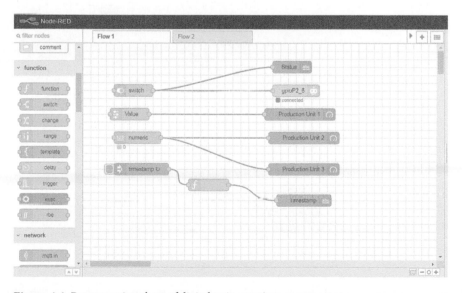

Figure 4.4 Programming chart of digital twin creation.

The production monitoring dashboard design is done through Node. js scripting language in SBC. The SBC is connected with the network and can able to deploy remote GPIO and programming logic through network programming methodology. The production is verified and the status is updated within microsecond delay to the cloud environment. Figure 4.4

Figure 4.5 Digital twin design of production monitoring unit.

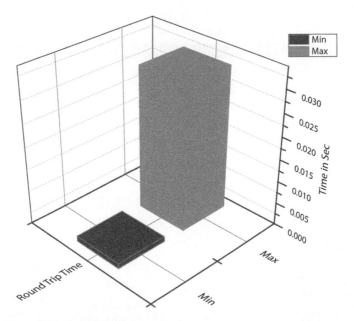

Figure 4.6 Network round trip delay time.

illustrates the digital twin creation using Node.js with gauge and dashboard design.

Figure 4.5 illustrates the application interface both monitor and android-based application design.

Figure 4.6 illustrates the minimum and maximum delay time to update the data in private cloud. The delay caused is due to various network traffic conditions inside the network.

4.5   Conclusion

A digital twin design is modeled through IoT SBCs. A battery manufacturing process is mimicked in thispaper. The data is also routed to the private cloud through securechannel. The sensor production to PLC circuitis tapped and programming is done to monitor the working of PLC logic. The time delay in uploading the data in the cloud is also calculated in this approach. The model is efficient and can be interfaced with any Industrial PLC circuits.

References

1. Tao, F., Zhang, L., Hu, Y.F., Resource service optimal-allocation system in MGrid, in: *Resource Service Management in Manufacturing Grid System*, pp. 27–41, Wiley, Hoboken, NJ, USA, 2012.
2. Kanagachidambaresan, G.R., Anand, R., Balasubramanian, E., Mahima, V., *Internet of Things for Industry 4.0*, EAI Springer, India, 10.1007/978-3-030-32530-5, 2020.
3. Tao, F., Zhang, L., Venkatesh, V.C., Luo, Y.L., Cheng, Y., Cloudmanufacturing: A computing and service-oriented manufacturing model. *Inst. Mech. Eng., B, J. Eng. Manuf.*, 225, 10, 1969–1976, Aug. 2011.
4. Tao, F., Lai, Y., Li, L., Xu, Zhang, L., FC-PACO-RM: A parallel methodfor service composition optimal-selection in cloud manufacturing system. *IEEE Trans. Industr. Inform.*, 9, 4, 2023–2033, Nov. 2013.
5. Tao, F., Zhang, M., Cheng, J., Digital twin workshop: A new paradigm for future workshop. *Comput. Integr. Manuf. Syst.*, 23, 1, 1–9, 2017.
6. Monostori, L., Cyber-physical production systems: Roots, expectations and R&D challenges. *Proc. CIRP*, 17, 9–13, Jan. 2014.
7. Mourtzis, D., Vlachou, E., Milas, N., Xanthopoulos, N., A cloud-basedapproach for maintenance of machine tools and equipment based on shopfloor monitoring. *Proc. CIRP*, 41, 655–660, Jan. 2016.

8. Zhu, H.H., Gao, J., Li, D.B., Tang, D.B., A Web-based product servicesystem for aerospace maintenance, repair and overhaul services. *Comput. Ind.*, 63, 4, 338–348, May 2012.

9. Hu, T.L., Li, P., Zhang, C.R., Liu, R.L., Design and application ofa real-time industrial Ethernet protocol under Linux using RTAI. *Int. J. Comput. Integr. Manuf.*, 26, 5, 429–439, 2013.

10. Regulin, D., Glaese, A., Feldmann, S., Vogel-Heuser, B., Enablingflexible automation system hardware: Dynamic reconfiguration of a realtime capable field-bus, in: *Proc. 13th Int. Conf. Ind. Informat.*, Cambridge, U.K., pp. 1198–1205, 2015.

11. Felser, M., Real time ethernet: Standardization and implementations, in: *Proc. IEEE Int. Symp. Ind. Electron.*, Bari, Italy, Sep. 2010, pp. 3766–3771.

12. Cena, G., Bertolotti, I.C., Hu, T., Valenzano, A., Seamless integration of CAN in intranets. *Comput. Stand. Interfaces*, 46, 1–14, May 2016.

13. Sauter, T. and Lobashov, M., How to access factory floor information using Internet technologies and gateways. *IEEE Trans. Industr. Inform.*, 7, 4, 671–699, Nov. 2011.

14. Mourtzis, D., Vlachou, E., Milas, N., Dimitrakopoulos, G., Energy consumption estimation for machining processes based on real-time shopfloor monitoring via wireless sensor networks. *Proc. CIRP*, 57, 637–642, Dec. 2016.

15. Liu, Q., Zhang, H., Wan, J., Chen, X., An access control model forresource sharing based on the role-based access control intended formulti-domain manufacturing Internet of Things. *IEEE Access*, 5, 7001–7011, Apr. 2017.

16. Zhang, Y.F., Zhang, G., Du, W., Wang, J.Q., Ali, E., Sun, S.D., An optimization method for shopfloor material handling based on realtime and multi-source manufacturing data. *Int. J. Prod. Econ.*, 165, 3, 282–292, Jul. 2015.

17. Edrington, B., Zhao, B.Y., Hansel, A., Mori, M., Fujishima, M., Machine monitoring system based on MTConnect technology. *Proc. CIRP*, 22, 92–97, Dec. 2014.

18. Zarte, M., Pechmann, A., Wermann, J., Gosewehr, F., Colomboet, A.W., Building an Industry 4.0-compliant lab environment to demonstrate connectivity between shop floor and IT levels of an enterprise, in: *Proc. 42th Annu. IEEE Ind. Electron. Soc. Conf.*, Oct. 2016, pp. 6590–6595.

19. Hoffmann, M., Büscher, C., Meisen, T., Jeschke, S., Continuous integration of field level production data into top-level information systems using the OPC interface standard. *Proc. CIRP*, 41, 496–501, Jan. 2016.

5

Generation of Two-Dimensional Text-Based CAPTCHA Using Graphical Operation

S. Pradeep Kumar* and G. Kalpana

Dept. of CSE, Saveetha School of Engineering, Saveetha Nagar, Thandalam, Chennai, India

Abstract

Text-based CAPTCHA is used as a standard security method to prevent the websites from bots and phishing attacks. However, nowadays, hackers are writing a false program to break the text-based CAPTCHA scheme due to their poor strength. In the proposed two-dimensional text-based CAPTCHA approach, the number of characters is dynamic, i.e., changes with every attempt, and all the characters are tilted and rotated in some specific angle, using graphical operation. To further intensify the security, the characters will collide with each other forming a parabolic shape and each will be of different sizes and colors, creating multiple permutations and combinations of size and pixel intensity. The resultant CAPTCHA thus generated is highly secure and can be used in sensitive applications such as defense, inventory management, social media, and banking services.

Keywords: Web security, graphical operation

5.1 Introduction

In the year 2000, researchers from Carnegie Mellon University designed a text-based CAPTCHA approach to restrict attackers entering the Yahoo Chat Rooms [1]. CAPTCHA, Completely Automated Public Turing Test to Tell Computers and Humans Apart [2], are also called as a Reverse Turing Test; subsequently, they were and are envisioned to enable a computer to

Corresponding author: spradeepkumar272@gmail.com

Shalli Rani, R. Maheswar, G. R. Kanagachidambaresan, Sachin Ahuja and Deepali Gupta (eds.) *Machine Learning Paradigm for Internet of Things Applications*, (75–96) © 2022 Scrivener Publishing LLC determine whether a remote client is a human or machine [3]. There are many types of the same such as Character Recognition Based, Optical Character Recognition (OCR), and Non-OCR (using hypermedia such as acoustic and video).

In the recent years, CAPTCHA have evolved and found its application in major websites such as Google, Microsoft, Hotmail, Yahoo, and E-Bay [4]. Below are the key applications of CAPTCHA in multiple platforms.

Nowadays, CAPTCHA is commercially used to block unwanted person to enter into the corresponding websites. The representation of various CAPTCHA in different sites is shown below. Table 5.1 shows the usage of text-based CAPTCHA in web applications with drawbacks.

From the above table, the design of the CAPTCHA in various sites is not convenient for the user to attempt in CAPTCHA screening test [5]. However, the solution has failed to last long, as architecture of bots are improved with sophisticated software programs to break the poorly designed text-based CAPTCHA. The hackers now increase the incoming traffic of a site with scripts to perform false registrations, with misleading information, at high volumes causing spike in the usage of the website. This, in turn, affects the experience of a target user of the site with it being non-responsive, slow, or down. Further, the most commonly used CAPTCHA approach is one of the distorted characters with complex notations, which makes it difficult for the end users to comprehend the characters [5].

There are some rules to be followed for design the CAPTCHA.

(i)   Computer program can able to produce the CAPTCHA character at that time and there.
(ii) User can able to distinguish these CAPTCHA characters with a rational amount of time.
(iii) Hackers wrote malicious program using sophisticated software to detect CAPTCHA character at any time.

In this work, Section 5.2 gives the type of CAPTCHA information, and Section 5.3 tells the designing of CAPTCHA problems in older days. Section 5.4 designates the new proposed technique for employing the graphical operations-based CAPTCHAs. Section 5.5 stretches the features of a text-based CAPTCHA character scheme. Section 5.6 describes the breaking methodology of the text-based CAPTCHA scheme. Section 5.7 shows the performance of text-based CAPTCHA using graphical operation. Section 6.8 shows the proposed graphical-based CAPTCHA used

Table 5.1 Text-based CAPTCHA used in commercial website.

S. no.	Text-based CAPTCHA	Website	Problem faced
1		Wikipedia	Segmentation can be easily done by the hackers.
2		Discuz	Some interface problems are taken place in the texture background.
3		Facebook	In the back ground view, the same black and white color can be used. So, the human user gets confused to predict the correct user.
4		Sina	Some interface lines cause the hallow effect to make adhesion operation.
5		Yandex	Some interface lines cause the distortion effect to make adhesion operation.

(Continued)

Table 5.1 Text-based CAPTCHA used in commercial website. (*Continued*)

S. no.	Text-based CAPTCHA	Website	Problem Faced
6	diandeokay	Google	Due to the collision of similar color collide character, human user got confuse to recognize CAPTCHA character.
7	X,T NM SYRE	Microsoft	Same color can be used for cracking and CAPTCHA character.
8	N9SBEW	Hot Mail	Due to the collision of similar color collide character, human user got confuse to recognize CAPTCHA character.

in online applications. Finally, Section 5.9 designates the conclusion and future enhancement on graphical operation CAPTCHA scheme.

5.2   Types of CAPTCHAs

A wide classification of CAPTCHA mechanisms [3] is labeled as follows.

5.2.1   Text-Based CAPTCHA

Many websites (like Google, Yahoo, and Microsoft) use the own style of text-based CAPTCHA representation. It is easily implemented in the programming language like JavaScript, Python, and ASP.net. There are 26 alphabets and 10 digits to generate a distorted combination of numeric and alphabets in a text-based CAPTCHA. These methods produce a casual arrangement of characters and entrench them in an image that is highly one-sided and designed in a distorted (by computer programs) form so that only the correct user can identify the characters entrenched in the image (see Figure 5.1). The manipulator has to recognize the characters and inscribe them in the allocated area to provide and submit. The operator is defensible as a correct user when the characters competition with that used by server and CAPTCHA producer system. However, many practices contain use of single image only, a performance [3] brands use of set of 12 pictures and enquires operator to find four pictures that contain English language word by just marking onto them instead of only if the fillings of the pictures as the response.

These methods are inhibited by problems such as follows:

- In Figure 5.1, distortion made a confusion to recognize the correct character to the user. The sequences characters such S and P, E and R, and E and Q impose observing problems as shown (see Figure 5.1) [4].

A method has been planned [5] that is able to produce alike CAPTCHA images as that made by Google, Yahoo, and Hotmail with precisions ended 85% for individually. Also, they have referred the pre-processing, subdivision, and post-dissection that work till finding out the totality of characters as shown (see Figure 5.1).

These practices are susceptible to OCR attacks as their safety is reliable upon the grade of distortion while maintaining the ease of determining the characters by human users [6].

Additional issues are such as linguistic reliance because some users not have fluency in English and they have not a clear idea to type the characters. They do not know the English alphanumeric characters have problems to identify the characters. These effects indicated that language does disturb the efficiency of a CAPTCHA's application for worldwide users.

Figure 5.1 Example of text CAPTCHA.

5.2.2   Image-Based CAPTCHA

The methods used in the image-based CAPTCHA referred as Image Recognition CAPTCHA (IRC). HumanAuth solver made the trial from a website implementing HumanAuth IRC and recognized the solution correctly. So, it is decided that IRCs are identifiable. IRCs are also susceptible to AI attacks.

Additional issues related with IRCs that prevent their usage are follows:

(i)   Huge database is essential to generate a test because active formation of images from which an operator can deduce some meaning is not possible as of now.

(ii) A solitary trial needs a huge number of images and, thus, enforces a bound on the recurrence of similar image for the consecutive test.

(iii) Adequately big images needs so that they can take a meaning perceivable by human user.

Hence, the IRC become complex, because maximum of the techniques refers to the user to identify, either the landscape or type of the image(s) being displayed and then reply with the precise answer. Newest instance of such techniques is Anomaly CATPCHA [2] (see Figure 5.2). Identification of image by the user that does not belong to the feature/category depicted by rest of the images. In the image-based CAPTCHA, usually 8 to 16 images are loaded in the given grid layout. These images are collected from the database available in the restricted website. The user has to select an image based on the information available on the test and then go for submission. This test is evaluated for the extreme of four times in order to restrict the bots to contact the evidence from the web. The sample figure has been collected from the web link for the user entry image-based CAPTCHA screening test. Some users have the problem to identify the image due to the low version and blurring images.

5.2.3   Audio-Based CAPTCHA

Audio-based CAPCHA is a sound-based system (ability between the computer and the user to recognize the spoken language) and it is mainly designed for the visually challenged user. The users have the tendency to put more effect to recognize the spoken word and also the end user must be

Figure 5.2 Image-based captcha.

good in English vocabulary. Then, the distorted sound clip is accessible to the user to enter the correct number or word. Some words have the similar sounds.

Such methods the users need to put much more effect to recognize a noisy audio narrated by a speech that references some characters. Operators have to recognize those characters and enter them to server in order to show themselves as persons. The voice motion is slanted by added noise so that the fonts are not effortlessly identifiable by artificially intellectual systems or AI bouts.

5.2.4   Video-Based CAPTCHA

This CAPTCHA method shows the category of video and animation based on showing a clip to the user. The system asks the users to type what they have seen or what information the users have perceived. This CAPTCHA method is so complex and expensive compared to other methods. Due to the large size video, the user struggles to download the video and to find the CAPTCHA test. The implementation of video CAPTCHA makes it difficult to support for the multiple input interface with different devices such as keyboard, touch screen, and a speaker. Another potential issue is that for the screen reader to provide a support for the interface which element may have the chance for the bot to allow and play the game.

5.2.5   Puzzle-Based CAPTCHA

The system enables the user to load any CAPTCHA image containing mathematical equation. The user must solve the expression and answer them for the entry process. This CAPTCHA test provides a greater solution to restrict the bots to clear the screening test. These CAPTCHA tests are not convenient to the user to solve the puzzle quickly. Due to the ambiguities which are arising in the puzzle-based CAPTCHAs, the end users get confused to solve them.

5.3   Related Work

Gimphy method uses the CAPTCHA word for the screening test. Most of the words are offered from the glossary, and it is easily broken by the hackers. It is found in the Yahoo website and to find the CAPTCHA word simply. In a disorderly image, the task is to find three of the roughly seven words [6].

Using machine learning algorithm, Chellapilla and Simard had successfully attempt to break a number of visual CAPTCHA taken from the web—Google and Yahoo—and lead a success rate of around 66% [7].

Elie Bursztein has recommended that using DeCaptcha tools to interrupt most of the text-based or visual-based CAPTCHA and found in a well-known websites such as Digg, eBay, and Wikipedia [8].

Using modern technology, it is possible to improve the security of prevailing CAPTCHA by adding clatter and distortion for ordering the CAPTCHA character more forcefully. But it is harder for the user to identify the CAPTCHA character in higher rate and network load [9].

In this connection, the other researcher Yan has fragmented a most of the visual CAPTCHA as collected from Captcha service.org with a high success rate of 100%. Also, the character segmentation can be easily done with the help of current available OCR software, and it merely counts the number of pixels in each segment. Hence, it is necessary to propose a new policy that can consider all the above discussed issues while displaying the CAPTCHA in securable manner.

5.4   Proposed Technique

The development trends has introduced a CAPTCHA screening test that was designed based on the graphical operation. This proposed work shows the interaction of convince to the user entry and harder for the bots. The separate window screening test will be displayed during the execution of user entry test. In the proposed two-dimensional text-based CAPTCHA approach, the number of characters is dynamic, i.e., changes with every attempt, and all the characters are tilted and rotated in some specific angle, using graphical operations such as scaling, rotation, and translation. To further intensify the security, the characters will collide with each other forming a parabolic shape and will each be of different size and colors, creating multiple permutations and combinations of size and pixel intensity.

The technique is free from OCR and segmentation attacks. The parabolic representation makes it difficult for the hackers to projections and segmentations to extract the correct CAPTCHA. At the same time, readability of the characters is kept intact in order to enhance the user experience.

5.5 Text-Based CAPTCHA Scheme

In the beginning stage, hackers used a different type of pattern matching algorithms and identify a similarity index of all each CAPTCHA characters. Pattern matching algorithms to find the similarity index of CAPTCHA characters was used to crack the CAPTCHA codes in the initial days. Hence, the researchers focused on arresting segmentation of characters, resulting CCT (Crowding Character Together) technique. However, the CAPTCHA generated were posing a challenge to users, causing confusions due to colliding characters [10] as shown below. The problems mainly occur due to the space between the allocated CAPTCHA characters (as shown in Figure 5.3).

Figure 5.1 show how some characters are in complete collision with each other. This was intended to create ambiguity to make the similarity index algorithms fail. Meanwhile, the user got confused to recognize and predict the correct CAPTCHA character.

A good text-based CAPTCHA screening test must hold [11].

(i) The CAPTCHA screening test must have a large enough space to carry out the entry process. The number of characters used in the screening test may vary.

Figure 5.3 Confusing character in a Google CAPTCHA.

Table 5.2 Breaking methodology and success rate of various sources.

Source	Sample CAPTCHA image	Breaking methodology	Breaking success rate
Glimpy-R		Using shape context matching algorithm (color matching algorithm) to segment the CAPTCHA character.	Breaking 78% in the year 2004
EZ-Gimpy		Correlation algorithm use the segmentation technique for connected region: Recognition: distortion evaluation	Breaking 97% in the year 2004
Captcha-service		Vertical projection can be done to do segmentation.	Breaking 100% in the year 2007
Ego-share		Segmentation: connected region Recognition: SVM (Support Vector Machine)	Breaking 92% in the year 2009
Slide share		Large space between the individual characters. More chance can have to do segmentation of each character.	Breaking 93% in the year 2010

(ii)   Must contain graphical operations such as distortion, adhesion and overlap of distorted characters, making it difficult for segmentation.

(iii) Different size, width, and font types of characters to reduce recognition accuracy.

(iv)   Allocating random lengths to shield against breaking CAPTCHA at fixed lengths.

(v)   The same color of the background and text, creating noise that would be very difficult to reduce, hence failing detection accuracies.

The safety of displaying a text-based CAPTCHA mainly depends on the visual interfering effects including rotation, scaling, adhesion, and overlapping. Table 5.2 shows the breaking methodology and success rate of various sources [12].

5.6   Breaking Text-Based CAPTCHA's Scheme

The basic idea is to break the segmentation techniques for individual character features such as font size, varying pixel count, distortion of individual character, and blurring rotation of each character [13]. Text-based CAPTCHA uses an anti-segmentation technique to arrest segmentation of individual character [14].

From the above table, there are no adherent characters, and thus individual characters are easily obtained. Hence, this is a wrong way for designing CAPTCHA [15]. Below are examples of breaking text-based CAPTCHA schemes.

5.6.1   Individual Character-Based Segmentation Method

This method is helpful in analyzing the number of pixels in different positions to find out each character. It is completely based on the character position and is helpful to determine the optimal segmentation position. The approach is highly effective in breaking non-adherent and distorted CAPTCHA types [16]. These typical methods used a vertical projection segmentation operation can be easily do in order to extract individual segmented CAPTCHA character (as shown in Figure 5.4).

Bar code is used to segment the re-CAPTCHA image:

Light blue color pixel intensity value, for $N\Sigma(x)$ $= 0.586$
White color pixel intensity value for $N_{\Sigma}(x)$ $= 1$

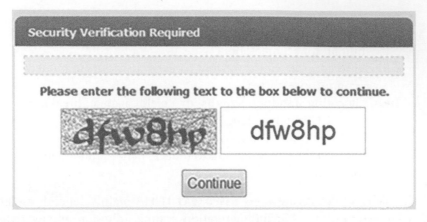

Figure 5.4 Segmentation method based on individual character.

Dark blue color pixel intensity value for N_Σ (x) = 0.287
$N\Sigma$ (x): Total number of objects hold for pixel intensity value.

Based on the above pixel values (as shown in Table 5.3), all the dark blue color is converted into black color pixel (intensity value 0) and light blue color is converted into white (intensity value 1). Thus, it completely removing the noise and making a clear image of CAPTCHA set. The extracted image allows furthermore segmentation based on the color and the gap between the characters in the given CAPTCHA.

5.6.2   Character Width-Based Segmentation Method

Segmentation-based character width is not easy method for segmenting to get an individual character. There are different widths for each character and the range is in between 0.75 and 1.6. Thus, each character primes

Table 5.3 Pixel value changed entry.

$N\Sigma$ (x)->0.586/ 0.287	$N\Sigma$ (x)->0.586/ 0.287	$N\Sigma$ (x)->0.586/ 0.287
$N\Sigma$ (x)->0.586/ 0.287	$N\Sigma$ (x)->1	$N\Sigma$ (x)->0.586/ 0.287
$N\Sigma$ (x)->0.586/ 0.287	$N\Sigma$ (x)->0.586/ 0.287	$N\Sigma$ (x)->0.586/ 0.287/

Figure 5.5 Segmented CAPTCHA image.

to four gratitude results [17], from which an optimal division as the final acknowledgment result is uncovered [18]. The enhanced dynamic programming approach is to determine the optimal segmentation between the minimum and maximum width of several CAPTCHA characters (as shown in Figure 5.5).

5.7 Implementation of Text-Based CAPTCHA Using Graphical Operation

All the CAPTCHA characters are represented in different shapes, widths, and pixel intensity (by changing the color). For example, pixel intensity of letter "s" may vary as shown in Table 5.4. Every CAPTCHA character will collide with the center of adjacent characters [19]. The graphical operation helps show the characters in a parabolic format (as shown in Figure 5.6). The number of CAPTHA character used in the screening test from 6 to 8.

5.7.1 Graphical Operation

The various graphical operations have made in each character in order to represent a parabolic format. The operation used are scaling, rotation, and

Table 5.4 Look up table entry.

Letter	Color used	Pixel count	CAPTCHA character
S	Violet	169	
S	Blue	175	
S	Green	184	

translation; each pixel that is in the position P(x,y) is shifted to a new position P'(x,y) [20].

(i) **Scaling:** The method is used to increase or reduce in size the CAPTCHA character with reverence to "X" or "Y" axis. It can be diverse up to 20%. The transformation for the successive scaling operations produces a composite scaling matrix [Equation (5.2)]. Scaling function is defined in Equation (5.1).

$$S(s_{x2}, s_{y2}).S(s_{x1}, s_{y1}) = S(s_{x1}.s_{x2}, s_{y1}.s_{y2})$$ (5.1)

The matrix for the translation [Equation (5.2)] is as follows:

$$\begin{bmatrix} X' \\ Y' \\ 1 \end{bmatrix} = \begin{bmatrix} Sx & 0 & 0 \\ 0 & Sy & 0 \\ 0 & 0 & 1 \end{bmatrix} \begin{bmatrix} X \\ Y \\ 1 \end{bmatrix}$$ (5.2)

(ii) **Rotation:** Some of the CAPTCHA characters that may spin in dissimilar angles can slander between 20° and −20°. Two successive rotations (θ_1, θ_2) are applied to produce a transformed operation. Scaling function is defined in Equation (5.3).

$$P' = R(\theta_2).[R\theta_1].P]$$
$$P' = R(\theta_1 + \theta_2).P]$$ (5.3)

The matrix equation [Equation (5.4)] can be represented by

$$\begin{bmatrix} X' \\ Y' \\ 1 \end{bmatrix} = \begin{bmatrix} Cos\theta Cos\varphi - Sin\theta Sin\varphi & -(Cos\theta Sin\varphi + Sin\theta Cos\varphi) & 0 \\ Sin\theta Cos\varphi + Cos\theta Sin\varphi & -Sin\theta Sin\varphi + Cos\theta Cos\varphi & 1 \\ 0 & 0 & 1 \end{bmatrix} * \begin{bmatrix} X \\ Y \\ 1 \end{bmatrix}$$

$$\begin{bmatrix} X' \\ Y' \\ 1 \end{bmatrix} = \begin{bmatrix} Cos(\theta + \varphi) & -Sin(\theta + \varphi) & 0 \\ Sin(\theta + \varphi) & Cos(\theta + \varphi) & 0 \\ 0 & 0 & 1 \end{bmatrix} * \begin{bmatrix} X \\ Y \\ 1 \end{bmatrix}$$ (5.4)

(iii) Translation: Using a matrix revolution method, a finicky CAPTCHA character in a specified text box is translated.

The corresponding pixels are translated to some other position from p to p'.

The two consecutive translation vectors (t_{x1}, t_{y1}) and (t_{x2}, t_{y2}) are applied to a

Coordinate position p, then $p' = T(t_{x2}, t_{y2}).[T(t_{x1}, t_{y1}).p$

p'->new position

The translation matrix equation can be represented in Equation (5.5).

$$
\begin{bmatrix} 1 & 0 & t_{x1} \\ 0 & 1 & t_{y1} \\ 0 & 0 & 0 \end{bmatrix} + \begin{bmatrix} 1 & 0 & t_{x2} \\ 0 & 1 & t_{y2} \\ 0 & 0 & 0 \end{bmatrix} = \begin{bmatrix} 1 & 0 & t_{x1} + t_{x2} \\ 0 & 1 & t_{y1}\, t_{y2} \\ 0 & 0 & 0 \end{bmatrix}
$$

(5.5)

Using all the above geometric graphical calculation, the entire set of CAPTCHA character has changed the position and shape with respect to different pixel coordinate position (as shown in Figure 5.6). Hence, the collectivization of all CAPTCHA characters is shown like a curve shape in parabolic formats.

5.7.2 Two-Dimensional Composite Transformation Calculation

In this CAPTCHA set, each and every CAPTCHA character can have the chance to signify in dissimilar colors and dissimilar shapes [21]. So, every character can have the fixed pixel count with respect to a particular color. The two-dimensional transformation has the combination of translation, scaling, and rotation to scale about P1 (x1,y1); the following sequence of the essential transformations is required [as define in Equation (5.6)]:

| Initial CAPTCHA In database | translation & Rotation | Rotation & scaling | Final CAPTCHA image contains cracks |

Figure 5.6 Graphical operation made CAPTCHA image.

1. Translate the object by (t_x, t_y)
2. Rotate the object by (θ)
3. Scaling the object by (s_x, s_y)

This sequence of stages can be achieved as follows:

$$
\begin{array}{cccc}
\text{New point} & \text{Translate}(x,y) & \text{Rotate}(\theta) & \text{Scaling} \\
\begin{bmatrix} X' \\ Y' \\ 1 \end{bmatrix} = & \begin{bmatrix} 1 & 0 & X+t_x \\ 0 & 1 & y+t_y \\ 0 & 0 & 1 \end{bmatrix} * & \begin{bmatrix} \cos\theta & \sin\theta & 0 \\ \sin\theta & \cos\theta & 0 \\ 0 & 0 & 1 \end{bmatrix} * & \begin{bmatrix} s_x & 0 & 0 \\ 0 & s_y & 0 \\ 0 & 0 & 1 \end{bmatrix}
\end{array}
\tag{5.6}
$$

$$
\begin{bmatrix} X' \\ Y' \\ 1 \end{bmatrix} = \begin{bmatrix} s_x\cos\theta & -s_y\sin\theta & x \\ s_x\sin\theta & s_y\cos\theta & y \\ 0 & 0 & 1 \end{bmatrix}
\tag{5.7}
$$

Now, the new coordinate point can be represented in Equation (5.7)
Consider a starting coordinate pixel position of an object is P(10,20) and do the translation by (5,10) with a rotation of an angle 30° and a scaling factor of $(s_x = 1.1, s_y = 1.3)$.

(i) Translation of vertex (20, 10): It is defined in Equation (5.8).

New point

$$
\begin{bmatrix} X' \\ Y' \\ 1 \end{bmatrix} = \begin{bmatrix} 1 & 0 & 5 \\ 0 & 1 & 10 \\ 0 & 0 & 1 \end{bmatrix} * \begin{bmatrix} 20 \\ 10 \\ 1 \end{bmatrix} = \begin{bmatrix} 1*20+0*10+5*1 \\ 0*20+1*10+10*1 \\ 0*20+0*10+1*1 \end{bmatrix} = \begin{bmatrix} 25 \\ 20 \\ 1 \end{bmatrix}
\tag{5.8}
$$

(ii) Rotation of a pivot point to some angle. It is defined in Equation (5.9).

New point

$$
\begin{bmatrix} X' \\ Y' \\ 1 \end{bmatrix} = \begin{bmatrix} 0.866 & -0.5 & 0 \\ 0.5 & 0.866 & 0 \\ 0 & 0 & 1 \end{bmatrix} = \begin{bmatrix} (0*25)+((-0.5)*20+(0*1) \\ 0*25+(0.866*20)+(0*1) \\ 0*25+0*20+(1*1) \end{bmatrix} = \begin{bmatrix} 11.65 \\ 17.32 \\ 1 \end{bmatrix}
\tag{5.9}
$$

(iii) Scaling function to a pivot pixel point [round of value (11.65, 17.32) to (12, 17)].

It is defined in Equation (5.10).

New point

$$\begin{bmatrix} X' \\ Y' \\ 1 \end{bmatrix} = \begin{bmatrix} 1.1 & 0 & 0 \\ 0 & 1.3 & 0 \\ 0 & 0 & 1 \end{bmatrix} * \begin{bmatrix} 12 \\ 17 \\ 1 \end{bmatrix} = \begin{bmatrix} (1.1*12)+(0*17)+(0*1) \\ (0*12)+(1.3*17)+(0*1) \\ (0*12)+(0*17)+(1*1) \end{bmatrix} = \begin{bmatrix} 13.2 \\ 18.9 \\ 1 \end{bmatrix}$$

$$(5.10)$$

Thus, the initial coordinate pixel position (20, 10) is shifted to (13, 19) position using the above graphical operation calculation. Moreover to do all remaining pixel position of an object to retrieve the correct accurate position.

All the tradition characters are exhibited inside the CAPTCHA screening test of a user typed web application form. Each character clutches a distinct grid layout. So, there are 36 separate {(a, b, ..., z,), (0, 1, ..., 9)} grid layout for the characters used. In each and every CAPTCHA test, all the arrangement of usage characters is to differ. There are preserving 10 different orders to confuse the bots for predicting the correct characters.

Advantages

(i)   Hackers using modern software cannot have the coincidental to analysis the CAPTCHA character at any time.
(ii)   Restrict to various attacks such as online guessing attacks, OCR attacks, and dictionary attacks.
(iii) Even using graphical operation, user never gets confused to recognize a CAPTCHA character in the screening test.

5.8   Graphical Text-Based CAPTCHA in Online Application

User filled all the essential details in the presently used online application form and then the system permits to allow for the CAPTCHA screening test. If the user is not able to give the correct details in the application form as on time, then a new set of graphical CAPTCHA character will be generated. Each and all character may have the possibility to show in dissimilar colors.

Implementation
The picture of CAPTCHA must be a user friendly to the user and strongly restrict the bots to enter into the profitable websites. In the database, it maintains nearly a 600 CAPTCHA character set. Using the random number creator, collect the CAPTCHA character from the database and allotted in the screening test. The working algorithm (mouse clicked CAPTCHA) embraces the working process of a CAPTCHA transmission test. The proposed procedure is undergoing a different objective based on the user entry and representation of CAPTCHAs.

(i)   User Entry
Since our technique is based on the grouping of text and imaged, the user does not enter the characters as it is in the screening test.

(ii) Image Recognition
A separate window is allotted in the CAPTCHA screening test. The user clicked all the familiar character based on dynamic order CAPTCHAs.

(iii) Less Storage
Small-sized window is maintained during the screening test. Typically, users use mouse cursor and provide easily visible to the user.

(iv) OCR and Dictionary Attack
CAPTCHA character is represented on the curve-based format. All the CAPTCHA character is represented in different colors. It does not lead to the OCR and dictionary attack.

The time required to solve the clickable CAPTCHA cursor is to identify the English letter and numerical in the screening test is less. The regularity of repetitive challenge lead to the variability in the number of CAPTCHs character used (6 to 8) in the screen text, representation (upper/lower curve), and useable character. Curve-based CAPTCHA were solved with the help of a mouse, and traditionally, CAPTCHA was solved with the help of the keyboard.

In adding up to that, some graphical operation has prepared in the CAPTCHA character along with some clatter (black curve lines are there in the text box). This leads to the stronger safety level for their CAPTCHA refreshment. In this graphical-based design CAPTCHA screening test, the background texts demote in white color and foreground texts refer in distorted ordered of different colors of CAPTCHA characters (as shown in Figure 5.7). The user can give all the sufficient details in the web application

Figure 5.7 Graphical sesign CAPTCHA in online application.

form and then only the system permits for graphical-based CAPTCHA screening test. After that, the entire screening test can hold only for 25 seconds in the online application form. Thus, fixed time graphical-based CAPTCHA is helpful and not give chance for the hackers to guess the correct characters on time.

5.9   Conclusion and Future Enhancement

This planned method shows all the CAPTCHA characters that have been given in dissimilar colors. Each character is colliding in middle of the neighboring character and creates a parabolic shape format. Vertical line segmentation has not feasible to identify a single character alone. Using graphical operation and take a longer time process to allocate the entire CAPTCHA letter in the screening test. At any situation, user never gets confused to recognize the CAPTCHA character in the online applications. The achievement rate on a model test has been boosted to 97% for the human user and 0% for the hackers regarding the recognition. In future, this technique is helpful to design a different cure-based format and enrolled in various applications like inventory, banking, and commercial websites, thus making the generation of two-dimensional text-based CAPTCHA using graphical operation approach as a secure and user-friendly way of CAPTCHA generation.

References

1. Hasan, W.K.A. and AlGharb, A., A Survey of Current Research on CAPTCHA. *Int. J. Comput. Sci. Eng. Sur. (IJCSES)*, 7, 3, June 2016, https://aircconline.com/ijcses/V7N3/7316ijcses01.pdf

2. Yadava, P.S., Sahu, C.P., Shukla, S.K., A Framework for Devanagari Script-Based Captcha. *Int. J. Adv. Inf. Technol. (IJAIT)*, 1, 4, August 2011, https://www.academia.edu/14911658/A_FRAMEWORK_FOR_DEVANAGARI_SCRIPT_BASED_CAPTCHA

3. Chen, J., Luo, X., Guo, Y., Zhang, Y., Gong, D., A Survey on Breaking Technique of Text-Based CAPTCHA. *Secur. Commun. Netw.*, 2017, Article ID 6898617, https://doi.org/10.1155/2017/6898617.

4. Jeng, A.B., Tseng, C.C., Tseng, D.F., Wang, J.C., A Study of CAPTCHA and Its Application to User Authentication, in: *Computational Collective Intelligence. Technologies and Applications. ICCCI 2010. Lecture Notes in Computer Science*, vol. 6422, J.S. Pan, S.M. Chen, N.T. Nguyen (Eds.), Springer, Berlin, Heidelberg, 2010.

5. Roshanbin, N. and Miller, J., A Survey and Analysis of Current Captcha Approaches. *J. Web Eng.*, 12, 1&2, 2013, 001–040© Rinton Press.

6. Azad, S. and Jain, K., CAPTCHA : Attacks and Weaknesse against OCR Technology. *Glob. J. Sci. Technol. Neural Artif. Intell.*, 13, 3, version 1.0, May 2013.

7. Bursztein, E., Martin, M., Mitchell, J.C., Text based CAPTCHA Strengths and Weaknesses. *ACM Computer and Communication security (CCS)*, pp. 1–14, 2011.

8. Mori, G. and Malik, J., Recognizing Objects in Adversarial Clutter:Breaking a Visual CAPCTHA, in: *Proceeding of IEEE Conference on Computer Vision and Pattern Recognition*, USA, June16-22, 2003, vol. 1, pp. 134–141.

9. Chellapilla, K. and Simard, P., Using Machine Learning toBreak Visual Human Interaction Proofs (HIPs), in: *Advances in Neural Information Processing Systems 17, Neural Information Processing Systems (NIPS)*, MIT Press, USA, 2004.

10. Jawane, V. and Rath, V., Survey Paper on Secure Text-Based CAPTCHA. *Open Access Int. J. Sci. Eng.*, 3, Special Issue 1, ISO3297:2007 Certified, March 2018.
11. Tariq Banday, M. and Shah, N.A., A Study of CAPTCHAs for Securing Web Services. *Int. J. Secur. Digit. Inf. Age*, 1, 2, December 2009.
12. Tang, M., Zhang, Y., Liu, Y., Zhang, P., Research on Deep Learning Techniques in Breaking Text-Based Captchas and Designing Image-Based Captcha, vol. 3, no. 3, pp. 572–577, 2018.
13. Sandeep, H. and Raghavendra, B.K., A New Security Primitive Model Based on Artificial Intelligence Using Captcha as Graphical Passwords. *Int. J. Comput. Eng. Appl.*, ICCSTAR-2016, Special Issue, May 16, 2016.
14. Kumar, D. and Sharma, S., Highly Secured Intellectual Graphical CAPTCHA. *Int. J. Modern Eng. Manage. Res.*, 6, 1, 2018.
15. Chandavale, A.A., Sapkal, A.M., Jainkar, R.M., A frame work to analysis the security Of text based CAPTCHA. *Int. J. Comput. Appl.*, 27, 2010, No. 27, Article 19, 2010.
16. Sinha, A. and Tarar, S., Review Paper on Different CAPTCHA Techniques. *Int. J. Comput. Sci. Technol.*, 7, 1, Jan - March 2016.
17. Moy, G., Jones, N., Harkless, C., Potter, R., Distortion Estimation Techniques in Solving Visual CAPTCHAs. *IEEE Conference on Computer Vision and Pattern Recognition (CVPR'04)*, June 2004, vol. 2, pp. 23–28, 2004.
18. Oleg Starostenko Claudia Cruz- Perez Fernando Uceda-Ponga, Breaking text-based CAPTCHAs with variable word and character orientation, 48, 1101–1112, 2015.
19. Wu, X., Dai, S., Guo, Y., Fujita, H., A machine learning attack against variable- length Chinese character CAPTCHAs. 14, 4, pp. 1548–1565, 2018.
20. http://www.cs.cityu.edu.hk/~helena/cs31622000A/Notes02.pdf
21. Ye, Chen, Y., Zhu, B., The Robustness of a New 3D CAPTCHA. *2014 11th IAPR Workshop on Document Analysis Systems*, Tours, pp. 319–323, 2014.

6

Smart IoT-Enabled Traffic Sign Recognition With High Accuracy (TSR-HA) Using Deep Learning

Pradeep Kumar S.[1]*, Jayanthi K.[1]† and Selvakumari S.[2]‡

[1]*Department of IT Department, Vel Tech Rangarajan Dr. Sagunthala R&D Institute of Science and Technology, Avadi, India*
[2]*Department of ECE, Sri Venkateshwara College of Science and Technology, Tiruvallur, India*

Abstract

Several types of signs in the road traffic available are nowadays to control the speed limits. Often, the drivers in heavy traffic failed to follow the traffic rules because of this busy world. In other points of view, the drivers may not have a clear knowledge about the traffic signs, and this causes many accidents and leads them to pay fine amounts. More or less a huge number of accidents may lead to death because of not following the traffic rules. All may have self-driving cars that mean all the passengers can completely depend on the car alone for traveling. The successful way of controlling 5 levels will leads the vehicle to understand and follow all the traffic rules. In the smart world, Artificial Intelligence (AI) development helps researchers and big companies. The toughest thing is reaching accuracy in this technique of the vehicles it interrupt with the traffic signals and able to take the decisions accordingly. In this chapter, deep neural network model is built that can classify traffic signs presented in the image into different categories with new models that able to understand the traffic signs which are a very important task for all autonomous vehicles. Deep learning helps us to train the machine to predict all kinds of traffic signals with huge datasets for more accuracy. By implementing concepts we can quietly reduce the accidents, simultaneously traffic problems which helps us to avoid the pay the fine amount.

Corresponding author: pradeepkumars@veltech.edu.in
†*Corresponding author*: jayanthi2contact@gmail.com
‡*Corresponding author*: ashamariya95@gmail.com

Shalli Rani, R. Maheswar, G. R. Kanagachidambaresan, Sachin Ahuja and Deepali Gupta (eds.) Machine Learning Paradigm for Internet of Things Applications, (97–112) © 2022 Scrivener Publishing LLC

In this project, it successfully classified the traffic sign classifiers with the accuracy of 98% and also visualized how the accuracy and loss changes with time, with the best results from a simple CNN model.

Keywords: IIoT, IoT, deep learning, deep neural network, R-CNN

6.1   Introduction

A huge number of ideas have been implemented in machine learning and deep learning concepts. In this chapter, deep learning with the platform of Python has been discussed [1–3]. In this chapter, all can have a clear idea about the concepts of the Convolutional Neural Network (CNN), with the image processing on the deep learning. The concept of traffic signals with the classification and recognition techniques with the help of the dataset is used to train our own custom traffic sign with classifiers [3, 4]. Traffic signs classification is the normal process of automatically recognizing traffic signs along the road, which also includes the speed limits signs, especially yield signs, merge signs, stop sign, and parking sign. Because of this, it is able to automatically recognize traffic signs that enable us to build "smart cars".

6.1.1   Internet of Things

For past few years, it is noticed that the unique technique called as IoT (Internet of Things) has started becoming a more and more important component in day-to-day life [4–6]. Only few IoT devices are used by people, commonly known and also unknown; for example, in smart homes, smart lamps; in the wearables, smart watch; in the big cities, smart cities; and in big company and retail shop, smart retail. As it is said, IoT is widely used. In the above mentioned concept, autonomous vehicles are going to be implemented. In general, the IoT is the extension of the internet connectivity into the physical devices and everyday new objects. This is well embedded with the electronics and internet connectivity with the other forms of hardware [7–10]. Most of the IoT devices may impact to produce in great variety of time series data which are of huge interest in AI.

6.1.2   Deep Learning

Business leaders must know about deep learning—what it is and how it works. It is high end of what machines, developers, and business leaders can do. Only deep learning works with the unique type of algorithm that has far surpassed any previous benchmarks for detecting and classification of images, text, and voice. Traffic signs have some constant characteristics of traffic signs,

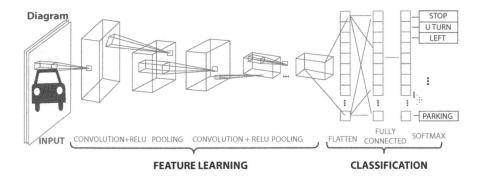

Figure 6.1 CNN feature extraction structure diagram in deep learning.

for example, colors, may be implemented for identification and classification. Form and shape are the most common attributes that can assist drivers in obtaining details on highways [12, 13, 15]. In all over the world the colors used in traffic signs are nearly identical, usually embodying basic colors (red, blue, yellow, etc.) as well as fixed forms (ring, triangles, rectangles, etc.).

6.1.3 Detecting the Traffic Sign With the Mask R-CNN

In this observation part, the basic operation is to remove the traffic sign and the segment is extended with many numbers using the Mask R-CNN detector extended enhancements. In next diagram, original Mask R-CNN is shown. Trainer provides our adaptation to traffic sign learning and categories, and finally, this is the way of detecting the augmentation technique. From Figure 6.1, the areas of interest and planning for the stage of classification are shown. The details of color and shape for traffic signs are two essential pieces of information. There is a particular color and defined form for the traffic sign; hence, this chapter will analyze the identification of traffic signals based on the two signs of knowledge [11]. The area of interest extraction based on color information is transformed into HSV color space by extracting H and S image components [15–17]. Hue plays a crucial role in the segmentation process because it demonstrates more invariance in the alteration of lighting order and color saturation in the background of highlights or shadows.

6.1.3.1 Mask R-Convolutional Neural Network

In this stage, the location of Mask R-CNN and the peruser [14] for additional short portrayals are noticed. The Mask R-CNN is the quicker organization model for the two modules made. The absolute first module is profoundly completely associated with a convolutional network known as Regional Proposal Network (RPN) [18–20]. This takes an info picture and creates a progression of recommendations for rectangular items, each with an article positioning. A subsequent module, called Quick R-CNN, is a locale-based CNN, which groups the districts that are proposed into a bunch of predefined classifications. As it shares convolutions across solitary recommendations, Fast R-CNN is profoundly powerful. To additionally advance the yield of the proposed regions, it likewise directs bouncing box relapse. The whole framework is a solitary firm organization where, by trading their convolutional qualities, RPN and Fast R-CNN are coordinated. The RPN module advises the Swift R-CNN module where to look, receiving the, as of late, normal language of neural organizations with the "consideration" system. Then, at that point, by incorporating the fundamental organization engineering with a Function Pyramid Network (FPN) [42], Mask R-CNN reinforces this technique [21, 22]. The identifier can help productivity on little articles with the FPN, since the FPN gathers data from the lower layers of the organization before down-examining the fundamental information from little items. Design of the hidden organization, which is VGG16 [39] in the R-CNN, supplants with a lingering organization (ResNet) in the cover R-CNN.

The training is done based on the region proposal tasks for speedy and Mask R-CNN by the classification tasks. The stochastic gradient descent is obtained by this performance. Both networks of the Mask R-CNN can be learned simultaneously using the technique of end-to-end learning. Normally, four steps for the optimization process are performed to implement the original faster R-CNN technique in between two tasks [23, 24]. A new end-to-end learning scheme is applicable for R-CNN to Faster R-CNN. Before they are trained with the specific domain, both webworks are initialized with the ImageNet pre-trained model.

6.1.3.2   Color Space Conversion

The very common kind of color space is RGB colors, namely, Red-Green-Blue components that represent the values of the colors in the image:

$$C = R(r) + G(g) + B(b) \tag{6.1}$$

It is a common formula to visualize the RGB space as defined by the basis of the primary colors; the major three components (R, G, and B) are closely related with each other. Each and every component will lead to a change in pixel color value in the image. But the change of the color does not help us to detect the traffic signs [25–27]. Why? Because it will be viewed outdoors, either in the open sunlight and dark moon light at night time. So, in this chapter, the HSV color space is used, which contains the hue, saturation, and value with the three components of the RGB; HSV is brilliancy of the picture [11]. When it is compared with the common RGB, HSV is nearer to the image, which is actually viewed by the man eyes, and it also contains a wider range of color than RGB of color space, which is termed as the disposed to the external light color changes.

6.2 Experimental Evaluation

In this part of the trial assessment, deep learning strategies are the most ideal path for suitable traffic sign discovery and acknowledgment. The interaction is executed with two significant states, specifically R-CNN and Mask R-CNN. With the connected work, first execution is finished with existing datasets to build up a pattern correlation with the connected work. The dataset, which is our own dataset, is performed with the thorough investigation of the proposed enhancements.

6.2.1 Implementation Details

The implementation process is done by our own training datasets with a number of input images with traffic signs. The deep learning concepts help to detect the image with some pooling techniques. This process is done by the convolution layers, and the output can be predicted with the R-CNN process. The main stop sign is implemented, and the output is verified.

6.2.2 Traffic Sign Classification

Traffic signs are detected through the camera that should be classified for identification. In this type of detection and classification, CNN is mainly used here for classification in the both process of training and testing data as an input with respective output. Hence, this comes under supervised learning. In this chapter, the dataset is our own dataset, which is directly collected as images through a camera. By the help of the dataset, only the machine is going to be trained and to be tested. The human brain function is similar to the working process of the CNN, which is multi-layered with neurons. Every single neuron will receive an input to perform a task, and only some of them will be passed as an input to the other neurons. Among these layers, the convolutional layer is the major core part of the CNN. The main function of this function is the feature selection. The output from this process will be compared with the general machine learning.

CNN is used in this document to identify the symptoms found. A lightweight CNN classifier is being created. The lightweight style CNN consists of two layers of convolution, two layers of pooling, and two layers of total relation. Here, the kernel size of the convolution layer is set to 5 × 5, the convolution kernel quantity is set to 32, and the phase size is set to 1. In the first convolution layer, the number of hidden layer nodes is 16, and in the second convolution layer, it is 32. The function graphs are 32 × 32 and 16 × 16 in dimension, respectively. The pooling layer size is 2 × 2; the total hidden nodes of the full nodes 512 and 128 are the link layer and the sum of secrets. The nodes for the last layer of production are 43. In order to avoid over-fitting, data from certain nodes is randomly discarded during the training process. Dropout sets the node data to 0 in order to discard any values of its own. This method of extraction of features and R-CNN classification is shown in Figure 6.1, for more brief understanding.

6.2.3   Traffic Sign Detection

As shown in Figure 6.1, the input data is given from the dataset or feed from the camera automatically. By the above process of convolutional layers that contain the pooling, which means the features from the some tiny part of the image are extracted, this may be done many times based on the pooling layers. The proposed CNN layers use the ReLU as the activating function to learn about the complex features of the image. In the Neural Network, the most common activation function is used. The learning network model is faster and conducive when compared to the real learning method. At the same time, in order to prevent the over-fitting, this is done. The over-fitting is a kind of error where the dropout layer is additionally added in the randomness of the network. Throughout the network, the dataset is developed to train and test by itself. The datasets contain 100%, meaning, out of that, 90% of the dataset is used for the training process and the rest of the 10% of the dataset is used to test the entire process. Whenever the loss rate decreases gradually as the accuracy of training increases, this may be done due to the increase of the training time. This is shown in the input image and with their respective images.

6.2.4 Sample Outputs

Here, the real-time output of identifying the traffic signs from the input images is given. The invented device clearly identifies the traffic sign, which is located on the roadside of traveling, and based on that, the training data in the process of identification can be done here. Based on the identification of the further action which supposes to be taken by the driver or any alarm, any further notifications can be triggered using the relay, which is connected with the single-board computer (SBC).

6.2.5 Raspberry Pi 4 Controls Vehicle Using OpenCV

In this chapter, the said concept is implemented in the SBC. Coding is written in Python 3 programming. Commonly, the SBC is used to some projects, for example, the easy and flexible kinds of IoT projects. Here, the Raspberry Pi 4 is also used to make this project implementation successful. A Pi camera is connected with IoT device with relay to enable and control the vehicle. The Pi camera runs continuously to detect the traffic signs. Once the captured image matches with the dataset, the label for that particular input is triggered and that action is done within nanoseconds (Figure 6.2 a-h). This helps to control the vehicle with some alert messages. The entire process can be connected, as shown in Figure 6.3.

6.2.5.1 *Smart IoT-Enabled Traffic Signs Recognizing With High Accuracy Using Deep Learning*

Smart IoT-enabled traffic signs are recognized with more accuracy using the deep learning concept. The IoT device is trained with a huge number of datasets using the concepts of R-CNN. The Pi camera captures the video or image and sends it to the device. The device that is implemented with deep learning concept tests the data with the training data and, based on the classification of R-CNN, will trigger the respective steps of the car to take the further steps in traffic, in which most human beings failed.

The following packages are in-built in the Python to implement the above that connects the basic import packages as list below:

Figure 6.2 (a) Input image; (b) Output image. (*Continued*)

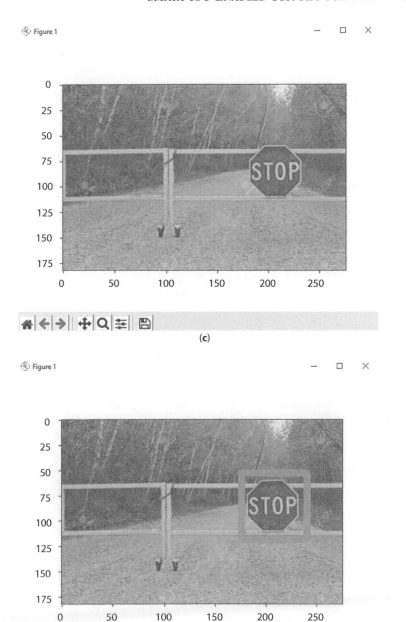

Figure 6.2 (Continued) (c) Input image; (d) Output image.   (*Continued*)

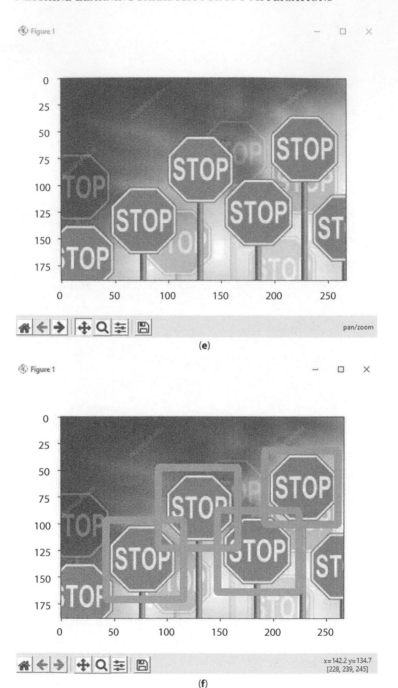

Figure 6.2 (Continued) (e) Input image; (f) Output image.   (*Continued*)

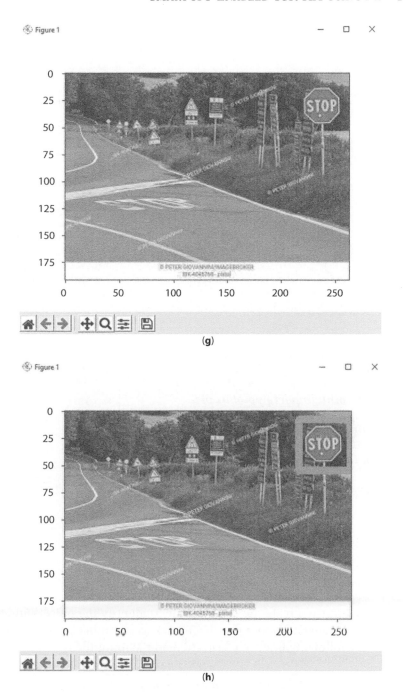

Figure 6.2 (Continued) (g) Input image; (h) Output image.

Diagram

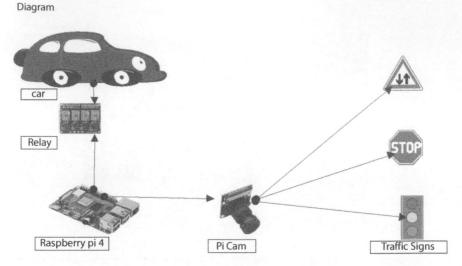

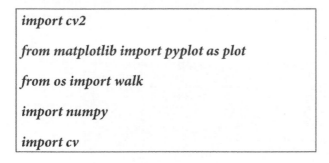

Figure 6.3 Smart IoT-enabled traffic signs recognizing with high accuracy using deep learning.

```
import cv2

from matplotlib import pyplot as plot

from os import walk

import numpy

import cv
```

The above packages are essential to run the above concept with the following code.

6.2.6 Python Code

Here, some hints to create the Python code to identify the objects and the traffic signs are given. As per the above packages, it must be imported in Python. The following line code helps to read the input file.

```
img = cv2.imread("file name with extension")
```

The above code to open the image

```
img_gray = cv2.cvtColor(img, cv2.COLOR_BGRtoGRAY)

img_rgb = cv2.cvtColor(img, cv2.COLOR_BGRtoRGB)
```

The above code, OpenCV, opens the image as the BRG, but we want it as RGB, and we also need a grayscale with version.

```
plt.subplot(1, 1, 1)

plt.imshow(img_RGB)

plt.show()
```

The above code is to create the environment of the given input image and to display it.

```
stop_data = cv2.CascadeClassifier('stop_data.xml')

found = stop_data.detectMultiScale(img_gray,minSize =(30,30))
```

The above code is used to minimize the size because, with the extra small dots, that would look like stop signs. Instead of importing all other identification of the sign, here, stop is used and output is shown. If needed, all other data xml file is executed to detect all other signs. This way, it can implement all the datasets of the traffic signs to be executed in real-time process.

6.3   Conclusion

In this chapter, deep learning helps to propose the traffic sign recognition method. The main aim of the article is to detect the traffic signs and to control the vehicle automatically. The R-CNN concepts are used to detect the signs with the major components of deep learning. Based on this output, further enhancement can be made by using the object detection with the depth of the objects to travel along the roadside. Instead of the Pi camera, the stereo vision camera is used to find the depth of the object to make the automatic driving 96% accident-free.

References

1. Pradeep Kumar, S. and Selvakumari, S., Deep Learning Enabled Smart Industrial Workers Precaution System Using Single Board Computer (SBC) Chapter from, in: *Internet of Things for Industry 4.0 EAI-2020*.
2. Rani, S., Maheswar, R., Kanagachidambaresan, G.R., Jayarajan, P., *Integration of WSN and IoT for Smart Cities*, Springer.
3. Saranraj, G., Selvamani, K., Kanagachidambaresan, G.R., Optimal energy-efficient cluster head selection (OEECHS) for wireless sensor network. *J. Inst. Eng. (India): Ser. B*, 100, 4, 349–356.
4. Saranya, V., Shankar, S., Kanagachidambaresan, G.R., Energy efficient data collection algorithm for mobile wireless sensor network. *Wireless Pers. Commun.*, 105, 1, 219–232.
5. Wang, C.Y., Research and application of traffic sign detection and recognition based on deep learning. *International Conference on Robots & Intelligent System (ICRIS)*, 2018.
6. Sheikh, M.A.A., Kole, A., Maity, T., Traffic sign detection and classification using colour feature and neural network. *International Conference on Intelligent Control Power and Instrumentation*, 2016.
7. Chen, T. and Lu, S., Accurate and Efficient Traffic Sign Detection Using Discriminative Adaboost and Support Vector Regression. *IEEE Trans. Veh. Technol.*, 65, 6, 4006–4015, 2016.
8. Xing, M., Chunyang, M., Yan, W. *et al.*, Traffic sign detection and recognition using color standardization and Zernike moments. *Chinese Control and Decision Conference*, 2016.
9. Liu, W., Lu, R.G., Liu, X.L., Traffic sign detection and recognition via transfer learning. *Chinese Control And Decision Conferenc*, pp. 5884–5887, 2018.
10. Yuan, Y., Xiong, Z., Wang, Q., VSSA-NET: Vertical Spatial Sequence Attention Network for Traffic Sign Detection. *IEEE Trans. Image Process.*, 99, 1–1, 2019.
11. Chen, W.W. and Wu, W., Linear and circular extraction method based on Hough transformation. *Electron Mass*, 383, 02, 25–27, 2019.
12. Zhu, Z., Liang, D., Zhang, S. *et al.*, Traffic-Sign Detection and Classification in the Wild. *IEEE Conference on Computer Vision and Pattern Recognition (CVPR)*, 2016.
13. Sheikh, M.A.A. and Mukhopadhyay, S., Noise tolerant classification of aerial images into manmade structures and natural-scene images based on statistical dispersion measures. *IEEE India Conference*, pp. 653–658, 2012.
14. Gomez-Moreno, H., Maldonado-Bascon, S., Gil-Jimenez, P. *et al.*, Goal Evaluation of Segmentation Algorithms for Traffic Sign Recognition. *IEEE Trans. Intell. Transp. Syst.*, 11, 4, 917–930, 2010.
15. Zhu, Y., Zhang, C., Zhou, D. *et al.*, Traffic sign detection and recognition using fully convolutional network guided proposals. *Neurocomputing*, 2016:S092523121630741X.

16. Zhao, G.F., *Traffic sign recognition Based on Machine Learning*, Hangzhou University of Electronic Science and Technology, 2015.
17. Din, S., Paul, A., Ahmad, A., Gupta, B.B., Rho, S., Service orchestration of optimizing continuous features in industrial surveillance using big data based fog-enabled internet of things. *IEEE Access*, 6, 21582–21591, CrossRefGoogle Scholar, 2018.
18. Krüger, J., Lien, T.K., Verl, A., Cooperation of human and machines in assembly lines. *CIRP Ann.*, 58, 2, 628–646, 2009, [2].CrossRefGoogle Scholar.
19. Haddadin, S., Albu-Schäffer, A., Hirzinger, G., Requirements for safe robots: Measurements, analysis and new insights. *Int. J. Rob. Res.*, 28, 11–12, 1507–1527, CrossRefGoogle Scholar, 2009.
20. Asadi, E., Li, B., Chen, I.M., Pictobot: A cooperative painting robot for interior finishing of industrial developments. *IEEE Rob. Autom. Mag.*, 25, 2, 82–94, CrossRefGoogle Scholar, 2018.
21. Krizhevsky, A., Sutskever, I., Hinton, G.E., Imagenet classification with deep convolutional neural networks, in: *Advances in neural information processing systems*, pp. 1097–1105, 2012, Google Scholar.
22. Xia, F., Campi, F., Bahreyni, B., Tri-mode capacitive proximity detection towards improved safety in industrial robotics. *IEEE Sens. J.*, 18, 12, 5058–5066, CrossRefGoogle Scholar, 2018.
23. Martin, A. and Voix, J., In-ear audio wearable: Measurement of heart and breathing rates for health and safety monitoring. *IEEE Trans. Biomed. Eng.*, 65, 6, 1256–1263, Google Scholar, 2018.
24. Lazzerini, B. and Pistolesi, F., Multiobjective personnel assignment exploiting workers' sensitivity to risk. *IEEE Trans. Syst. Man. Cybern.: Syst.*, 48, 8, 1267–1282, CrossRefGoogle Scholar, 2018.
25. Lazzerini, B. and Pistolesi, F., An integrated optimization system for safe job assignment based on human factors and behavior. *IEEE Syst. J.*, 12, 2, 1158–1169, Google Scholar, 2018.
26. Tsukada, K., Tomioka, T., Wakabayashi, S., Sakai, K., Kiwa, T., Magnetic detection of steel corrosion at a buried position near the ground level using a magnetic resistance sensor. *IEEE Trans. Magn.*, 54, 11, 1–4, Google Scholar, 2018.
27. Rybczyński, A., Wolska, A., Wisełka, M., Matusiak, J., Pfeifer, T., Welding arc ignition and photobiological hazard evaluation, in: *2018 IEEE International Conference on Environment and Electrical Engineering and 2018 IEEE Industrial and Commercial Power Systems Europe (EEEIC/I&CPS Europe)*, IEEE, Google Scholar, pp. 1–6, 2018.
23. Doan, D.R., Unrecognized hazards [electrical safety]. *IEEE Ind. Appl. Mag.*, 24, 5, 5–5, MathSciNet, 2018.

7

Offline and Online Performance Evaluation Metrics of Recommender System: A Bird's Eye View

R. Bhuvanya* and M. Kavitha

Vel Tech Rangarajan Dr. Sagunthala R&D Institute of Science and Technology, Chennai, India

Abstract

Recommender system (RS) plays a major role in e-commerce sites and social media. In today's world, the usage of data has increased with a large database, and it is becoming a difficult task for people, to find a relevant item of their interest. So, the RS helps the people to find the most relevant item from the available database, and there exist various algorithms for prediction and recommendation. To determine the effectiveness of algorithms in RS, there are numerous ways to evaluate the goodness of recommendation and a recommender algorithm. The efficiency of the recommendation can be evaluated through various performance evaluation metrics. This paper analyzes various evaluation methods and metrics and demonstrated the ranking prediction and top-N movie recommendation for the users with different algorithmic approaches which will help the designers to understand the ways to choose a good recommendation algorithm under various scenarios. In addition to the above, this paper presents the accuracy calculation of our system based on real-world data.

Keywords: Evaluation metrics, offline, online, recommender system, user study, SVD, SVD++

Corresponding author: bhuvanyaraghunathan@gmail.com

Shalli Rani, R. Maheswar, G. R. Kanagachidambaresan, Sachin Ahuja and Deepali Gupta (eds.) Machine Learning Paradigm for Internet of Things Applications, (113–146) © 2022 Scrivener Publishing LLC

7.1 Introduction

The influence of the recommender system (RS) has started in the mid-1990s, and it is still active in the area of research field as it provides a solution to the information overload problem. The major application areas of the RS are Amazon, Flipkart, Netflix, YouTube, and Facebook. The goal of the RS is to build a predictive model based on the preferences and interests of each user to successfully recommend new products, songs, videos, and persons which will, in turn, increase the engagement level of each user with the service. A key purpose of the RS is to help users to discover items which they would not find easily by themselves. As suggested in the previous work, M. Balabanovic and Y. Shoham [30], the most common filtering techniques are Collaborative Filtering (CF), Content-Based Filtering (CBF) [38], and Hybrid techniques [1, 39]. The recommendation will be generated in CF by analyzing the historical interaction of user-item whereas CBF recommends the product by analyzing the content of items and creates a profile. The recommendation results could be enhanced by combining the features of CF and CBF which is known as the Hybrid technique. In addition to the CF and CBF, there exists a content-based recommendation that analyzes the demographic information and timestamp. Another method known as temporal recommendation which generates the recommendation list by consider time as a significant factor. Since the user's interest and item's popularity gets vary over time. As suggested by Trewin [45], another popular recommendation technique, called knowledge-based recommendation, recommends the item by identifying the needs of the user, and it is considered as the intelligent one among all the other techniques as the scope of the recommendation is user satisfaction and increased revenue of e-commerce site.

7.1.1 Modules of Recommender System

The modules of the RS are listed below.

- Collecting the user's behavior
- Predicting user preferences by the algorithm
- Ranking and recommending the items
- Evaluating the performance of RS.

This paper completely aims at the elaborated study of evaluation metrics in the RS. Apart from that, it is essential to know about the difference between the prediction and recommendation. Often the above two come together since both the approaches encourage user engagement in e-commerce sites. Prediction helps to quantify the item and it is based on data models while the recommendation helps the users to discover the items by analyzing the user-item interaction history.

7.1.2   Evaluation Structure

The evaluation of the RS algorithm can be performed in three modes such as Offline, User Study, and Online [40]. Figure 7.1 displays the evaluation structure of the RS where the complete data set is split into two parts train and test. The test set will be hidden from the recommender algorithms and based on the train data set the recommender algorithms produces the result of either prediction or recommendation. From the result, the evaluation will be done by comparing it against the test set. Creating multiple randomly allocated training sets, often known as k-fold cross-validation, can improve the performance of offline evaluation. The RS is trained using an individual training set and the user ratings can be predicted accurately by considering the score of each fold and averaging them together. Finally, the accuracy of the result can be measured against the test set. The major advantage of k-fold cross-validation is that it will not end up in overfitting. But it may consume a lot more computational power to predict the user ratings. The existing works by Cremonsi, Hua Zheng, and Said [7, 17, 41] focused on the comparison of offline evaluation, user studies, and online evaluation, and this work relies on the performance analysis of offline evaluation and user studies with different algorithms in the RS.

7.1.3   Contribution of the Paper

The main contributions of this work are as follows:

- Modules of RS and the evaluation structure of RS.

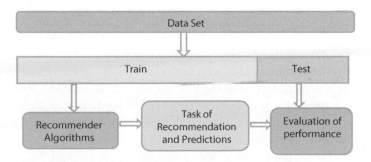

Figure 7.1 Evaluation structure of recommender system.

- A detailed study about the offline, user study, and online evaluation metrics of the RS.
- A detailed narration of data mining techniques in the RS.
- Experimentation of MovieLens dataset to produce top-N recommendation along with its accuracy calculation through offline evaluation.

7.1.4   Organization of the Paper

This chapter is organized as follows. Section 7.2 deals with the offline, user study, and online evaluation metrics where the offline metrics are further divided into prediction accuracy metrics, decision support metrics, and rank aware top-N metrics. All the above metrics are explained elaborately which helps the users to calculate the accuracy in their designed RS. Section 7.3 describes the algorithmic approaches in the RS. Finally, Section 7.4 infers the way to predict top-N recommendation items and the analysis of offline evaluation metrics with the explored algorithms.

7.2   Evaluation Metrics

7.2.1   Offline Analytics

In general, the recommendation system collects user behavior and model the algorithm to provide recommendations. This is usually done by analyzing the user's historical interaction with the item and then the system will make predictions or recommendations. As the technology evolves, there are plenty of recommendation algorithms available; hence, it needs to be evaluated. Table 7.1 summarizes the overview of the offline metrics which is given below.

7.2.1.1   Prediction Accuracy Metrics

It falls under the mode of offline evaluation, which is about calculating the error in the user's prediction. It is an important metric in the offline analysis. The dataset is divided into training and test sets and the dataset should contain user ratings for the product. The user's rating prediction model is trained on the training set and the prediction of new users is computed against the test set. The deviation between the actual and predicted ratings [12] is termed as an error. The metrics such as Mean Absolute Error (MAE), Mean Square Error (MSE), and Root Mean Square Error (RMSE) are used to measure the

Table 7.1 Offline evaluation metrics.

S. no.	Category	Evaluation content	Metrics
1.	Prediction Accuracy Metrics	Prediction Accuracy	Mean Absolute Error (MAE), Mean Squared Error (MSE), Root Mean Squared Error (RMSE), Hit Ratio (HR)
2.	Decision Support Metrics	Performance Measurement	Receiver Operating Characteristic (ROC), Area Under the Curve (AUC), Precision, Recall
3.	Rank Aware Top-N Metrics	Ranking Precision	Mean Reciprocal Rate (MRR), Normalized Discounted Cumulative Gain (nDCG), Mean Average Precision (MAP), Spearman Rank Correlation Coefficient (SRCC)

prediction accuracy. The formula to calculate the MAE, MSE, and RMSE is defined in (7.1), (7.2), and (7.3), respectively, where the first parameter (P) denotes the predicted rating and the second parameter (R) denotes the actual rating. These metrics are used to calculate the regression error.

7.2.1.1.1   Mean Absolute Error
The absolute error also known as Absolute Accuracy Error is the amount of error in the measurement [14]. The difference between the expected and actual rating is being used to compute the absolute error whereas the MAE is the average of all absolute errors which is given below.

$$\mathrm{MAE} = \frac{1}{n}\sum\nolimits_{j=1}^{n}|P-R| \qquad (7.1)$$

7.2.1.1.2   Mean Square Error
It is the default metric for most of the regression algorithms. MSE is calculated by taking the difference between the actual and predicted ratings and squaring them. The squaring is done to remove the negative signs. Also, MSE paves the way to understand and calculate RMSE.

$$MSE = \frac{1}{n} \Sigma_{i=1}^{n} (P-R)^2 \qquad (7.2)$$

7.2.1.1.3   Root Mean Square Error

The major issue with the MSE is that the loss function is high. Hence, the RMSE is intended to reduce the loss function by taking the root value from the obtained value of the MSE [12].

$$RMSE = \sqrt{\frac{1}{n} \Sigma_{i=1}^{n} (P-R)^2} \qquad (7.3)$$

7.2.1.1.4   Hit Ratio

The test set generates the top-N recommendation for all of the users. A hit is always defined as the percentage of observations that is correctly predicted by the recommendation model. The hit rate (HR) can be computed by finding all items in the training data and to apply the method intentionally known as Leave-One-Out Cross-Validation (LOOCV) [32]. The remaining items will be fed to the recommender and top-N recommendations will be produced. If the intentionally removed item is present in the top-N list, then it is considered as a hit.

7.2.1.2   Decision Support Metrics

Decision support emphasizes that many RSs' ultimate objective is to assist individuals in making excellent decisions. Decision support metrics are also known as binary relevance metrics as it helps to know if the item is good or not. In general, the recommended items for the user will be displayed either horizontally or vertically. But most of the users will prefer the front parts of items and few users will consider the back parts of the item and this is known as top-N recommendation. Precision can be described in simple terms as "how many selected items are relevant?", whereas recall is defined as "how many relevant items are selected?" The formula to calculate precision, recall, and F1 score is defined below as in (7.4), (7.5), and (7.6), respectively [42]. The issue with the precision and recall is that it tends to cover the entire dataset and it is not targeted at the top-recommended items. These measures are used in the field of information retrieval, where

Table 7.2 Illustration of confusion matrix.

	Predicted class	
Actual Class	Positive	Negative
Positive	True Positive	False Negative
Negative	False Positive	True Negative

people go through very careful annotations of every item to infer whether the query made is relevant or not. Table 7.2 illustrates the confusion matrix which plays a key role in calculating precision and recall.

$$\text{Precision} = \text{True Positives} / (\text{True Positives} + \text{False Positive}) \quad (7.4)$$

$$\text{Recall} = \text{True Positives} / (\text{True Positives} + \text{False Negative}) \quad (7.5)$$

$$F1 = (2 * \text{Precision} * \text{Recall}) / (\text{Precision} + \text{Recall}) \quad (7.6)$$

7.2.1.2.1 ROC and AUC

ROC can also be abbreviated as Relative Operating Characteristic (ROC) curve that plots the performance of a filter or classifier at different thresholds [13, 15]. Figure 7.2 displays the ROC–Area Under the Curve (AUC) curve generated using the KNN classifier, and it is designed to plot true positive against false positive. AUC measures the effectiveness of the recommendation.

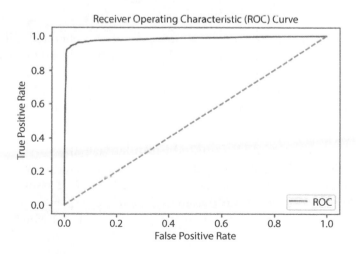

Figure 7.2 ROC-AUC curve.

If the value of AUC is higher, then the performance will be better when distinguishing between the positive and negative classes. The area covered between the curve and the axis is known as AUC.

7.2.1.3   Rank Aware Top-N Metrics

7.2.1.3.1   Mean Average Precision
The average precision (AP) of many recommendations is called the Mean Average Precision (MAP) [16]. The formula to calculate the MAP is defined as follows (7.7):

$$MAP = \frac{\sum_{q=1}^{Q} Avep(q)}{Q} \tag{7.7}$$

where Q is the number of queries in the set and Avep(q) is the AP for a given query, q.

7.2.1.3.2   Mean Reciprocal Rank
This is a very basic metric for determining if the RS has placed the user's favorite items at the top of the N(rank) suggestion list [16]. The formula to calculate MRR is defined below in (7.8).

$$MRR = \frac{1}{N} \sum_{i=1}^{N} \frac{1}{rank_i} \tag{7.8}$$

For each user, a list of recommendations will be generated. Then, the rank of the first relevant recommendation will be calculated. It always starts from one, so the recommendation to the top of the list has rank 1, then the reciprocal rank will be computed, 1 over the rank. For multiple queries, the mean of the reciprocal ranks will be calculated.

7.2.1.3.3   Normalized Discounted Cumulative Gain
To compute the efficiency of the RS, usually, the computation will be done based on how good the list is. Each item in the list will be associated with a value known as gain and the missing values will be replaced to zero. The summation of the score is known as cumulative gain (CG) which is given in (7.9).

$$CG = \sum_{i=1}^{P} rel_i \qquad (7.9)$$

The formula to calculate CG is mentioned in (7.9), where rel_i denotes graded relevance of result at index i. Since most of the users prefer top n items, before summing the scores, divide each by a growing number known as Discounted Cumulative Gain (DCG). The formula to calculate DCG is given in (7.10).

$$DCG = \sum_{k=1}^{n} \frac{rel_k}{\log_2(1+k)} \qquad (7.10)$$

If the performance of the search algorithm is compared from one query to the next, then the consistency of results cannot be achieved using DCG alone. So, the normalization of DCG takes place and it is denoted as nDCG, which is illustrated below (7.11)

$$nDCG_p = DCG_P / I\dot{D}CG_p \qquad (7.11)$$

where the formula to calculate IDCG is (7.12)

$$IDCG = \sum_{i=1}^{|REL|} \frac{2^{rel_i}}{\log(i+1)} \qquad (7.12)$$

where |REL| is the list of documents ordered by relevance to position p.

7.2.1.3.4 Spearman Rank Correlation Coefficient

It is a technique used to describe the direction of the relationship between two variables. The result of SRCC will always be in the range between +1 and −1. The formula to calculate the SRCC is given below (7.13)

$$\rho = 1 - \frac{6\sum d_i^2}{n(n2-1)} \qquad (7.13)$$

where n is the number of observations and d_i refers to the difference between the ranks.

Table 7.3 Overview of additional metrics.

S. no.	Metrics	Evaluation content
1.	Coverage	The percentage of products for which a recommender can make a prediction.
2.	Popularity	The metric used to check the popularity of the item.
3.	Personalization	It is a measure to examine, whether the system is providing the recommendation of the right product based on individual preference.
4.	Serendipity	It helps to explore and consume the less popular, unexpected items through recommendation.
5.	Diversity	A metric for determining the degree of similarity between items in a list.
6.	Churn	To know, how sensitive the recommender is to the user behavior, the churn metric is helpful.
7.	Responsiveness	This metric describes how new user's behavior influences the recommendation system.

7.2.2   Item and List-Based Metrics

RSs are fundamentally about recommending things that their users did not already know about. A recommender that only predicts what people will do regardless is not really useful. To deal with the idea of focusing on attributes that are more closely related to enhanced business objectives or customer happiness, the metrics to be considered are coverage, popularity, personalization, serendipity, and diversity. Table 7.3 presents the overview of additional metrics mentioned above.

7.2.2.1   Coverage

The percentage of products for which a recommender can make a forecast is referred to as coverage [24]. It is also used as a background metric when the things are comparing from the top-N end. It can be applied to both the item and the user known as item coverage and user coverage. The percentage of items in the recommendation that are covered compared to the total number of items is referred to as item coverage. User coverage, on the other hand, refers to the percentage of users for whom the recommender was able to provide a list of recommendations for the entire user population. The percentage of recommended user-item pairs over the entire number of pairs is known as catalogue coverage.

7.2.2.2   Popularity

Another simple metric is popularity, which can be applied to either individual recommendations or an average over a list of recommendations [19, 26]. It is measured as a percentage of users who buy or rate the item, and it is simply defined as "how popular the item is" and the inverse of popularity is "novelty". The novelty of the RS is that it is designed to recommend items to users that are not widely known. The novelty can be achieved in the RS by displaying the non-popular items to the users [35].

7.2.2.3   Personalization

It is a method to verify if the model recommends many of the same items to different users [51]. There are numerous ways to determine how personalized a recommender is; one method is to compute the prediction for each item across all users on an item-by-item basis. Then, the computed variance needs to be observed if the value is higher than the system which denotes it is more personalized and the model offers a personalized experience to each user whereas the lower value denotes the model is less personalized.

7.2.2.4   Serendipity

Serendipity's main business goal is to inspire customers to consume less popular things [14, 44]. The term "serendipity" was coined in the 18th century, and it is introduced by Pek Van Andel [37]. If the term is looked up in a dictionary, then it refers to the occurrence of events by chance happily or beneficially. A good RS should always suggest unknown things to the user and if the recommendation is defined from the user point of view, it should always offer surprise, delight, and non-expected results to the user. Hence, the serendipitous recommendation is getting the unexpected result but the user loves it in the end, and it can be measured through offline analytics and user survey.

7.2.2.5   Diversity

It is a metric for how dissimilar items in a list are [6, 19]. This can be applied only to the list of recommendations and for a single item there is no diversity score exists which means an item is not diverse. In general, the user will always pick the first item in the recommended list but if later times the items in the top-N list are similar to the already chosen product then the recommendation is not the stimulating one. So, the items which are too similar to the chosen product could be replaced to get a more diversified list. The diversification can also be achieved through clustering. It can be done by taking three or four clusters which will show a few items from the user interesting things. Scatter-gather is a set of the interface which can do this effectively by displaying few items as a representative of each cluster. It will let the user select their interested items and gather those items together and then re-cluster and re-scatter. This is perceived as an interactive method of finding items of interest to users [33].

7.2.2.6   Churn

Churn measures how sensitive the RS is, for new user behavior. If the recommendation system shows completely the same set of items then it is not an effective one. Hence, a little bit of randomization can be included in the top-N recommendation. But if the churn is compared with diversity and novelty, a high churn value is not a good thing. The churn metric can be maximized by recommending items completely at random and of course, those would not be considered as good recommendations.

7.2.2.7   Responsiveness

The next metric to be considered is responsiveness which measures how quickly does new user behavior influences the recommendations. More responsiveness would always seem to be a good thing but from the developer's point of view, they need to decide how responsive the RS needs to be. Since expecting the RSs to be instantaneous responsive is complex, difficult to maintain, and expensive to build.

When all these metrics are observed, accuracy is the topmost metric in which users are highly concerned about but experimentally analyzed, users would prefer to compromise a little bit of accuracy to achieve some serendipity, diversity, and to meet other parts of the search goals. The offline metrics discussed above will always deal with the ground truth while the item and list-based metrics dealt with the lab and real-world studies. Both the above metrics will not evaluate the recommendation during the live session of users. The success of a recommendation system can be declared only it has a real impact on real users. In online evaluation, recommendations will be displayed to the real users during their live session and the system will observe the users through the acceptance rate. Beel, Joeran *et al.* [4]

proved that the efficiency of the RS can be well measured in user studies and online evaluation, compared to the offline evaluation.

7.2.3   User Studies and Online Evaluation

The offline evaluation deals with the rating prediction task will always support user browsing and search. However, if there is a change in the user behavior over time, then the items in the recommendation list need to be updated. Hence, the online evaluation focuses on live users with real-time observations. User studies measure the satisfaction of users through the analysis of explicit ratings given to the item [40]. When dealing with the recommendation it is important to know the data sources. A RS begins with information about each user that can be used to determine the user's preferences and interests. One way to understand the user is through ratings and it is divided into explicit and implicit. Writing comments, thumbs up and down, giving a rating on the scale of 1 to 5 are considered as the explicit rating. User view, User clicks, and Bookmarks are considered to be the implicit rating. The percentage of user clicks calculated by the RS when it is online is known as the online accuracy metric [3]. Figure 7.3 shows the classification of user study.

7.2.3.1   Usage Log

To know about the user preference of items and how it is related to the recommended list, the construction of usage logs will be helpful. It comprises the information of items displayed to the user, user click, and also about what the user purchased. Hence, the usage logs are a great way of evaluating the user roughly. If the recommendation system is constructed based on hybrid filtering, then the resultant recommendation will be produced from the combination of some filtering algorithms (e.g., content-based and item-item CF). To predict which is more successful the usage logs will play a predominant role. It gives the ability to measure the accuracy not only based on some ground truth but also based on the actual recommendations

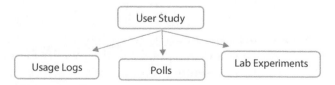

Figure 7.3 Types of user study.

that the system made. It is a nice way to understand whether the system is doing its intended work.

7.2.3.2   Polls

The best way to understand what a person wants is to ask them. When the new user or item enters the site cold start problem occurs and the recommendation system will not be aware of the new user and item and the suggestion can be provided by creating a questionnaire that helps to understand the users and items as well. Zhao, Wayne [50] implemented one such solution for the cold start problem by collecting users' detail through the social network where the demographic attributes such as age, gender, profession, and marital status are considered, and the recommendation can be obtained without considering the previous purchase pattern. Z.K.A Baizal [52] implemented another sort of solution for the cold start by implementing a conversational RS.

7.2.3.3   Lab Experiments

There are a lot of ways to do the lab experiments where the first idea is that the evaluations can be carried out in the lab by bringing the participants in and the experience can be obtained by asking them to do things, whereas the second way is that the lab experiments can be conducted online. Participants in lab studies are aware that they are taking part in a user study and behavioral change may probably affect the evaluation results thereby.

7.2.3.4   Online A/B Test

The personalized recommendation has become a core part of most e-commerce sites. A/B tests or massive A/B test allows gathering user-item interactions which could be used to train for personalized recommendations. The major objective of the online A/B test is to compare two different items and to decide which is the most interesting item for the user by observing the behavior of users. It will take some time to implement and the following observations about the user will be inferred. Do the people take as many recommendations? Do they come back to the system more or less? Do they end up liking the things that they rate more or less?

The goal of an online experiment is to analyze whether the changes made in the system improve the responses of the user. It is a measure to assess whether the way of presenting recommendations help the users to buy more recommended items. Machmouchi and Buscher [47] presented

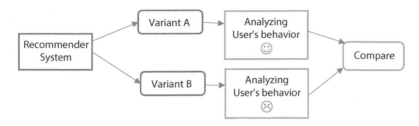

Figure 7.4   Basic structure of A/B test.

an in-depth study of online A/B metrics. However, Alexandre Gilotte, Clement Calauzènes *et al.* [2] exploited the offline A/B evaluation.

Figure 7.4 displays the basic structure of A/B Test where two variants are involved. Variant A is the current system, and it recommends few items to the user with the assumption of popularity-based item retrieval and the variant B is constructed, for instance, through CF or CBF and recommends few items to the user. One group of users sees Version A and other groups of users see version B and the responses will be measured differently by observing which group of users buys more items as it is recommended [25].

7.3   Related Works

In this section, an extant literature review on algorithmic approaches to RS is provided. There are two predominant approaches in the RS CF, and CBF. CF [5, 23] works based on user similarities. The assumption here is that two users who liked the same items in the past probably may like the same items in the future, and the CF is further divided into memory-based CF and model-based CF. Memory-based CF always deals with the history of recorded values, whereas the model-based CF will generate a user model based on the user ratings for recommending a product. On the other hand, CBF [36] learns the user preference by considering the item features. It saves the history of a user's favorite products in the past and uses that information to create a model that can recommend comparable products in the future. The recommendation is also divided into push, pull, and passive. "Push" is a direct method of providing recommendations through emails and notifications. "Pull" is considered to be the indirect method where the recommendations are displayed to the user only when the users ask for them. Finally, the related products are displayed in the "passive" method which has a resemblance to the product that the user currently viewed. All the above-described methods have advantages and disadvantages. Table 7.4 explains the input and real-time examples of filtering techniques.

Table 7.4 Overview of filtering techniques.

S. no.	Method	Input	Example
1.	Collaborative	Ratings given by the user and community ratings	E-commerce sites such as Amazon and Flipkart provide the recommendation by considering the user's shopping cart, purchase history, and the user ratings given for the product.
2.	Content-based	Ratings given by the user and attributes of the item	YouTube will always provide the personalized recommendation to the users. Personalization can be enhanced by combining the user information which creates a series of videos that the user will watch next.
3.	Knowledge-based	Specification of the user combined with attributes of the item and domain knowledge	It works based on the user query. The knowledge-based recommendation is applicable for products that are not purchased often, e.g., house and cars.
4.	Demographic	Demographic information of users and their ratings of items	In real-time movie recommendations, the movie can be recommended to the user by utilizing the demographic data.

7.3.1   Categories of Recommendation

RSs are classified into three classes as designed by McNee *et al.* [44]. The first category is *Recommending good items* to users. The system will provide a list of items that the user is predicted to prefer. But the user will not prefer all the suggested items instead the user can choose one or more suggested items. For instance, the e-commerce sites will provide the recommendation for list of items that the user may be interested in. Another category is *Recommending some good items* which will recommend only a part of the preferred item set and the most important thing to consider is not to include any disliked item for the recommendation, and the final category is *Recommending all good items* which recommend all the important items to the user.

7.3.2   Data Mining Methods of Recommender System

The process of data mining in RS is data preprocessing, analysis, and interpretation of data [40]. To recommend a product based on real-life data, it needs to be preprocessed. The major preprocessing techniques are sampling and dimensionality reduction. Figure 7.5 depicts the stages of recommendation in RS.

7.3.2.1   Data Pre-Processing

7.3.2.1.1   Sampling
The main technique for selecting a subset of data from a large data set. When the algorithms in RS suffer from the scalability issue then preprocessing the entire data set may be expensive hence the sampling technique plays an important role in data mining methods. It can also be used to partition the data set to create training and test sets. The simplest sampling technique will have an equal probability of selecting items from the dataset known as "random sampling". Sampling may lead to overfitting to the

Figure 7.5 Process of data mining in RS.

specific subset of training and testing data sets hence the training process may be iterated several times. The performance of offline evaluation will be enhanced by creating many randomly assigned training sets instead of a single train and test split which is named k-fold cross-validation. The RS is trained using the individual training set, and the system's accuracy is assessed against the test set. Although it demands a significant amount of computer power, the benefit is that it avoids overfitting.

7.3.2.1.2   Dimensionality Reduction

Curse of dimensionality [34] refers to the set of problem arises when working with high-dimensional data. When the dataset contains a large number of attributes it is known as high-dimensional data. Another important issue to deal with the RS is sparsity [5] which defines the limited amount of information. Hence, the dimensionality reduction techniques can be applied as a solution to overcome the curse of dimensionality and sparse matrix. There exist various methods for dimensionality reduction such as Principal Component Analysis (PCA) [31], Linear Discriminant Analysis (LDA) [21], Singular Value Decomposition (SVD) [48], Matrix Factorization, and Independent Component Analysis (ICA). Out of all the methods, PCA and SVD play an important role in dimensionality reduction.

PCA is a dimensionality reduction technique that helps to reduce the dimensionality of large datasets. The dimensionality will be reduced by applying the transformation method which transforms the large set of variables into a smaller one but still preserves as much information as possible. The major reason behind PCA is if the dimensionality of the data is reduced the exploration and visualization of data become much easier. PCA is a statistical method that also helps to identify the patterns in the high-dimensional data sets. The first step in PCA is "standardization" which will transform all the variables into the same scale. Mathematically, it can be computed by subtracting the mean and dividing the standard deviation for each value of each variable.

$$z = \frac{value - mean}{standard\ deviation} \tag{7.14}$$

To identify if the variables contain redundant information, the next step is to perform the covariance matrix. It is measured between two dimensions to check if there exists a relationship between the two dimensions.

$$\text{covarinace}(X, Y) = \frac{1}{n-1} \sum_{i=1}^{n} (x_i - x)(x_i - x)^T \qquad (7.15)$$

Finally, the computation of eigenvalue and eigenvectors from the covariance matrix needs to be calculated to determine the principal components of the data. The outcome of PCA is the set of new variables that can be constructed either through linear combinations or a mixture of initial variables. The new variables should not be correlated to each other and most of the information will be compressed in the first component and the remaining information in the second and so on.

SVD is a method that decomposes a rectangular matrix into three other matrices. It is a powerful tool for matrix factorization. It is widely applied in statistics, machine learning, and computer science. This methodology is often applicable in the real-life scenario since the rectangular matrix always represents a wide variety of data. Equation (7.16) represents the mathematical illustration of SVD.

$$A = USVT \qquad (7.16)$$

where A is an m × n rectangular matrix, U is an m × n unitary matrix, S is an n × n diagonal matrix, and V is an n × n unitary matrix. A unitary matrix is a matrix whose inverse equals its conjugate transpose. Usually, when both train and test data are available in the beginning, SVD can be applied to both of training and test set as a single matrix. The outcome of SVD is, reduced dimension data which is further divided into train and test sets. The major advantage of SVD is, it simplifies data, removes noise, and improves the results. In the RS, SVD is applied as a CF technique, which uses a matrix structure where each row represents a user and each column represents an item.

7.3.2.2 Data Analysis

When observing the part of data analysis, it can be classified into the tasks that come under supervised and unsupervised machine learning. The most dominant method of classification and clustering comes under supervised and unsupervised learning, respectively. Both the techniques of classification and clustering get differed with the type of dataset we are exploring. Classification technique utilizes the labeled dataset and clustering uses the unlabeled dataset. The broadly used classification algorithms are Logistic

Table 7.5 Overview of classifier algorithm.

S. no.	Classifier algorithm	Description	Advantages	Disadvantages	Application
1.	Logistic Regression	It helps to predict a binary outcome based on set of independent variables.	Easy to implement	May not be accurate if the sample size is too small.	Spam email detection, Prediction of fraudulent transaction.
2.	Naïve Bayes	Naïve Bayes is a supervised learning algorithm which is based on Bayes theorem.	It can be used for binary and multiclass classification problem.	It assumes all the features are independent; hence, it cannot learn the relationship between the features.	Text classification such as sentiment analysis and spam filtering.
3.	Decision tree classifier	It has a flowchart like structure, where the internal node represents the feature and the branch represents the decision rule. It selects the best attribute using Attribute Selection Measures.	It is easy to interpret and visualize.	It is sensitive to noisy data.	Engineering, civil planning and law.

(Continued)

Table 7.5 Overview of classifier algorithm. (*Continued*)

S. no.	Classifier algorithm	Description	Advantages	Disadvantages	Application
	K-Nearest Neighbor	It is also known as the lazy learner algorithm because it does not learn anything from the training set; instead, it saves the data to the dataset and executes a classification operation. It can be applied to both classification and regression problem.	It is more effective when the training data is large.	The computation cost is bit high as it needs to calculate the distance between the data points for all the training samples.	Pattern recognition, intrusion detection.

(*Continued*)

Table 7.5 Overview of classifier algorithm. (*Continued*)

S. no.	Classifier algorithm	Description	Advantages	Disadvantages	Application
	Random forest	Type of ensemble learning method which can be used for classification and prediction. It generates decision trees from randomly picked data points and uses each tree to make predictions. The best solution can be chosen by implementing a voting rule.	The result is accurate and it prevents overfitting.	Difficult to implement. Slow in nature.	E-commerce, Banking, and Stock Market Analysis.
	Support Vector Machine	SVM constructs the hyperplane that separates the two classes very well.	It is effective in high-dimensional spaces.	It may lack with large datasets as the training time required is high.	Face detection, Image classification, and Bio informatics.

Regression [9], Naïve Bayes [43], Decision Tree Classifier [46], K-Nearest Neighbor [20], Random Forest Algorithm [46], and Support Vector Machine. The overview of the classification algorithms in machine learning is depicted in Table 7.5.

Clustering is the process of unsupervised learning which group the similar data points. Clustering algorithm divides the data points into different groups such that each data point is similar to the data points in the same point and dissimilar to the data points in the other groups. By applying the similarity and dissimilarity measures, the data points will be assigned. The popular clustering algorithms are partitional clustering algorithm, hierarchical clustering algorithm and density-based algorithm. The partitional algorithm [22] decomposes the dataset into disjoint clusters. It constructs K partitions based on N points and (K ≤ N). The hierarchical clustering algorithm [29] divides the dataset into tree like structure which is also known as dendrogram. The hierarchical clustering is further divided into agglomerative and divisive clustering. The agglomerative clustering follows the bottom-up merge approach and divisive clustering follows the top-down split approach. Another popular clustering technique is density-based clustering [28] which cluster the regions based on the density. The lower dense regions will form a cluster and the high-density regions will be categorized into another cluster.

This section narrates the data mining techniques of RS which reviews the classifier and clustering algorithms. Choosing the appropriate data mining technique in RS is a tedious task that covers many constraints. However, the short description of algorithmic approaches included in this section will be helpful to have a collective information.

7.4   Experimental Setup

The above metrics are experimented with the MovieLens dataset [10] which comprises around 9,000 movies. The overview of the explored dataset is mentioned in Table 7.6. The minimum rating threshold is set which saves the recommendation list by avoiding the movies that fall below the threshold value. The explored dataset is experimented with two different recommender algorithms known as Random and SVD. SVD was used widely during the Netflix competition and it achieved a lot.

Matrix decomposition is also known as the matrix factorization [8] technique which decomposes a matrix into its constituent elements. This factorization technique reduces the number of features of a dataset by reducing the space dimension, for instance, N-dimension to K-dimension

Table 7.6 Overview of the explored dataset.

Dataset	Movies	Users	Ratings	Time stamp	Internet Movie Database ID (IMDb ID)	Genres	Tags	Demographic information
MovieLens	9125	671	100,004	✓	✓	✓	✓	×

where K < N. The SVD approach [48] predicts the user ratings through the term defined in (7.17), where R is the missing rating, U denotes the user, and M denotes the movies.

$$R = U\Sigma M^T \tag{7.17}$$

The unknown values of R can be constructed through the known values of U and M. The training data set will always be represented in terms of a smaller matrix that are factors of the ratings to be predicted, and the sigma matrix in the middle is used to scale the values. The unknown values of R can be easily constructed by multiplying these factors together. Figure 7.6 illustrates the way of computing the missing user rating "Alexa" for the movie "Avengers".

By assuming the known ratings of a given row and column in U and M, if the unknown values of those complete rows and columns are found, then the error will be much reduced and this is one of the better ways for rating prediction. From the obtained dataset, a single train and test split are created where 70% of the data is used to train and 30% of the data is used to test. One of the standard methods in CF is K-Nearest Neighbor (KNN) algorithm which computes the item similarity. The SVD recommender algorithm with a fixed random seed is employed here to get consistent results. The random recommender algorithm and the SVD algorithm is applied to the train set to produce a recommendation. Further, the test set is processed on this algorithm which produces a set of rating predictions for all of the test ratings that it was fed. Figure 7.7 illustrates the workflow of generating and evaluating the top-N recommendation using the MovieLens dataset.

To measure how good those predictions are, prediction accuracy metrics such as RMSE and MAE metrics are used. To evaluate the items in the top-N recommendations, the LOOCV [32] method is used and it is

Users	Titanic	Liar-Liar	Star Wars	Avengers
Alexa	5	4	3	?
Siri	3.5	?	?	5
George	5	3.5	4	?

$$R_{Alexa, Avengers} = U_{Alexa}.M^T Avengers.$$

Figure 7.6 Rating prediction through matrix factorization.

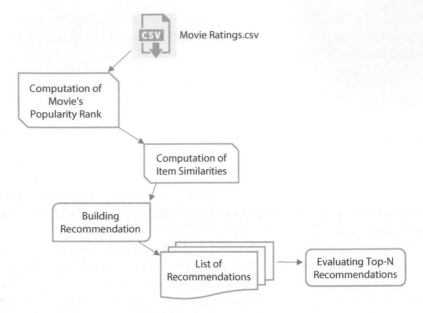

Figure 7.7 Process flow of offline evaluation.

processed with the single train and test split. LOOCV [18] always set aside one rating per user, which is randomly selected for the test set and the major task is to predict top-N recommendations including the left-out movie. Since LOOCV works on a per user basis, the way the train and the test set created is utterly different; hence, the split has to be performed again, which means that the SVD algorithm needs to be trained with the new training set, and the testing will be carried out again with the test set of left-out ratings for each user.

In general, to evaluate the complete list of top-N recommendations of each user, the rating prediction will be carried out for every movie which the user has not already rated. This is one of the common approaches for rating prediction in the top-N RS. Instead of using the common approach here considered the ratings from the movies the user has not already seen. Since, the recommendation should focus more on the movies that the user has not seen. So, the test set is built by considering all the possible user-movie pairs that are not present in the training set. Thus, the process of rating prediction will be carried out with the Random and SVD algorithm. After the rating prediction stage is built, a new recommendation list will be created where the results will be sorted based on the ranks and top-N movies will be recommended to the user. Then, the metrics of HR, coverage, diversity, and novelty of the proposed system is evaluated.

The performance of the proposed RS is evaluated against the SVD and a random recommender algorithm. SVD is one of the best algorithms under the CF; hence, there would not be a wonder if the SVD performs better than the random recommender algorithm. CF predicts the rating for the user-movie pair by analyzing the history of the ratings given by the user for the movies present in the training set. Instead of finding similar people and recommend the stuff based on their likings, item-based CF (IBCF) [39] analyzes the individual user and recommends similar movies to the user by observing the previous pattern. In the existing work, Zhang and Hurley [33] implemented the IBCF to construct the item-item similarity matrix and the recommended things maximized the diversity and preserved a certain level of accuracy. The working style of IBCF also known as item-item CF is depicted in Figure 7.8.

The detailed results of RMSE, MAE, coverage, diversity, and HR obtained through Random and SVD are depicted in Table 7.7.

In general, lower RMSE and MAE scores are better, as they are measuring errors, and it is good to get the lower RMSE and MAE value in SVD. Also, SVD does a better job in the HR. Further, the metrics of coverage, diversity, and novelty scores are better with the random compared to the SVD. If the coverage is considered, then SVD is recommending quality items using the threshold value on the top-N recommendations whereas the random is predicting the ratings based on the normal distribution and fill the recommendation list with the average rating threshold value. Hence, it produces 100% coverage.

Though the diversity is lower with SVD, users may get the expected thing as the value is comparatively good. Finally, novelty is lower with SVD but it is good and expected. Since picking the random movies for recommendations will always result in good novelty while SVD discovers the good popular movie for recommendations. Also, it can be clearly stated that the

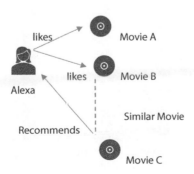

Figure 7.8 Illustration of IBCF.

Table 7.7 System generated metric results using MovieLens with Random and SVD when n = 10.

S. no.	Metric	Random	SVD
1.	RMSE	1.4414	0.9066
2.	MAE	1.1503	0.6990
3.	HR	0.0119	0.0298
4.	Coverage	1.0000	0.9553
5.	Diversity	0.0704	0.0445
6.	Novelty	545.6599	491.5768

novelty is a measure of the obscure recommendation. Figure 7.9 depicts the performance analysis of both the algorithm in a graphical manner.

Though the SVD results in good accuracy and high novelty, the performance can be further enhanced by SVD++ [11] which is the extension

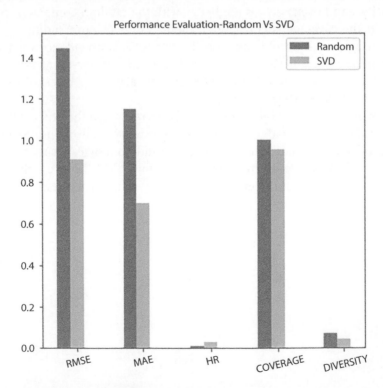

Figure 7.9 Performance evaluation of Random vs. SVD.

of SVD. SVD++ played a major role in the winning system of the Netflix competition [27, 49]. Compared to the SVD, SVD++ will rate the movies by even considering the implicit feedback which makes the system more successful and it results in improved accuracy and novelty. The comparison result of SVD and SVD++ is shown in Table 7.8. Figure 7.10 depicts

Table 7.8 System generated metric results using MovieLens with SVD and SVD++ when n = 10.

S. no.	Metric	SVD	SVD++
1.	RMSE	0.9066	0.9009
2.	MAE	0.6990	0.6923
3.	HR	0.0298	0.0283
4.	Coverage	0.9553	0.9419
5.	Diversity	0.0445	0.0967
6.	Novelty	491.5768	632.0025

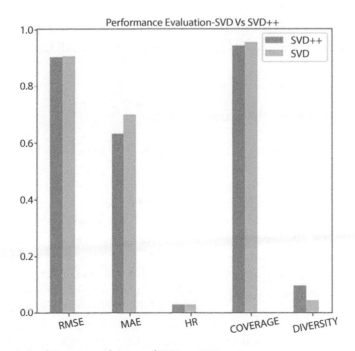

Figure 7.10 Performance evaluation of SVD vs. SVD++.

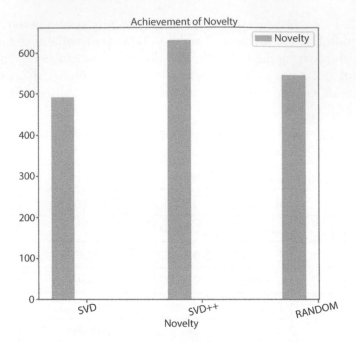

Figure 7.11 Novelty calculation of Random, SVD, and SVD++.

the performance analysis of SVD and SVD++, and Figure 7.11 represents the graphical illustration of achieved novelty score through Random, SVD, and SVD++.

7.5 Summary and Conclusions

The major goal of the RS is increased customer satisfaction. For instance, Amazon and Flipkart users are benefitted by presenting with many choices, and they spend their money through e-commerce sites. Considering Netflix and YouTube, their target is to help the users to find relevant movies that fit their preferences and it may lead to the subscription of the site. By considering all these, RS indirectly increases the revenue of commercial sites. As mentioned in Section 7.2, this paper discusses various evaluation metrics that include offline, online, and user study. By considering the available metrics designers of the RS can choose the evaluation metrics based on the specific task and can evaluate the performance of the recommendation algorithm which can further help to optimize the algorithm. Next, the paper experiments with the MovieLens data with three different algorithmic approaches known as Random, SVD, and SVD++ for ranking prediction and recommendation. From this study, we can conclude that the SVD++ performs better than the other two approaches with a better accuracy score and achieved the highest novelty rate. Evaluation of the recommender algorithm is one of the important research aspects in the RS as there exist plenty of algorithms that help to find the best one among all the candidates. Finally, we have presented a framework for the evaluation and it is hoped that this work helps the designers to choose the algorithms and metrics under various scenarios.

References

1. Adomavicius., G. and Tuzhilin, A., Toward the next generation of recommender systems: a survey of the state-of-the-art and possible extensions. *IEEE Trans. Knowl. Data Eng.*, 17, 6, 734–749, 2005.
2. Gilotte, A., Calauzènes, C., Nedelec, T., Abraham, A., Dollé, S., Offline A/B Testing for Recommender Systems, in: *Proceedings of the Eleventh ACM International Conference on Web Search and Data Mining Association for Computing Machinery*, pp. 198–206, 2018.
3. Maksai, A., Garcin, F., Faltings, B., Predicting online performance of news recommender systems through Richer evaluation metrics, in: *Proceedings of the 9th ACM Conference on Recommender Systems*, pp. 179–186, 2015.
4. Beel, J. and Langer, S., *A Comparison of Offline Evaluations, Online Evaluations, and User Studies in the Context of Research-Paper Recommender Systems*, in: *Proceedings of the 19th International Conference on Theory and Practice of Digital Libraries (TPDL)*, vol. 9316, pp. 153–168, 2015, 10.1007/978-3-319-24592-8_12.
5. Alhijawi, B., Al-Naymat, G., Obeid, N., Awajan, A., Novel predictive model to improve the accuracy of collaborative filtering recommender systems. *Inf. Syst.*, 96, 101670, 2021.
6. Ziegler, C.-N., McNee, S.M., Konstan, J.A., Lausen, G., Improving recommendation lists through topic diversification, in: *Proceedings of the 14th international conference on World Wide Web Association for Computing Machinery*, New York, NY, USA, pp. 22–32, 2005.
7. Cremonesi, P., Garzotto, F., Negro, S., Papadopoulos, A.V., Turrin, R., Looking for "Good" Recommendations: A Comparative Evaluation of Recommender Systems, in: *INTERACT 2011. Lecture Notes in Computer Science*, vol. 6948, Springer, Berlin, Heidelberg, 2011.
8. Gurini, D.F., Gasparetti, F., Micarelli, A., Sansonetti, G., Temporal people-to-people recommendation on social networks with sentiment-based matrix factorization. *Future Gener. Comput. Syst.*, 78, Part 1, 430–439, 2018.

9. Fan, Y., Bai, J., Lei, X., Zhang, Y., Zhang, B., Li, K.-C., Tan, G., Privacy preserving based logistic regression on big data. *J. Netw. Comput. Appl.*, 171, 102769, 2020.

10. Maxwell Harper, F. and Konstan, J.A., The MovieLens Datasets: History and Context. *ACM Trans. Interact. Intell. Syst. (TiiS)*, 5, 4, Article 19, http://dx.doi.org/10.1145/2827872, 1–19, 2015.

11. Guan, X., Li, C.T., Guan, Y., Enhanced SVD for collaborative filtering, in: *Advances in Knowledge Discovery and Data Mining: 20th Pacific-Asia Conference, PAKDD 2016*, vol. 9652 LNAI, pp. 503–514, (Lecture Notes in Computer Science (including subseries Lecture Notes in Artificial Intelligence and Lecture Notes in Bioinformatics), Springer-Verlag London Ltd, 2016, https://doi.org/10.1007/978-3-319-31750-2_40

12. Gunawardana, A. and Shani, G., A Survey of Accuracy Evaluation Metrics of Recommendation Tasks. *J. Mach. Learn. Res.*, 10, 2935–2962, 2009, 10.1145/1577069.1755883.

13. Haley, J.A. and Mcneil, B.J., The meaning and use of the area under a receiver operating characteristic (roc) curve. *Radiology*, 143, 29–36, 1982.

14. Herlocker, J., Konstan, J., Terveen, L., Lui, J. C.s., Riedl, T., Evaluating collaborative filtering recommender systems. *ACM Trans. Inf. Syst.*, 22, 5–53, 2004.

15. Hernández-del-Olmo, F. and Gaudioso, E., Evaluation of recommender systems: A new approach. *Expert Syst. Appl.*, 35, 790–804, 2008.

16. Liu, H., Kong, X., Bai, X., Wang, W., Bekele, T.M., Xia, F., Context-Based Collaborative Filtering for Citation Recommendation. *IEEE Access*, 3, 1695–1703, 2015.

17. Zheng, H., Wang, D., Zhang, Q., Li, H., Yang, T., Do clicks measure recommendation relevancy? an empirical user study, in: *Proceedings of the fourth ACM conference on Recommender systemsAssociation for Computing Machinery*, New York, NY, USA, pp. 249–252, 2010.

18. Konstan, J.A., McNee, S.M., Ziegler, C.N., Torres, R., Kapoor, N., Riedl, J., Lessons on applying automated recommender systems to information-seeking tasks, in: *Proceedings of the TwentyFirst National Conference on Artifical Intelligence*, 2006.

19. Jannach, D., Lerche, L., Gedikli, F., Bonnin, G., What Recommenders Recommend – An Analysis of Accuracy, Popularity, and Sales Diversity Effects, in: *User Modeling, Adaptation, and Personalization. UMAP 2013. Lecture Notes in Computer Science*, vol. 7899, Springer, Berlin, Heidelberg, 2013.

20. Gou, J., Ma, H., Ou, W., Zeng, S., Rao, Y., Yang, H., A generalized mean distance-based k-nearest neighbor classifier. *Expert Syst. Appl.*, 115, 356–372, 2019.

21. Nam, J.H., Kim, D., Chung, D., Sparse linear discriminant analysis using the prior-knowledge-guided block covariance matrix. *Chemometr. Intell. Lab. Syst.*, 206, 104142, 2020.

22. Jin, X. and Han, J., Partitional Clustering, in: *Encyclopedia of Machine Learning*, C. Sammut and G.I. Webb (Eds.), Springer, Boston, MA, 2011, https://doi.org/10.1007/978-0-387-30164-8_631.

23. Breese, J.S., Heckerman, D., Kadie, C.M., Empirical analysis of predictive algorithms for collaborative filtering, in: *UAI: Uncertainty in Artificial Intelligence*, pp. 43–52, 1998.

24. Kaminskas, M. and Bridge, D., Diversity, Serendipity, Novelty, and Coverage: A Survey and Empirical Analysis of Beyond-Accuracy Objectives in Recommender Systems. *ACM Trans. Interact. Intell. Syst.*, 7, 1–42, 2016.

25. Kohavi, R., Longbotham, R., Sommerfield, D., Henne, R., Controlled experiments on the web: Survey and practical guide. *Data Min. Knowl. Discovery*, 18, 140–181, 2009.

26. Majbouri Yazdi, K. *et al.*, Improving Recommender Systems Accuracy in Social Networks Using Popularity. *20th International Conference on Parallel and Distributed Computing, Applications and Technologies (PDCAT)*, Gold Coast, Australia, pp. 301–307, 2019.

27. Koren, Y., The BellKor solution to the Netflix Grand Prize, 2009, http://www.netflixprize.com/assets/GrandPrize2009_BPC_BellKor.pdf

28. Kriegel, H.P., Kröger, P., Sander, J., Zimek, A., Density-based clustering. *Wiley Interdiscip. Rev.: Data Min. Knowl. Discovery*, 1, 3, 231–240, 2011.

29. Kuchaki Rafsanjani, M., Asghari, Z., Emami, N., A Survey of Hierarchical Clustering Algorithms. *J. Math. Comput. Sci.*, 5, 229–240, 2012.

30. Balabanovic, M. and Shoham, Y., Fab: content-based, collaborative recommendation. *Commun. ACM*, 40, 3 (March 1997), 66–72, 1997.

31. Aaldering, L.J., Leker, J., Song, C.H., Recommending untapped M&A opportunities: A combined approach using principal component analysis and collaborative filtering. *Expert Syst. Appl.*, 125, 221–232, 2019.

32. Meijer, R. and Goeman, J., Efficient approximate k-fold and leave-one-out cross-validation for ridge regression. *Biom. J. Biom. Z.*, 55, 141–155, 2013.

33. Zhang, M. and Hurley, N., Avoiding monotony: improving the diversity of recommendation lists, in: *Proceedings of the 2008 ACM conference on Recommender systems Association for Computing Machinery*, New York, NY, USA, pp. 123–130, 2008.

34. Aremu, O.O., Hyland-Wood, D., McAree, P.R., A machine learning approach to circumventing the curse of dimensionality in discontinuous time series machine data. *Reliab. Eng. Syst. Saf.*, 195, 106706, 2020.

35. Celma, O., *Music Recommendation and Discovery in the Long Tail*, Ph.D. Dissertation, Universitat Pompeu Fabra, Spain, 2009.

36. Sánchez, P. and Bellogín, A., Building user profiles based on sequences for content and collaborative filtering. *Inf. Process. Manage.*, 56, 1, 192–211, 2019.

37. Van Andel, P., Anatomy of the Unsought Finding. Serendipity: Orgin, History, Domains, Traditions, Appearances, Patterns and Programmability. *Br. J. Philos. Sci.*, 45, 2, 631–648, 1994.

38. Lops, P., de Gemmis, M., Semeraro, G., Content-based recommender systems: State of the art and trends, in: *Recommender Systems Handbook*, pp. 73–105, Springer, Boston, MA, USA, 2011.
39. Bhuvanya, R. and Kavitha, M., Recommendation System: A Systematic Overview on Methods, Issues and Solutions. *Int. J. Adv. Trends Comput. Sci. Eng.*, 9, 5, 8851–8859, 2020.
40. Ricci, F., Rokach, L., Shapira, Chapter 8 Evaluating recommender systems, in: *Recommender Systems Handbook*, figure pp. 257–294, Springer, US, 2011.
41. Said, A., *Evaluating the Accuracy and Utility of Recommender Systems*, 2013, http://dx.doi.org/10.14279/depositonce-3563
42. Sarwar, B.M., Karypis, G., Konstan, J.A., Riedl, J.T., Analysis of recommendation algorithms for e-commerce, in: *Proceedings of the 2nd ACM conference on Electronic commerce (EC '00)*, ACM, New York, pp. 158–167, 2000.
43. Chen, S., Webb, G.I., Liu, L., Ma, X., A novel selective naïve Bayes algorithm. *Knowledge-Based Syst.*, 192, 105361, 2020.
44. Mcnee, S., Lam, S.K., Guetzlaff, C., Konstan, J.A., Riedl., J., Confidence displays and training in recommender systems, in: *Proceedings of the 9th IFIP TC13 International Conference on Human Computer Interaction INTERACT*, IOS Press, pp. 176–183, 2003.
45. Trewin, S., Knowledge-based recommender systems. *Encyclopedia Lib. Inf. Sci.*, 69, 32, 180, 2000.
46. Lan, T., Hu, H., Jiang, C., Yang, G., Zhao, Z., A comparative study of decision tree, random forest, and convolutional neural network for spread-F identification. *Adv. Space Res.*, 65, 8, 2052–2061, 2020.
47. Machmouchi, W. and Buscher, G., Principles for the Design of Online A/B Metrics, in: *Proceedings of the 39th International ACM SIGIR conference on Research and Development in Information Retrieval*, Association for Computing Machinery, New York, NY, USA, pp. 589–590, 2016.
48. Yuan, X., Han, L., Qian, S., Xu, G., Yan, H., Singular value decomposition based recommendation using imputed data. *Knowledge-Based Syst.*, 163, 485–494, 2019.
49. Koren, Y., Bell, R., Volinsky, C., Matrix Factorization Techniques for Recommender Systems. *Computer*, 42, 8, 30–37, 2009.
50. Zhao, W., Li, S., He, Y., Chang, E., Wen, J.-R., Li, X., Connecting Social Media to E-Commerce: Cold-Start Product Recommendation On Microblogs. *IEEE Trans. Knowl. Data Eng.*, 28, 1–1, 2015.
51. Zhou, T., Kuscsik, Z., Liu, J.-G., Medo, M., Wakeling, J., Zhang, Y.-C., Solving the apparent diversity-accuracy dilemma of recommender systems. *Proc. Natl. Acad. Sci. U. S. A.*, 107, 4511–4515, 2010.
52. Baizal, Z.K.A., Widyantoro, D.H., Maulidevi, N.U., Design of knowledge for conversational recommender system based on product functional requirements. *2016 International Conference on Data and Software Engineering (ICoDSE)*, Denpasar, pp. 1–6, 2016.

8

Deep Learning–Enabled Smart Safety Precautions and Measures in Public Gathering Places for COVID-19 Using IoT

Pradeep Kumar S.[1*], Pushpakumar R.[1] and Selvakumari S.[2]

[1]IT Department, Vel Tech Rangarajan Dr. Sagunthala R&D Institute of Science and Technology, Morai, India
[2]ECE Sri Venkateswara Institute of Science and Technology, Tiruvallur, India

Abstract

The security dimensions of public gathering cannot be breached and periodic reporting is compulsory in most public gathering places. The Internet of Things (IoT) serving for human safety is widely used nowadays. This methodology incorporates the safety aspects verification of people were entering and traveling from one place to other public places with very high risk. The suggested approach is working on deep learning concepts verifies the presence of the safety things like mask, gloves, and also help to detect temperature to the public who enter in public places like working environments and open places. A camera is positioned in front of the door, entry door, and then from camera with temperature sensor connected with single-board computer (SBC) verifies the mask and gloves presence by the help of image processing. This project deals on low cost safety precautions that ensure the public safety inside the public gathering places. This device also have the sanitizer sprayer to auto spray when hand placed in front of it. This device includes sensor, Raspberry Pi 3, or any kind of SBC a locking actuators. The public gathering in common places may affect by COVID-19 and may not but safety precautions are important. Wearing of mask after entering into common gathering places is needed. In such a case, ensuring these safety precautions helps the public to travel in common place with safety. The obstacle sensor triggers the camera sensor, verified by the image processed by deep learning and the required safety requirements. Once the security elements are verified, the GPIO command opens

Corresponding author: pradeepkumars@veltech.edu.in

Shalli Rani, R. Maheswar, G. R. Kanagachidambaresan, Sachin Ahuja and Deepali Gupta (eds.) Machine Learning Paradigm for Internet of Things Applications, (147–166) © 2022 Scrivener Publishing LLC

the locks. If the safety aspects are not met, then the reputation of individuals is remembered by the supervisor for more safety measures and disciplinary acts.

By this methodology, above 95% object detection using the principle of deep learning and image processing is done with precision, and the overall output leads mainly to the worker's safety of public places to install the safety measures of workers in less cost and also leads to reduce the workload of the supervisors and to reduce the man power.

Keywords: IoT, prevention and safety measures, deep learning method, image processing, low money for automation

8.1   Introduction

The common part of view the safety measures for the public is mandatory and that can be checked in routine bases. Nowadays, we are moving toward to technology world, and many kind of changes are keep on occurring in the medical field to safeguard the public before they became as a patient [1]. Huge IoT technology had been implemented to help medical field for shorting out the spending time for patient in testing, scanning, x-rays, and other kind of investigations. When the COVID-19 blasted in spreading in world, each and every one in the globe had been stunt to face these issues and struggled to stop the spreading virus. At last, the research scientist and doctors had find out that the issues cannot be stopped but prevention can be done to control COVID-19.

For preventing from COVID-19, the safety measure that made compulsory globally includes safety clinic mask, gloves, distance among crowd, and especially the sanitizer. Nowadays, each and every public gathering place had an employee for checking the people wearing mask or not. Because of this, man power is needed if the staff is not doing the work properly and the people may be affected by the COVID-19. It is not at all possible to maintain this kind monitoring using human [2]. For this reason, this project paper helps to resolve this kind of problem by using IoT concept.

8.2   Prelims

8.2.1   Digital Image Processing

This is a kind of task on image to upgrade the image or it is also done to remove some valuable data from the image. The image processing is the process that may lead us to make changes over the original image to digital formats. Many ways are introduced for signal agreement in the way of gathering the input data that is image and video edges. The image or requirements for the image may be picture or photo yield [14]. Digital image processing is wide range of technique that was spreading among the research field; this technique may be used to perform the many operations on the image, in order to obtain an enhanced image or to extract to get huge useful information about the data which is given in the format of image or video.

8.2.2 Deep Learning

Deep learning is widely used in technical research fields, machine learning fields, and mainly in IoT filed [5, 7, 21]. The deep learning concepts make us to consider the number of layers from which the data is obtained [3] that is altered to reach the goal of exact output which overcomes the drawbacks of the traditional algorithm of the machine learning [34–40, 46]. Almost all the quantity of the layers may be changed for which the given information may also be changed. More or less the deep learning systems are more important. In the fields of computer vision of version numbers, speech recognition, Natural Language Processing, audio recognition, social network filtering (SNF), machine translation, medical image analysis, and other forms of machine learning principles, the same learning concepts have been applied [32, 37, 41, 42]. Deep Learning designs are also constructed with these deliberations with a voracious layer-to-layer technique and helps to select which highlights improve in the execution section [4].

8.2.3 WSN

For sensor used for wireless network, it is referred as a network of huge point of equipment and devices that communicate the data and as well as various information that are combining and collected by the supervised field through the numbers of links using wireless network. From the beginning, wireless sensor networks (WSNs) have been recognized as key enablers of the Internet of Things (IoT) paradigm [8, 38]. WSNs are a resilient and efficient distributed data collection technology, but their large-scale use is still limited by issues related to reliability [6], autonomy, cost, and accessibility to application domain experts. Commercial solutions can tackle vertical application domains effectively, but they also lead to lock-ins in technology that hinder horizontal compensability and reuse. The huge varieties of sensors are available nowadays; each one differs based on their speed, size, cost, bandwidth, and memory commonly that vary based on the usage of the user need.

Table 8.1 Raspberry Pi history with version and configuration.

Family	Model	Form factor	Ethernet	Wireless	GPIO	Released	Discontinued
Raspberry Pi	B	Standard[a]	Yes	No	26-pin	2012	Yes
	A		No			2013	No
	B+		Yes		40-pin	2014	
	A+	Compact[b]	No			2014	
Raspberry Pi 2	B	Standard[a]	Yes	No		2015	
Raspberry Pi Zero	Zero	Zero[c]	No	No		2015	
	W/WH			Yes		2017	
Raspberry Pi 3	B	Standard[a]	Yes	Yes		2016	
	A+	Compact[b]	No			2018	
	B+	Standard[a]	Yes			2018	

(Continued)

Table 8.1 Raspberry Pi history with version and configuration. (*Continued*)

Family	Model	Form factor	Ethernet	Wireless	GPIO	Released	Discontinued
Raspberry Pi 4	B (1 GiB)	Standard[a]	Yes (Gigabit Ethernet)	Yes		2019 [35]	Yes
	B (2 GiB)						
	B (4 GiB)						
	B (8 GiB)						
	400 (4 GiB)	Keyboard				2020	

8.2.4   Raspberry Pi

The generation of the Raspberry Pi was started in the year of 2012, when it was introduced in the model of simple and cheaper model A. Later in the year of 2014, it was ARM11 processors that are used to produce the updated version. From that, continuously, the updated new version is available till date. Because of this, huge projects and new IoT and machine learning projects are invited and introduced [24–26]. Not only because it is cheaper, it also contains the huge number of features in newly invited versions. The clear configuration is displayed in Table 8.1. In Table 8.1, the family of the Raspberry Pi and configuration is available in initial state to till date. The single-board computer (SBC) is the common name called for these kinds of computers. Most of the common IoT patent and projects in 2020 common research people are going with the Raspberry Pi versions only. The common factor is cheaper and so easy to carry from place to another. Table 8.1 shows the version of the Raspberry Pi history and the configuration like model name with the GPIO pin numbers.

The Raspberry Pi 3 and Raspberry Pi 4 model may vary due to some model difference like 400 (4 GiB). In this project, Raspberry Pi 3 is used. The form factor is standard, and it is allowed to connect the pi camera and USBs. Ethernet is also allowed in this feature of SBC with the Gigabit of Ethernet connection. The Raspberry Pi 4 was introduced in the year of 2020, with high level of configuration.

8.2.5   Thermal Sensor

The thermal sensor is the small device which is used to measure the degree of both hotness and coolness in any kind of object. The process is made possible by the voltage across the diode. The coolness of the temperature will be automatically changed according to the diode's resistance. This will be vice-versa for the temperature that changes directly proportional to the diode. Mainly two types of thermal sensors are "Contact Type Temperature Sensors" and "Non-Contact Type Temperature Sensors". Based on the need, it may be used for the IoT projects.

8.2.6   Relay

The relay is a kind network which is used to transfer a kind of information between two devices over some distance. The source and destination are interconnected with nodes; in this case, the source and destination cannot communicate with each other directly because the distance is greater than transmission range. For this reasons, the relay network is used to share and exchange the information between the source and destination with short time lapse without any interruptions.

Because of this, the wireless networks take advantage of the relay network system. The basic concept of the relay can use in different topologies, from a base line to a ring type of tree shape structure to pass over the information with fast and more efficient way as possible.

8.2.7   TensorFlow

TensorFlow is the main technical tool used for the writing of machine learning applications [52–57]. One of the libraries commonly used to execute machine learning and various calculations, which includes a large account of scientific activities, is TensorFlow [8]. TensorFlow was created by famous IT Company Google and is one of machine learning's best among the popular libraries. TensorFlow's central component is the computational graph and tensors that move through edges between all the nodes. TensorFlow is a versatile artificial open source.

According to the flow of data construction a wide range of templates are implemented in the Graphical model, in the intellect library. It is often used to identify, interpret, comprehend, discover, anticipate, and construct.

TensorFlow excels in numerical computation, which is critical to profound learning. In most of the major languages and environments needed for deep learning projects, it has a rich set of application programming interfaces. A set of primitive values formed into an array of any number of dimensions which contain a TensorFlow. The reason why GPUs and various processors designed to perform end point arithmetic exceed expectations in initiate these cluster calculations and algorithms is because of these monstrous amounts of massive clusters' calculations and algorithms.

8.2.8   Convolution Neural Network (CNN)

The most successful is image classification using CNN. We need a sequence of pictures, main, and leading. We take pictures in this shell, as our initial training data collection [9]. The total amount of images, image dimension, channel quantity, and the number of levels per pixel are the most common reflective data input parameters.

Figure 8.1 clearly shows the operating process of the convolutional neural network with effective development and classification models [43]. From Figure 8.1, the input is carried out via the camera [9], the convolution and the counting process is processed into the pooling process, and the same

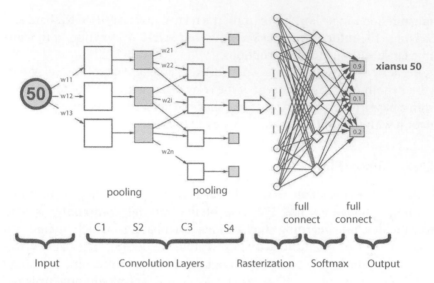

Figure 8.1 Convolutional Neural Network (CNN).

process is replicated again. Some of the algorithms are used to characterize the safety equipment method on the basis of the above procedure [44]. The safety equipment is identified, and with the aid of this input, the other process will begin [10]. Then, the output is compared to what is called deep learning based on the output (SBC) that will perform the rest of the process.

8.3 Proposed System

The anticipated system methodology of working is in deep learning terminology and this ensures as well as verifies the presence of safety precautions of COVID-19 like mask, gloves, and social distance among the people who want to enter into public gathering places like shopping malls, colleges, schools, and traditional places to ensure the safety to the public in common place [11]. The proposed line for the people is affected by the COVID-19 and incorporates the protection aspects confirmation of people in groups, either they are all maintaining the social distance or not [50, 51]. The proposed device also provides the automatic spraying of the sanitizer to the people who are all entering into the automatic gate which allowed them to enter into the place after ensuring them with mask and hand gloves; it is made possible by image processing as shown in the Figure 8.2. TensorFlow using Raspberry Pi 3 and Raspberry Pi 4 deep learning technique commonly used

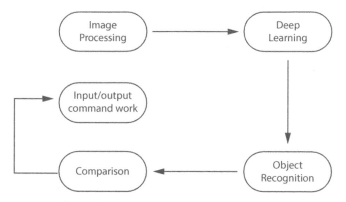

Figure 8.2 Dataflow diagram.

to do the verification time is measured with huge different subjects and the mask, gloves, and mainly social distance [12]. The camera is placed in the entrance gate which is facing the people who wants to enter via gate or main door and the feed from the IVR or IVSS from Pi-camera attached with the SBC ensures the mask presence through the image dispensation [13].

The key features of this job are deep learning and object detection servers. Inside the Raspberry Pi (SBC) style board, the python program code used to detect objects is run to identify objects [14]. The camera sensor is used to activate the mechanism, which is an obstacle detection sensor. The data for the system is from a camera sensor. The single-board machine named Raspberry Pi is attached as a USB to the camera [15]. The computer is connected to a laptop or any monitor via Wi-Fi.

Figure 8.3 is the process of ensure the safety masks, gloves, and social distance, allowing smart locking and opening the automated door [17]. From Figure 8.3, the fixed pi-camera is used to recognize the safety things of the people if they are not wearing the mask and gloves and they are not allowed in the public gathering places like schools, colleges, theaters, and traditional places [47, 49]. After measuring the safety equipment, the door will be opened and they will do their works.

The camera is attached with the SBC and that is completely trained device by the concept of the deep learning with the image processing. To process the above, all the said technique is executed by the programming language called as python.

Above proposed method includes the temperature sensing by the help of the thermal sensing sensors. Often, due to COVID-19, huge amount of man power are needed to keep on monitoring and to check the body temperature of public while they are entering in public places. This technology

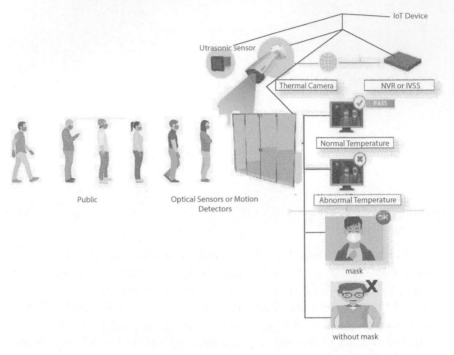

Figure 8.3 Safety equipment detecting.

also helps to prevent the spreading of viruses from country to country. The invited methodology also helps to mandatory checking and monitoring of this process, while in the other country, people enter into our country. By the help of deep learning in machine learning concepts [27–29], this kind work obtains the best results and leads us achieve concepts results.

8.4   Math Model

Contradictory to YOLO, SSD follows a various type of scale system which means that the element maps that are used to classify different objects are at various scales. While each component guide is generated from convolution results at a similar level, the convolution open platform of the various levels must be dissimilar in size [18–20]. In particular, the receptive fields of the sophisticated convolution layer are much larger than those of the lower layers, and the separate data of the abnormally high-level convolution layer lay out [33, 35]. The splitting of data comparing to an abnormal state mentioned highlighted layers is more short form of the entire data. The detail abstract of the extract features of the data is not as much detailed information will be; SSD discovery is similar to the heartless toward little articles.

The computation of the receptive field of convolution is according to the following formula:

$$Z_{CRF}(i) = (Z_{CRF}(i-1)-1)L_s + Z_f \tag{8.1}$$

where $Z_{CRF}(i)$ Ls is the size of the i-th layer's convolution receptive region, and Ls is the length of phase.

The filter size is Th and Zf.

$$s\,min = \frac{Cs - \dfrac{Pt}{2}}{P\,feature} \quad Pimg = \left(\frac{i+0.5}{|Fr|} - \frac{pr}{2}\right) \tag{8.2}$$

$$t\,min = \frac{Ct - \dfrac{ht}{2}}{h\,feature} \quad himg = \left(\frac{j+0.5}{|Fr|} - \frac{hr}{2}\right) \tag{8.3}$$

$$s\,max = \frac{Cs - \dfrac{Pt}{2}}{P\,feature} \quad Pimg = \left(\frac{i+0.5}{|Fr|} - \frac{pr}{2}\right)Pimg \tag{8.3}$$

$$t\,max = \frac{Ct - \dfrac{ht}{2}}{h\,feature} \quad h\,img = \left(\frac{j+0.5}{|Fr|} - \frac{hr}{2}\right) \tag{8.5}$$

where (cs, ct) Ht is the height of the default bouncing box, wt is the width of the default bouncing box, h is the size of the part map, $w_{feature}$ is the width of the element map, $|f_t|$ is the size of the r th highlight map, w_{img} is the size of the first image, and w_{img} is the width of the first image, centered on (i+0.5 $|f_r|$),(j+0.5 $|F_{zr}|$). In the event that the model SSD 300 × 300 is adopted, with the end goal that the size of the information image is 300 × 300, the component maps of the model are mostly made from layers [23]. The sizes of the convolution open field and the mapping region of the default bouncing box for each element map

$$O_{overlap} = (O_1 \cap O_2) / (O_1 \cup O_2) \qquad (8.6)$$

In order to assess the recovery potential of the techniques, their ability to retrieve issues in each image was first assessed and a standard estimate of these outcomes was then calculated. Usually, the recovery potential is surveyed using the W-measure, which is the weighted normal of accuracy and review and communicates as follows:

$$W = \frac{(s^2 + 1) \times B \times C}{s^2 \times (B + C)} \qquad (8.7)$$

8.5   Results

In our work, we have created a safe gathering environment for people using the deep learning method and image processing, ensuring the well-being of people and, at the same time, as working in the any organization. In addition,

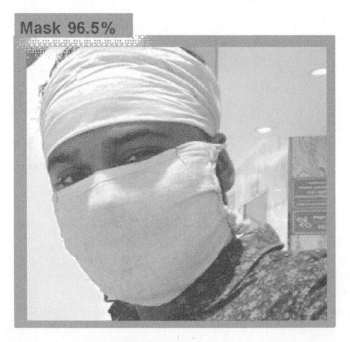

Figure 8.4 Detecting mask using deep learning.

our work allows us to prevent major spreading for not only COVID-19; it also saves people in working places and to minimize manpower for monitoring [16]. In future, by this project, we can point out the particular people who remove the mask after entering into the common places by some color identifications. We also accomplish this approach at a minimal rate. The incentive for future work could be applied to other wearable safety materials with identifying the affected people by the diseases.

Figure 8.4 shows the detecting mask using the deep learning using our device.

Figure 8.5 shows the detecting temperature of the human using the deep learning using our device with the help of the thermal sensor. If the body temperature is more the normal temperature, then the automatic door will open and allow the human to enter into the particular place [22, 48].

Figure 8.5 Detecting body temperature using thermal sensor.

If not, it would not allow above 5 seconds, if the man stands in front of the door, then the alarm will be on and the security will ask him to leave. This is made possible using thermal sensor and deep learning in wide range.

Figure 8.6 clearly shows the smart locking door system of the entrance door. After verifying the safety equipment like mask and gloves, the device enables the power supply to enable to open the smart locking door. When the trained device scans the people who stands and want to walk into the main door, as soon as the mask and gloves is detected, the green light glows and the doors open [43–45]. If the red light glows, it means the worker is not wearing the safety measures like mask, gloves, and social distance.

After ensuring that the mask and gloves are worn by the people, the smart device will open the door; meanwhile, if the people try to remove the mask and gloves, the smart device will alarm automatically [31–33]. So that the major spreading infection of COVID-19 can also be avoided. This may be the precautions for the people safety.

Another program extension is to recognize when staff and public people are keeping social distance and to detect the people who are all affected

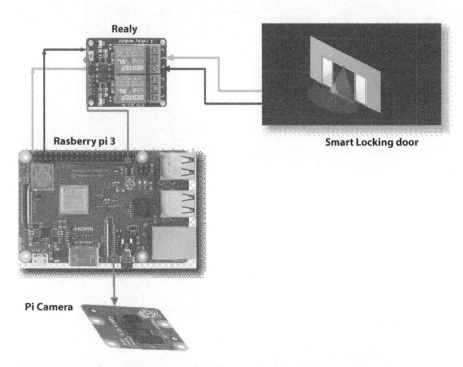

Figure 8.6 Raspberry Pi 3 connected with smart Locking door.

by not only COVID-19 but also by any other diseases; a third increase involves adding a program to identify a specialist based on the structure of a specialist and ordinary developments in the distance of the leg while walking using OpenCV and database like YOLO [41, 42]. This work also helps us to determine the temperature of the people who are all entering into the main door of all kinds of common places. In addition, the use of the board's YOLO database for each people is being investigated with the ultimate aim that the software will record any one of the chronicles of the specialists in terms of violation of security law. Further research will continue until all the PPEs (gloves, sanitizer, and so on) can be sufficiently distinguished by the software [47–49]. When using this application, it would be easier to identify gloves and infected people than to differentiate and hand in packet and gloves since the cameras will not reliably capture the condition of the social distance and gloves because of their small size relative to safety measures [50, 51].

8.6   Conclusion

In this work, using the deep learning method and image processing, we built a healthy working and safety atmosphere for the people. This ensures the safety of public in the common gathering, unsafe environment, and working places, or while purchasing and traveling. This ensures the well-being of people. In addition, our work allows us to prevent wide range spreading of COVID-19 and reduce the monitoring capacity of humans, and we also accomplish this strategy at minimal cost. The work can be applied to other wearable protection materials in the future.

References

1. Kanagachidambaresan, G.R., Anand, R., Balasubramanian, E., Mahima, V. (Eds.), *Internet of Things for Industry 4.0, Design, Challenges and Solution*, EAI/Springer Innovations in Communication and Computing, 2020.
2. Kanagachidambaresan, G.R., Maheswar, R., Manikandan, V., Ramakrishnan, K. (Eds.), *Internet of Things in Smart Technologies for Sustainable Urban Development*, EAI/Springer Innovations in Communication and Computing, 2020.
3. Pradeep Kumar, S., Selvakumari, S., Praveena, S., Rajiv, S., Deep Learning Enabled Smart Industrial Workers Precaution System Using Single Board Computer (SBC), *Internet of Things for Industry 4.0, Design, Challenges*

and *Solution-EAI/Springer Innovations in Communication and Computing*, 91–102, 2020.

4. Din, S., Paul, A., Ahmad, A., Gupta, B.B., Rho, S., Service Orchestration of Optimizing Continuous Features in Industrial Surveillance Using Big Data Based Fog-Enabled Internet of Things'- Digital Object Identifier. *IEEE Access*, 6, 21582–21591, 2018.

5. Krüger, J., Lien, T.K., Verl, A., Cooperation of human and machines in assembly lines. *CIRP Ann.-Manuf. Technol.*, 58, 2, 628–646, 2009.

6. Haddadin, A., Albu-Schäffer, Hirzinger, G., Requirements for safe robots: Measurements, analysis and new insights. *Int. J. Rob. Res.*, 28, 11–12, 1507–1527, Nov. 2009.

7. Asadi, E., Li, B., Chen, I.-M., Pictobot: A Cooperative Painting Robot for Interior Finishing of Industrial Developments. *IEEE Rob. Autom. Mag.*, 25, 2, 82–94, 2018.

8. Krizhevsky, A., Sutskever, I., Hinton, G.E., ImageNet classification with deep convolutional neural networks. *Proc. Adv. Neural Inf. Process. Syst.*, 1097–1105, 2012.

9. Xia, F., Campi, F., Bahreyni, B., Tri-Mode Capacitive Proximity Detection Towards Improved Safety in Industrial Robotics. *IEEE Sens. J.*, 18, 12, 5058–5066, 2018.

10. Martin, A. and Voix, J., In-Ear Audio Wearable: Measurement of Heart and Breathing Rates for Health and SafetyMonitoring. *IEEE Trans. Biomed. Eng.*, 65, 6, 1256–1263, 2018.

11. Lazzerini, B. and Pistolesi, F., Multiobjective Personnel Assignment Exploiting Workers' Sensitivity to Risk-. *IEEE Trans. Syst. Man Cybern.: Syst.*, 48, 8, 1267–1282, 2018.

12. Lazzerini, B. and Pistolesi, F., An Integrated Optimization System for Safe Job Assignment Based on Human Factors and Behavior. *IEEE Syst. J.*, 12, 2, 1158–1169, 2018.

13. Tsukada, K., Tomioka, T., Wakabayashi, S., Sakai, K., Kiwa, T., Magnetic detection of steel corrosion at a buried position near the ground level using a magnetic resistance sensor. *IEEE International Magnetic Conference (INTERMAG)*, pp. 1–1, 2018.

14. Rybczyński, A., Wolska, A., Wisełka, M., Matusiak, J., Pfeifer, T., Welding Arc Ignition and Photobiological Hazard Evaluation. *IEEE Explore*, 1–6, 2018.

15. Doan, D.R., Unrecognized Hazards [Electrical Safety]. *IEEE Industry Appl. Magazine*, 24, 5, 5–5, 2018.

16. Doan, D., Equipment Testing Safety [Electrical Safety]. *IEEE Ind. Appl. Mag.*, 23, 4, 6–7, 2017.

17. Doan, D., Dangers of Distractions [Electrical Safety]. *IEEE Ind. Appl. Mag.*, 23, 3, 5–72, 2017.

18. Jayawardena, A., Duffy, D., Manahan, J.M., Lighting Matters in Industrial Environments: A Framework Linking Workplace Safety to Lighting Quality Metrics. *IEEE Ind. Appl. Mag.*, 23, 3, 54–63, 2017.

19. Spang, R.J., Integrated Safety Management: Creating an All-Inclusive Electrical Safety Program. *IEEE Explore*, 23, 3, 64–70, 2017.

20. Mayer, S., Hodges, J., Yu, D., Kritzler, M., Michahelles, F., An Open Semantic Framework for the Industrial Internet of Things. *IEEE Intell. Syst.*, 32, 1, 13, 2017.

21. Doan, D., Workplace Hazards for the Electrical Worker' [Electrical Safety]. *IEEE Ind. Appl. Mag.*, 23, 2, 6–6, 2017.

22. Henriques, V. and Malekian, R., Mine Safety System Using Wireless Sensor Network. *IEEE Access*, 4, 3511–3521, 2016.

23. Khan, M., Silva, B.N., Han, K., Internet of Things Based Energy Aware Smart Home Control System'- Digital Object Identifier. *IEEE - Explore*, 4, 7556–7566, 2016.

24. Li, W., Zhao, R., Xiao, T., Wang, X., DeepReID: Deep filter pairing neural network for person re-identification, in: *Proc. IEEE Conf. Comput. Vis. Pattern Recognit*, Jun. 2014, pp. 152–159.

25. Luo, P., Tian, Y., Wang, X., Tang, X., Switchable deep network for pedestrian detection, in: *Proc. IEEE Conf. Comput. Vis. Pattern Recognit*, Jun. 2014, pp. 899–906.

26. Krizhevsky, A., Sutskever, I., Hinton, G.E., ImageNet classification with deep convolutional neural networks, in: *Proc. Adv. Neural Inf. Process. Syst.*, pp. 1097–1105, 2012.

27. Lawrence, S., Giles, C.L., Tsoi, A.C., Back, A.D., Face recognition: A convolutional neural-network approach. *IEEE Trans. Neural Netw.*, 8, 1, 98–113, Jan. 1997.

28. Chenand, C.F. and Hsiao, C.H., Haar wavelet method for solving lumped and distributed-parameter systems. *IEE Proc.-Control Theory Appl.*, 144, 1, 87–94, Jan. 1997.

29. Marjani, M., Nasaruddin, F., Gani, A., Karim, A., Hashem, I.A.T., Siddiqa, A., Yaqoob., I., Big IoT Data Analytics: Architecture, Opportunities, and Open Research Challenges. *IEEE Access*, 5, 5247–5261, 2017. Panetta, K., *Gartner's top 10 strategic technology trends for 2017*, 2016.

30. Mohammadi, M., Al-Fuqaha, A., Sorour, S., Guizani, M., Deep Learning for IoT Big Data and Streaming Analytics: A Survey. *IEEE Commun. Surv. Tutorials*, 20, 4, 2923–2960, 2018.

31. Kim, H.-G., Han, S.-H., Choi, H.-J., Discriminative Restricted Boltzmann Machine for Emergency Detection on Healthcare Robot. *IEEE*, 2017.

32. Fiore, U., Palmieri, F., Castiglione, A., De Santis, A., Network Anomaly Detection with the restricted Boltzmann machine. *Neurocomputing*, Elsevier, 2012.

33. Aldwairi, T., Perera, D., Novotny, M.A., An evaluation of the performance of Restricted Boltzmann Machines as a model for anomaly network intrusion detection. *Comput. Networks*, Elsevier, 144, 111–119, 2018.

34. Hongqing, F. and Chen, H., Recognizing Human Activity in Smart Home Using Deep Learning algorithm. *Proceedings of the 33rd Chinese Control Conference*, IEEE, China, 2014.
35. Mocanu, E., Larsen, E.M., Nguyen, P.H., Pinson, P., Gibescu, M., *Demand Forecasting at Low Aggregation Levels using Factored Conditional Restricted Boltzmann Machine*, Power Systems Computation Conference, 2016.
36. Song, W., Feng, N., Tian, Y., Fong, S., Cho, K., A Deep Belief Network for Electricity Utilisation Feature Analysis of Air Conditioners Using a Smart IoT Platform. *J. Inf. Process. Syst.*, 14, 2, 162–175, 2018.
37. Kim, H.-Y. and Kim, J.-M., A load balancing scheme based on deep-learning in IoT. *Cluster Comput.*, 2016.
38. Cheng, Y., Zhou, X., Wan, S., Choo, K.-K.R., Deep Belief Network for Meteorological Time Series Prediction in the Internet of Things. *IEEE Internet Things J.*, 14, 2015.
39. Zheng, W.-L., Zhu, J.-Y., Peng, Y., Lu, B.-L., EEG-Based Emotion Classification Using Deep Belie Networks. *IEEE conference on multimedia and Expo (ICME)*, 2014.
40. Sun, J., Wyss, R., Steinecker, A., Glocker, P., Automated fault detection using deep belief networks for the quality inspection of electromotors. *Tech. Mess.*, 81, 5, 255–263, 2014.
41. Alhussein, M. and Muhammad, G., Voice Pathology Detection Using Deep Learning on Mobile HealthcareFramework. *IEEE Access*, 2016.
42. Hsieh, Y.-Z. and Jeng, Y.-L., Development of Home Intelligent Fall Detection IoT System Based on Feedback Optical Flow Convolutional Neural Network. *IEEE Access*, 2017.
43. Granados, J., Westerlund, T., Zheng, L., Zou, Z., IoT Platform for Real-Time Multichannel ECG Monitoring and Classification with Neural Network, in: *IFIP International Federation for Information Processing*, Springer, 2018.
44. Islam, A., Hossan, Md T., Jang, Y.M., Convolutional neural network scheme–based optical camera communication system for intelligent Internet of vehicles. *Int. J. Distrib. Sens. Netw.*, 14, 4, 2018.
45. Pamela, D. and Chitoor, M.K., Smart Logistics Using Convolutioal Neural Networks and Sensor Data fusion. *International Conference on Intelligent Computing, Instrumentation and Control Technologies (ICICICT)*, IEEE, 2017.
46. Park, J., Jang, K., Yang, S.-B., Deep Neural Networks for Activity Recognition with Multi-Sensor Data in a Smart Home, *2018 IEEE 4th World Forum on Internet of Things (WF-IoT)*, 2018.
47. Du, S., Li, T., Gong, X., Yu, Z., Huang, Y., Horng, S.-J., A Hybrid Method for Traffic Flow Forecasting Using Multimodal Deep Learning, 2005.
48. Tornai, K., Oláh, A., Drenyovszki, R., Kovacs, L., Pinter, I., Levendovszky, J., Recurrent Neural Network Based User Classification for Smart Grids. *IEEE-Explore*, 2017.
49. Zhang, J., Wang, P., Yan, R., Gao, R.X., Long short-term memory for machine remaining life prediction. *J. Manuf. Syst.*, Elsevier, 2018.

50. Fouladgar, M., Parchami, M., Elmasri, R., Ghaderi, A., Scalable Deep Traffic Flow Neural Networks for Urban Traffic Congestion Prediction. *International Joint Conference on Neural Networks (IJCNN)*, 2017.
51. Cheng, Y., Xu, C., Mashima, D., Thing, V.L.L., Wu, Y., PowerLSTM: Power Demand Forecasting Using Long Short-Term Memory Neural Network, Springer Link, 2017.
52. Pham, T., Tran, T., Phung, D., Venkatesh, S., Predicting healthcare trajectories from medical records: A deep learning approach. *J. Biomed. Inf.*, *Elsevier*, 2017.
53. Kong, F., Li, J., Lv, Z., Construction of Intelligent Traffic Information Recommendation System Based on Long Short-Term Memory. *J. Comput. Sci.*, *Elsevier*, 2018.
54. Zhang, J., Zhu, Y., Zhang, X., Ye, M., Yang, J., Developing a Long Short-Term Memory (LSTM) based Model for Predicting Water Table Depth in Agricultural Areas. *J. Hydrol.*, 2018.
55. Garcia, F.C.C., Creayla, C.M.C., Macabebe, E.Q.B., Development of an Intelligent System for Smart Home Energy Disaggregation Using Stacked Denoising Autoencoders. International Symposium on Robotics and Intelligent Sensors, IRIS 2016, IEEE, Japan.390 Tausifa Jan Saleem et al. *Proc. Comput. Sci.*, 163, 2019, 381–390, 2016.
56. Ghosh, S., Asif, M.T., Wynter, L., Denoising autoencoders for fast real-time traffic estimation on urban road networks. *56th Annual Conference on Decision and Control (CDC)*, IEEE, Australia, 2017.
57. Gu, F., Khoshelham, K., Valaee, S., Shang, J., Zhang, R., Locomotion Activity Recognition Using Stacked Denoising Autoencoder. *IEEE Internet Things J.*, 5, 3, 2085–2093, 2018.

9

Route Optimization for Perishable Goods Transportation System

Kowsalyadevi A. K.[1]*, Megala M.[2] and Manivannan C.[3]

[1]Department of ECE, PSG Institute of Technology and Applied Research, Coimbatore, India
[2]Department of AMCS, PSG College of Technology, Coimbatore, India
[3]Department of Mechanical Engineering, Coimbatore Institute of Technology, Coimbatore, India

Abstract

The chapter aims to provide an optimal solution to find the most suitable routes for a fleet of vehicles performing the transportation of goods by visiting a set of market hubs. Additionally, the method concentrates to minimize the empty trips that tend to cost, vehicle usage, fuel consumption, manpower, travel time, and CO_2 emission, respectively, thereby avoiding long routes. Primarily, a clustering algorithm is used to classify the market hubs in the entire city and nearby cities based on a threshold time and distance. Subsequently, deciding the optimal group size, the supply depot, and the required number of vehicles to be transported at a particular time and distance is performed. The dynamic approach is possible for the entire region or state as the concluding procedure in distributing the perishable goods on time with the lowest of trash.

Keywords: Vehicle routing, clustering, perishable goods carrier system, shortest route

9.1 Introduction

- Logistics is not just transporting goods. The human effort involved in planning, managing, and tracking dispatches

*Corresponding author: kowsalyadevi.a.k@gmail.com

Shalli Rani, R. Maheswar, G. R. Kanagachidambaresan, Sachin Ahuja and Deepali Gupta (eds.) Machine Learning Paradigm for Internet of Things Applications, (167–180) © 2022 Scrivener Publishing LLC

often that leads to inefficiencies, complications, and unhappy customers. To simplify logistics, there is a need for an advanced algorithm that automates and optimizes deliveries. Through a smarter route planning and better tracking features, it is possible to achieve voluminous returns such as smart events, reporting and simulations, notifications and tracking, quicker and timely deliveries, and robust communication.

- Route optimization determines the most reliable cost-efficient route from one point to another vide a critical process. However, it is not the same in obtaining the shortest distance among the two or three points. Since, there are various relevant factors needs to be considered during route optimization. One of the factors is total number and location of all facilities on the route. Then, another factor is arrival or departure of a time gap, effective loading, etc. The vehicle routing problem (VRP) includes lot of constraints, such as number of vehicles, cost, and time.

9.2   Related Works

There is a significant increase in recognition to the importance of logistics management in present decade [1]. In recent years, a considerable increasing research interest is toward agribusiness that involves supply chain. Earlier, the revolution started in Europe and USA toward consolidation of organizations, along with government deregulation of agribusiness markets [2]. In addition to it, interest in food safety, competition in agribusiness markets, and quality management systems [3] were also increasing [4]. Agriculture logistics denotes handling the relationships between the businesses, which is accountable for efficient supply chain of products from farmers to buyers. Apart from the agriculture produces agriculture logistics should be consistent to meet the consumer requirements in relation with quantity, quality, and price. In spite of a sustainable agribusiness, current status of agriculture logistics in India is not effective and still complicated leading to reduction in the transport quality of the produces from the farmers to the consumer and thereby increasing the cost of produces [5]. Owing to high importance of the logistics in agriculture, researchers are trying for the integration of agricultural marketing system and logistics that starts from what to produce and how to produce [6]. Also, the recent work infers a strategy to reach the destination by ensuring high quality and quantity of the products.

Assuming the current state of Indian agriculture logistics sector discloses that various technical and structural changes lead to high requirements for quality management [7]. In agriculture logistics, there is a continuous change in the quality with respect to time. Additionally, the quality degradation begins as soon as the raw material leaves from the farmers to the consumer. Therefore, the management of the timely delivery of produces [8] and services at the lowest possible cost is an effective practice for achieving sustainable agribusiness success.

At present, the consumer expectation is in the direction of "fresh on demand" with higher supply. In addition to that, their specific need in terms of agriculture logistics is tracking and tracing on quality management systems [9]. Therefore, agriculture market is not only toward harvesting and consuming but also considering the effective transportation from harvesting area to consumer place. In Indian agriculture logistics, the produces are transported in an inappropriate way through the unorganized market [10].

Therefore, Indian agriculture logistics demands the need for implementing optimized agriculture logistics network [11]. In general, the distribution of fresh-agriculture produces such as vegetables, fruits, and cereals from farmer to consumer is complicated process, owing to the perishable nature of this agricultural produce [12]. Consequently, the development of proper agriculture logistics network is most important to retain freshness and reduce post-harvest losses [13].

In developing countries, post-harvest loss is about 24% and 40%. As in developed countries, the post-harvest losses are 2% and 20%. Therefore, this leads to increase in price and the farmer facing profit losses [14]. Mostly fresh produces are harvested by farmers, but those fresh produces do not reach the consumer with good quality. Likewise, those produces are transported to another market in the same way but in different packing. Intermediaries acquire variety of produces from farmers and offer to the consumers. The intermediaries consequently develop relationships with consumers and farmers. In addition to that, they are maintaining exchange relationships for which they compete with others [15]. Therefore, intermediaries practice the essential business functions of exploring market exchange chances [16]. The intermediaries play a major role in the economy by bridging the gap present in the market network. Intermediaries are specialized individuals' person in performing various marketing roles and interpretation participating in the marketing of agriculture produces [16].

The complexity of agriculture logistics network and mishandling by the intermediaries has significant role in agriculture logistics management and the post-harvest loss management [17]. The Indian agriculture logistics needs optimized network to retain freshness and reduce post-harvest loss. The above sections explained about the need of optimization in Indian agriculture logistics. Therefore, it is clear that agriculture logistics need to be optimized without eliminating markets. The optimization begins with modeling and ends with solutions. The modeling is a most powerful tool to optimize any system. That modeled system can be solved using many algorithms. The algorithms are nothing but optimizing tool for any modeling and are classified into heuristic and metaheuristic. The researcher can choose any one of the algorithm to solve their modeling.

9.2.1   Need for Route Optimization

It is essential to handle hundreds and even thousands of delivery points every day. For an assumption, a fleet contains 100 trucks and there is a need to draw a delivery plan for those trucks in "n" locations every day. The system needs to plan for minimizing the cost and, at the same time, maximizing the efficiency. It is possible to achieve and manage the system with appropriate vehicle routing planning. Solving mathematical model with many constraints like number of vehicle, vehicle capacity, time, distance, number of produces, number of depots, fragmented deliveries, human resources, and traffic and road conditions is challenging. Although finding a solution is challenging, it will be useful if the solution is found.

When the VRP is solved, it is certainly feasible to improve the utilization of vehicles. Scilicet means the possibility to transport more quantity of goods at the same time. Consequently, the traveling time of fleets will be reduced. So, it is possible to save lots of logistics cost which combining all these make customers more satisfied with services. As per the literature, routing problem can be solved in three approaches. The first manual approach is the most effective way to solve with the given constraints. But this approach takes several hours to find solution. The second approach is a bit faster by using pre-set solvers, but those solutions only meet some basic constraints. These can only be used in mathematical education systems that do not apply to the real world. The utilization of advanced computing is the final and efficient approach. Overall, the route optimization technique is needed to solve the route problem in instants. The chapter proposes the routing optimization which eliminates all manual planning and generates the optimal route automatically.

9.3   Proposed Methodology

The proposed method of routing is divided into three phases. Namely,

1. Hub Count Identification,
2. Key Hub Identification, and
3. Vehicle Route Identification

In the hub count identification phase, being the initial stage involves the process of collecting the details of the market hubs location for the entire city or state in the mode of a distance matrix vector. A distance matrix is the two-dimensional square matrix containing the distances, taken pair wise, between the elements of a set. As all diagonal values are zero, there will be no distance between the same location. Therefore the distance matrix is symmetric. Being the initial stage, the hub count identification phase involves the process of collecting the details of the market hub's location for the entire city or state in the mode of a distance matrix vector. A distance matrix is the two-dimensional square matrix which contains the distances, taken pair wise, between the elements of a set. This distance matrix is symmetric in nature and therefore all diagonal values are zero which means that the distance between the same location is zero. The distance matrix which holds the distances between different market hub locations is an array that is denoted with a measurement unit called meters. The term referred as num_locations which is the count of the number of market hub locations. The term num_vehicles denote the number of vehicles in the fleet, and the term depot represents the index or the unique id of the depot is for denoting the location where all vehicles start and end their routes. It is mandatory to assign the appropriate XY coordinates to the market locations in the state after the process of computation of the distance matrix. In the considered problem, the distance matrix is precomputed since the location coordinates are not included in the problem data which is required to solve the routing problem. The precomputed distances between the market locations are calculated using Manhattan distance by considering the distance between two points, (x1, y1) and (x2, y2) that is defined to be $|x1 - x2| + |y1 - y2|$. Google distance API can also be a handbook to acquire the relevant distance matrix for any given set of locations in the world. This phase involves a distance call-back which effectively return the distances between the market locations and passes it to the next step. The call-back method also sets the curve costs, which define the cost of travel, to be the distances of the curves.

Silhouette analysis is performed to obtain the optimal number of clusters. The separation distance between the resulting clusters trained using Silhouette analysis. Silhouette plot displays that each point of a cluster is closer to the points in neighboring clusters. This measure has a range from −1 to +1. It provides a way to visually estimate parameters such as multiple clusters. If the sample is far away from the neighboring clusters, then silhouette coefficients will be near the range +1. A value of zero indicates that the end between two neighboring clusters is near or significantly closer to the boundary. Negative values indicate that those samples may have been assigned to the incorrect cluster.

In the key hub identification phase (Table 9.1), clustering begins by calculating the distance between each pair of units facing the threshold distance. The method intends to the key hub optimization through city planning via clustering. The K-means clustering algorithm is preferred for grouping the market hubs based on the adequate distances for all market depot locations in the entire state/city region. The algorithm is necessary to reduce the sum of the distances between the points and the respective

Table 9.1 Phase 2: algorithm for key hub identification.

Step 1: Cluster assignment
    a.   Specify the number of clusters to assign
    b.   In the example, K = 3. The value of K is determined by means of silhouette analysis.
Step 2: Initialize the K points randomly called the cluster centroids.
Step 3: Move Centroid
            The centroid moves closer which means it actually moves toward the actual centroid.
Step 4: Optimization
            The migration happens iteratively within the model.
 	
    a.   **Repeat the previous two steps iteratively** till the cluster centroids stop changing their positions.
 	
            At some point, the centroid does not change for further computations. That is when the model converges.
Step 5: Convergence
            Finally, K-means clustering algorithms converges.

cluster centroid. These cluster centroids for each group becomes the key market hub of each cluster. Once the key market hub is identified from K-means algorithm, it is essential to optimize the routes at this centroid. Examples are customer segmentation (what people kind of belong together, group them together), social network analysis (might look at sentiments, what kind group of people like something and dislike something), and city planning (segmenting like industrial zone and commercial zone). Key market hubs in the middle of whole city and neighborhood cities or centroid point (location) of each group need to be identified for the requirement of route optimization centred on threshold distance.

Key market hubs in the middle of whole city and neighborhood cities or centroid point (location) of each group are identified.

Finally, it is necessary to work for an individual cluster and find the minimum length of the longest single route in a sufficient number of vehicles. The vehicle route identification phase (Table 9.2) should define the optimal routes to reduce the length of the longest single route between all vehicles. This is the perfect explanation if you want to complete all deliveries as soon

Table 9.2 Phase 3: algorithm for vehicle routing.

Function Call
Step 1: Distance from source to source is set to 0
distance[source] = 0
Step 2: **Initializations**
Step 3: Unknown distance function from source to each node set to infinity
distance[v] = infinity
Step 4: All nodes initially in X
Step 5: The **main loop**
Step 6: In the first run-through, this vertex is the source node
remove v from X
Step 7: where neighbor y has not yet been removed from X
for each neighbo.r y of v:
alternate = distance[v] + length (v, y)
Step 8: A shorter path to y has been found
if alternate < distance[y]
Step 9: Update distance of y
distance[y] = alternate
return distance []
end function

as possible with time and distance constraints. Vehicles are required to pick up goods at each market they visit, but capacity control and time window are required to visit each market. The vehicle should reach the market with maximum carrying capacity and reach within a specific time window are major constraints. To imitate the requirements, link state algorithm is applied. Each node creates a connection map with the network where the nodes are connected to the other nodes. The next best logical path is calculated from each independent node and at every possible point in the network. The routing table of the node is formulated from the collection of best paths. Dijkstra algorithm is used to identify the next node internally.

9.4   Proposed Work Implementation

The first phase of the proposed method is integrated with a .csv file containing the real-time market data of Tamilnadu state. A 282 × 282 data is being considered for simulation, i.e., distance matrix used for processing. By applying the silhouette method, it is possible to choose the optimum number of clusters.

If the cluster is further increased more than the optimum point, then cost would be increasing exponentially and the benefit decreases drastically. Since it is difficult to achieve more gains for higher clusters, hence K becomes the decision point.

From the result and Figure 9.1a, the highest value of s(i) exists for k = 3. Therefore, the optimal number of clusters for the worked out data is 3. For the reason that the cost would be large, whereas increasing the number of clusters and taking decisions at this point is essential for the case. Figure 9.1a illustrates that significant benefit is obtained at optimization of the cost when the K is 3. Optimum number of clusters is obtained from selecting the number of cluster with silhouette analysis.

The main aim of the key hub identification phase is to determine the key market hubs/centroid point from each group and utilize the cluster space. The determination of key market hubs is derived from the K-means clustering process. This process needs to visit its other submarket locations in a city represented using the identical rectangular blocks. Figure 9.2 shows an example city with the key market hub marked in red and the submarket locations to visit in blue. This red node acts an initial supply point, thereby proceeding to the vehicle routing phase.

In the vehicle route identification phase, it is necessary to create the distance dimension, which calculates the total distance each vehicle will travel in its path. In each case, cost proportional can be set to the maximum ratio

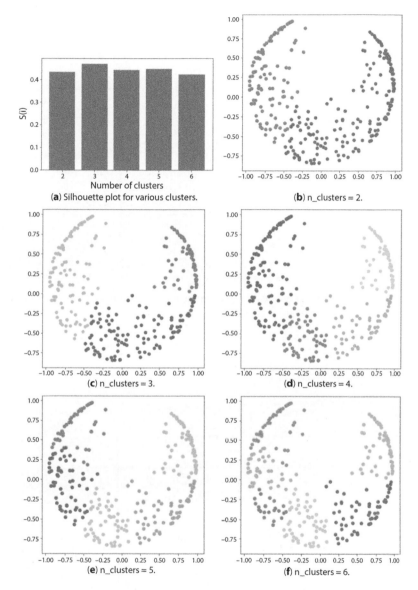

Figure 9.1 Silhouette analysis on K-means clustering on sample data with n_clusters = 2, 3, 4, 5, and 6, respectively.

of the total distances. Routing programs are used as dimensions to track the number of the vehicle accumulated in the path of a vehicle. Finally, the function shows the total distances of routes and direction to the vehicles. Alternatively, initial routes are saved a list or array and then can be printed.

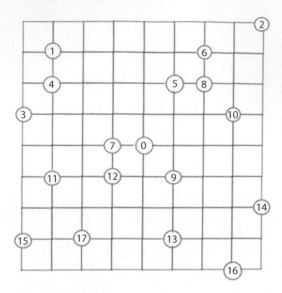

Figure 9.2 City market hub marked in red and the market locations to deliver goods in blue.

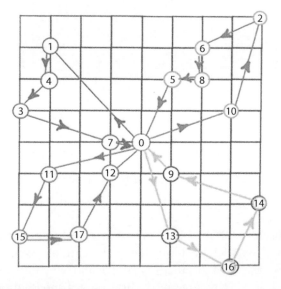

Figure 9.3 Assigned vehicle route for a key market hub.

The complete procedure is the one that minimizes the longest single route and the output is shown in Figure 9.3. The routing methodology is growing popularly in the transport and logistics industry. Since it reduces the time consumed traveling and at the same time lessens the incurred cost in the process. This should accomplish the optimal routes identified from a depot to a specific location. Each route has separate business-specific constraints, such as vehicle limitations, cost controls, time windows, and resource limitations concerning the loading process at the depot, etc.

Market locations along the routes are marked with their codes in the list of locations. All routes begin and end at the depot (0). The diagram above shows the assigned routes in which the location codes are converted to the corresponding x-y coordinates The above procedure is applied to all main market hubs along with the K-means clustering process. As a part the value of the maximum distance parameter in the distance dimension to the threshold value (e.g., in the region of 150 km) is set. When the modified program is executed, it returns the following output as in Figure 9.4.

Google distance matrix API can also be used to create the distance matrix for any set of locations defined by latitudes and longitudes. It is feasible to use the API to calculate the distance matrix for many types of routing problems. Additionally, if the threshold exceeds the value of 150 km, then new subclusters can be formulated inside the existing cluster group and can iterated with the second and third phase.

```
Route for vehicle 0:
 0 -> 8 -> 6 -> 2 -> 5 -> 0
Distance of the route: 142Km

Route for vehicle 1:
 0 -> 7 -> 1 -> 4 -> 3 -> 0
Distance of the route: 150Km

Route for vehicle 2:
 0 -> 9 -> 10 -> 16 -> 14 -> 0
Distance of the route: 148Km

Route for vehicle 3:
 0 -> 12 -> 11 -> 15 -> 13 -> 0
Distance of the route: 138Km

Maximum of the route distances: 150Km
```

Figure 9.4 Sample output for the depot (0).

9.5   Conclusion

The chapter solves the perishable good delivery problem with silhouette algorithm for identifying the optimal grouping of the sales depot. The key hub identification, i.e., the key sales depot is identified K-means algorithm, thereby leading to the vehicle routing solution. The optimum route is solved by the link state route protocol. The process provides a framework to combine the results, diversify and intensify the search process. The proposed system will be able to identify optimal routes for a set of vehicles traveling in different directions in the city and between states. The solution is much satisfactory for the delivery points ranging between hundreds and thousands. Heuristic approaches would be preferred for large sized applications with varied considerations and set of decision rules. The formulated methods must be robust in order to deal with varied constraints.

References

1. Bosona, T. and Gebresenbet, G., Food traceability as an integral part of logistics management in food and agricultural supply chain. *Food Control*, 33, 1, 32–48, 2013.
2. Wallenfeldt, J., *Agricultural revolution*, ed. Encyclopaedia Britannica, inc, 2015, https://www.britannica.com/topic/agricultural-revolution
3. Nordenskjöld, J., *Implementation of a quality management system in food production*, Master's Thesis, Swedish University of Agricultural Sciences, 2012, https://stud.epsilon.slu.se/4676/7/nordenskjold_j_120815.pdf
4. Haggblade, S., Modernizing African agribusiness: reflections for the future. *J. Agribus. Dev. Emerg. Econ.*, 1, 1, 10–30, 2011.
5. Sasmal, J., Food price inflation in India: The growing economy with sluggish agriculture. *J. Econ. Finance Adm. Sci.*, 20, 38, 30–40, 2015.
6. Li, J., Liu, Y.-C., Gao, H.-M., Requirement Analysis for the Collaborative Supply and Logistics Management of Fresh Agricultural Products. *The 4th Annual International Conference on Information Technology and Applications*, EDP Sciences, 2017.
7. Rais, M. and Sheoran, A., Scope of supply chain management in fruits and vegetables in India. *J. Food Process. Technol.*, 6, 3, 1–7, 2015.
8. Zarei, M., Fakhrzad, M.B., Jamali Paghaleh, M., Food supply chain leanness using a developed QFD model. *J. Food Eng.*, 102, 1, 25–33, 2011.
9. Zhong, R., Xu, X., Wang, L., Food supply chain management: systems, implementations, and future research. *Ind. Manage. Data Syst.*, 117, 9, 2085–2114, 2017.

10. Kitinoja, L., Saran, S., Roy, S.K., Kader, A.A., Postharvest technology for developing countries: challenges and opportunities in research, outreach and advocacy. *J. Sci. Food Agric.*, 91, 4, 597–603, 2011.
11. Mishra, A. and Gupta, S., Innovation of agriculture logistics managing food inflation', KPMG International, India, 2011.
12. Nunes, M.C.D.N., Nicometo, M., Emond, J.P., Melis, R.B., Uysal, I., Improvement in fresh fruit and vegetable logistics quality: berry logistics field studies. *Philos. Trans. R. Soc. A: Math. Phys. Eng. Sci.*, 372, 1–19, 2014.
13. Shukla, M. and Jharkharia, S., Agri-fresh produce supply chain management: a state-of-the-art literature review. *Int. J. Oper. Prod. Manage.*, 33, 2, 114–158, 2013.
14. Adepoju, A.O., Post-harvest losses and welfare of tomato farmers in Ogbomosho, Osun state, Nigeria. J. *Stored Prod. Postharvest Res.*, 5, 2, 8–13, 2014.
15. Haveripeth, K.D., *A critical study of law relating to agricultural produce marketing in india*, PhD Thesis, Karnatak University, 2013, https://shodhganga.inflibnet.ac.in/handle/10603/14594
16. Kishori, D., Management of regulated markets: A micro study of Duggirala regulated market, A.P., PhD Thesis, Acharya nagarjuna university, 2012, https://shodhganga.inflibnet.ac.in/handle/10603/9832
17. Negi, S. and Anand, N., Cold chain: A weak link in the fruits and vegetables supply chain in india. *IUP J. Supply Chain Manage.*, 12, 1, 48–62, 2015.

10

Fake News Detection Using Machine Learning Algorithms

M. Kavitha*, R. Srinivasan and R. Bhuvanya

Computer Science & Engineering, Vel Tech Rangarajan Dr. Sagunthala R&D Institute of Science and Technology, Chennai, India

Abstract

Any sorts of untrue information designed to mislead or defame any individual are termed as fake news. In this paper, we describe a technique to spot bogus news using machine learning (ML) architectures. The ever-increasing production and circulation of skewed news stories necessitates an immediate need for software that can automatically discover and detect them. Automated identification of fake news, on the other hand, is extremely difficult because it necessitates the model's understanding of natural language nuances. Binary classification method was used as a fake news detection technique in the existing methodologies, which restricts the ability of the model to discern how closely the reported news is connected to true news. To address these issues, this paper attempted to design a neural network architecture that could reliably predict the attitude between a given combination of headlines and article bodies. We have fused some advanced ML techniques together which includes the logistic regression and recurrent neural network technique particularly. The implemented approach is better than the existing architectures by 2.5% and achieved accuracy of 90.39% on test data.

Keywords: Machine learning, binary classification, logistic regression, recurrent neural network, fake news detection, natural language

10.1 Introduction

With the abundance of today's technology, there is unimaginable growth of information online; hence, there exists a necessity to identify the bogus

Corresponding author: mkavi277@gmail.com

Shalli Rani, R. Maheswar, G. R. Kanagachidambaresan, Sachin Ahuja and Deepali Gupta (eds.) Machine Learning Paradigm for Internet of Things Applications, (181–208) © 2022 Scrivener Publishing LLC

news from the original one. This section encompasses various machine learning (ML) algorithms [17] followed in the previous works to identify the fake news content. Fake news can be identified through both linguistic and non-linguistic cues. M. AlRubaian, M. Al-Qurishi *et al.* [6] explained that the integrity of data can be defined in terms of trustworthiness, accuracy, fairness, etc. The above-mentioned research developed a model for detecting incredible content on one of the social network Twitter to avoid the spread of dangerous information [15]. The model employs a user-based crawler to collect user information then the user aggregated features are also extracted. A pair-wise compression results in priority vector which will rank the instance features based on the relative importance. Finally, the Naïve Bayes (NB) classifier is adopted to classify the tweets in place of credible or non-credible. This method is considered to be the first work which considers the relative importance to identify the credibility of tweets in microblog analysis. The public opinion gets affected through fake news websites. Hence, Kushal Agarwala *et al.* [13] explored the natural language processing (NLP) techniques [5]. Natural Language Tool Kit (NLTK) was used to tokenize the body and headlines statement. Various ML algorithms [7] such as Support Vector Machine (SVM), Logistic Regression (LR) [1–3], and NB with Lidstone Smoothing were applied to evaluate the performance. Among the applied algorithms the NB with Lidstone Smoothing achieved with 83% result accuracy. Mahabub Atik [14] identified the fake news by creating an "Ensemble Voting Classifier". To validate the news, the researchers used a variety of ML classifiers, including NB, SVM, and K-Nearest Neighbor (KNN) [21], Ada Boost, LR, and many other approaches. A resampling procedure known as cross-validation was used, and the top three ML algorithms were selected using the best accuracy score and the chosen algorithms were processed with Ensemble Voting Classifier. A multiclassifier-based Ensemble Coding classifier results in deciding the real and fake news based on soft and hard voting. Nowadays, information can easily be accessible from anywhere. In the age of a technology where now an individual can access and have a detailed knowledge of various events happening around the world with the comfort of his/her own home, people are updating information with increasing inaccuracy and irrelevance, which is usually referred to as false news dissemination. Because the majority of people utilize social media to keep up with news, providing them with accurate and altruistic information is a responsibility that must be fulfilled. Because of the growing number of social media users, news can be quickly published by anyone from anywhere, putting the authorship of news in danger. Fake news is frequently circulated to mislead readers, causing tensions, mental stress, and plenty of other dangerous issues. It is a difficult task to detect those misleading facts based on the content of the news only. The news content is different in terms of styles, the subject form, and the way of delivering it. Thus, it becomes essential to bring an efficient system for its detection. Many researchers and developers have recently focused on detecting fake news. The stance recognition technique, which is the subject of our research, is a novel and innovative way to detect bogus news. The basic aspect of a series of methodologies for assessing the relationship between two pieces of text and, in particular, detecting fake news, is stance detection. With the recent introduction of social media platforms like Facebook and Twitter, it has become much easier to disseminate information to the masses in minutes. While the spread of information is proportional to the expansion of social media, the authenticity of these news articles has deteriorated.

In this study, we look at different methods for predicting the outcome of a news article and news feature pair. The positions between them can be classified as "concur", "deviate", "examine", or "inconsequential" which depends on the similarity content of news article. We looked at a few classic AI models to establish a baseline and then compared the results to cutting-edge deep organizations to determine the position of the article body and feature. We offer a model that can recognize fake news using test methods by exactly anticipating the position between the feature and the news article. We additionally concentrated what diverse hyperboundaries mean for the model presentation and summed up the subtleties for future work. The established model performs good while arranging between all the positions for certain varieties in exactness.

10.2   Literature Survey

In this segment, we will introduce the diverse sort of models, preprocessing strategies, and datasets utilized on the writing. In the time of 2017, two difficulties were proposed by RumorEval (SemEval 2017) and the Fake News Challenge. The previous had two subtasks: one for position identification of an answer to a news and another that endeavored to group the news as evident or bogus. The last is only a position recognition of a news, which groups the answer of a news in concur/dissent, talking about, and random. There are various locales for manual truth keeping an eye on the web like snopes.com and factcheck.org which are the most famous among all. What is more, there are some other particular destinations as well, for spaces like governmental issues, as politifact.com. Conversely, there are additionally a few locales, as theonion.com, that distribute news unequivocally announced phony. The majority of these locales are distributing this information as a parody, diverting, or as a pundit. Many exploration papers produced their dataset from these two sources. Wang submitted statements made by public figures via the LIAR dataset, which was labeled with their authenticity. Zubiaga *et al.* generated the PHEME dataset, which is suited for rumor research. This dataset compiles a huge number of rumor thread tweets and links them to news stories. Muhammad Syahmi Mokhtar *et al.* developed a web application that allows users to enter news material or URLs using the LR technique. The authors used model development methodology and proved that LR shows good performance in classification task. Stance detection technique was applied using TF-IDF feature which has shown greater accuracy. As per their research, LR detection model was found to work well in dealing with long and also short input text. It was found that the technique achieved around 79.0% to 89.0% accuracy based on the data used. Due to its capabilities, the Term Frequency–Inversed Document Frequency (TF-IDF) has been demonstrated to be a good feature to utilize in text preparation. After that, this model was combined with a web service that receives news URLs or text news items as input. The "FAKENEWS" app was also used to verify the news' legitimacy. Joseph Meynard Ogdol *et al.* tried to address the solution in a unique way of creating a classifier based on a logistic binary regression commonly prevalent in ML and Artificial Intelligence. The sentiments, neutrality, page rank, and content length were measured here to specifically find the structure error ratio for each data to create a model for the fake news classifier. The study used dataset of nearly 10,000 news data for the measurement purpose. The model was subjected to show an 80% accuracy rate and was found capable of classifying legitimate news apart from fake news. A labeled news dataset, third party API's and a mathematical software tool were used as the resources by the team members. Harika Kudarvalli *et al.* conducted their research by performing numerous Machine algorithms out of which, with over 92% accuracy, the findings of LR and SVM were promising.

According to their findings, NB and Long Short-Term Memory (LSTM) did not perform as well as they had anticipated. The applicability of the algorithms in photographs and videos for better identification of fake news is one of the most essential and interesting use cases for this model. They performed their analysis on Tweets datasets from Twitter by extracting the real time tweets using keywords. They then preprocessed it and retrieved important tweet features from the dataset. To reduce processing load, these features were separated and the tweet information column was removed. Fathima Nada *et al.* attempted to identify fake content from the news articles automatically. They started by introducing the task's dataset and then went over the pre-processing, feature extraction, classification, and prediction processes in depth. The preprocessing capacities played out certain activities which were tokenizing, stemming, and exploratory information investigation like reaction variable dispersion and information quality check. Furthermore, they utilized some element extraction methods like basic sack of words, n-grams, and TF-IDF. The model proposed by them researched distinctive element extraction and ML procedures which accomplished a precision of 72% around utilizing TF-IDF highlights and strategic relapse classifier. Abdullah-All-Tanvir and Ehesas Mia Mahir [9] actualized five distinct calculations. Notwithstanding the most widely recognized ML classifier calculations, NB, LR, SVM, and two profound learning strategies, for example, recurrent neural network (RNN) and LSTM were utilized. As the examination is about content information the accompanying thoughts, for example, Count Vectors, TF-IDF, and Word Embedding, were abused. Check Vectors structure a network information where each line addresses the corpus report, every section addresses the corpus term and every cell addresses the recurrence include of a particular term in the current archive. TF-IDF is utilized for data recovery and text mining. Term Frequency is a proportion of how regularly a particular term, for example, "t" shows up in an archive and IDF gauges the significance of a particular term "t". Lastly, the Word Embedding is a sort of word portrayal that addresses words with comparative importance to have a comparable portrayal. The proposed work investigated a model for perceiving false news from Twitter information. The previously mentioned portrayal procedures of Count Vectors, TF-IDF, and Word Embedding were applied with the ML calculations of NB, LR, and SVM, and further investigated with the profound learning models. While considering the above presentation examination SVM yields the most noteworthy precision of 89% with the portrayal procedure. S. Aphiwongsophon and P. Chongstitvatana [18] exploited the work of identifying the fake news based on Twitter data collected from October 2017 to November 2017. Twenty-two attributes of raw data such as ID, Name, Profile-Image, Friends count, Followers count, and many more are selected from the 948,373 messages. Then, the normalization process is applied which converts the text data into numbers. From the obtained result, replicated data is removed as a pre-processing which will reduce the size of the result to 327,784 messages. ML algorithms such as NB, Neural Networks, and SVM were used to classify the retrieved utterances as believable or unreal.

To detect fake news, Thota, Aswini *et al.* [19] used deep learning architecture. To anticipate the stance between the headline and the news article, TF-IDF, GloVe, and Word2Vec were combined with the Dense Neural

Network (DNN). TF-IDF with DNN resulted in the highest accuracy with 94% and another model based on BoW-DNN achieved the second-highest score. Pérez-Rosas, Verónica and Kleinberg *et al.* used two different data-sets FakeNewsAMT and Celebrity news which contain news about general views and celebrities, respectively. Several linguistic features such as N-grams, Punctuation, Psycholinguistic features, Readability, and Syntax are applied to build a model for detecting the fake news. The proposed work uses two different annotators to categorize real and fake news. Bajaj Samir *et al.* exploited various models such as LR, two-layer feed-forward Neural Network, Convolutional Neural Network (CNN), RNN, and Gated Recurrent Unit. The work mainly focuses on NLP which will identify the fake news by applying the linguistic features.

Wenlin Han and Varshil Mehta [20] applied conventional ML calculations and deep learning models [11–12] to identify counterfeit news. Relies upon the source, the phony news strategy is arranged into news and social setting models. The news content is additionally arranged into semantic-based and visual-based. Conventional AI strategies, for example, Deception Modeling, Clustering, NB, TF-IDF, and Probabilistic Context-Free Grammar (PCFG), are applied. Then, again, the profound learning model is misused with CNN, RNN, Hybrid RNN, and CNN. Further, the profound learning model is applied with three distinct variations, for example, LSTM, LSTM (with dropout regularization), and LSTM with CNN. By noticing the acquired outcomes, TF-IDF, Hybrid CNN, and RNN model accomplish better contrasted and different strategies. In order to improve one's understanding of the world, it is useful to keep up with current events. Fake news will fool people groups. Because the news is bogus, fake news is occasionally utilized to spread gossipy morsels about products or to affect some political administrative jobs. Deception, gossip, fraud, and other types of deception are sometimes related with the term "false news". Issues relating to such subjects are frequently noted, depending on the categorization. LR, NB, SVM, Random Forest (RF), and deep neural networks are all used to model fake news detection systems (DNN). The proposed model compared all the above ML methods to identify the fake news. After the data pre-processing, stemming and stop words removal is done then the important features are extracted from the text. Out of all the mentioned classification techniques, DNN is more capable of distinguishing between bogus and real news.

Anjali Jain and Avinash Shakya [10] devised a system for detecting bogus news. The NB classifier, SVM, and NLP approaches are all part of the model. Aggregator, News Authenticator, and News Suggestion System are the three key modules that make up the suggested model. Data gathering is the major task of the news aggregator and the news authenticator helps to verify the news by comparing the news with different sites and detect whether the given news is fake or real. The news suggestion system suggests the news to the user based on keywords that the user desires to authenticate. The proposed work achieved about 93% accuracy compared with the individual traditional machine algorithms. Michail Mersinias *et al.* demonstrated novel method by utilizing class label frequency distance-boosted LR classifier and deep learning methods [39]. In the 21st century impact of fake news has considerably increased, this is due to float of large amount information to the public without filtering. In today era, huge amount of data is produced and flooded in the internet as fake news, which is drawing the attention of the viewers [37]. Revenue is generated just by clicking which is affecting the major events like Political Elections. The government has framed a law to stop the fake news creation and spreading it through online. Due to this spread of fake news, viewers and readers are misguided, reports show that some fake accounts, and social bots are created by Russia. In 2013, there was a fake news floated in Twitter stating that Barack Obama was got injured in Explosion, due that stock value of around 130 billion dollars was wiped out. So, there is a greater demand [38] for stopping as well as detecting the fake news and it is a challenging task too. Using dimensionality reduction approaches like Principal Component Analysis (PCA) and Chi-square methods, Muhammad Umer *et al.* coupled CNN and LSTM algorithms. The model will classify the articles by giving the labels as unrelated, discuss, agree, or disagree. PCA and Chi-square methods reduce the nonlinear features and produces contextual features. The classification is based on the acceptance level between the headline and the body of the headline. The keywords are used to find the relevancy of the articles and with the help of it the whole content on the body can be identified. Initially, the feature set is converted into word vectors, and then, the feature set is reduced by applying the dimensionality reduction methods like PCA and Chi-square methods. Normally, PCA is the widely used techniques in various applications, which converts the new variable to subset of variable by calculating the correlation between the variables. The Principal Component is computed using co-variance matrix. The PCA features are fed into the embedding layer of the deep model, vectorized, and then fed back to the 1D CNN to extract the features.

These characteristics are filtered again in five dimensions with 64 filters, and then, some of them are returned to the max pooling layer to extract the most significant features. Some features are fed into the LSTM layer for series modeling to find the relevant keywords which is hidden. The model produced 97.8% accuracy by determining the comparative sentences from a news article. NLP has a well-defined task which is to detect the stance. Earlier studies show that target-specific stance detection is used in tweets and for online debates which is structural, lexical, and linguistic features. Initially, stance detection was kicked off in 2017. Fake News Challenge-1 (FNC-1) is based on ensemble method that combines both gradient boosted decision trees and deep CNN with Google News Pretrained vectors. The accuracy of the model was 82.02%. Another model used multilayer perceptron (MLP) methods which obtained 81.97% accuracy. Also, one of the existing techniques used Bags of Words (BOW), Term Frequency and TF-IDF as features and produced 81.72% accuracy. FNC-1 task combined RNN with max-pooling and neural attention mechanisms to produce 83.8% accuracy. The model used deep recurrent model to calculate statistical features and neural embedding, the method produced 89.29% accuracy. Preprocessing converts the raw data to system understandable format. It is performed on FNC-1 dataset, which will convert the characters to small case letters, removal of stop words, tokenization, and stemming. The difficulty in detecting false news stems from the fact that humans find it difficult to distinguish between fake and authentic news. Particularly, the use of language in fake news is complex. Rashkin explores the distinctions between fake news language usage and true news language usage in three forms of false news: satire, hoax, and propaganda. Her research demonstrates that subjective, intensifying, and hedging words, among other linguistic qualities, play a part in the creation of fake news, with the purpose of introducing imprecise, obscuring, dramatizing, or sensationalizing language. Consequently, applying feature-predicated approaches will be labor-intensive and time-consuming. R. Sandrilla *et al.* informed COVID-19 commenced to affect diverse people in different ways. People get infected and develop mild to mitigate illness.

So, the public from sundry places transpired to expose their cerebrations about COVID-19 on sundry platforms. This paved the way for the engenderment and development of fake news about COVID-19. When people are in desideratum of access to high quality evidence still, they face vigorous barriers to take suggested actions. To understand the bamboozling information WHO has developed to fortify infodemic to fight against the epidemic disease and to stop the reader from bamboozling evidence. The word "infodemic" was coined to describe the risks of distortion phenomena in virus outbreak management, because it has the potential to speed up the epidemic by inciting and collapsing gregarious replication. It is something with a surplus of information which can be either true to the evidence and some may not. The aim of the infodemic is not to eliminate but to manage the situation to avert and to respond to the bamboozling information.

Because amassing the data from the convivial media or the other news media platforms without fact checking may astringently affect the general public's lifestyle, harmony, the old one's emotional psychology and their noetic demeanors. In the expeditious spread of COVID-19, the globe is in grief and facing the situation of identifying the fictitiously unauthentic or the genuine news propagation. The authentic news avails to mitigate the calamity, whereas the unauthentically spurious one amplifies it. This erratic situation inspires the researcher to understand and to develop a model which will avail to apperceive the transmuting nature of news in convivial media cognate to COVID-19 pandemic.

This investigation will avail to analyze and detect fake news in convivial media with less effort. It mainly fixates on gregarious media fake news cognate to COVID-19 the opensource dataset has been accumulated for detection of misinformation. During the pandemic, a classifier based on ML is being created to detect falsehoods. We also put our model through rigorous testing in a range of challenging situations, indicating that it can attain extraordinarily high precision. The following article is divided into four pieces. The findings of prior relevant studies in this field are analysed and examined in the literature review. The methods part goes through data collecting, data annotation, data cleaning and prepossessing, and data exploration in great detail. The primary and minor findings of the study are highlighted in the relegation outcome section. The COVID-19 outbreak exposed a parallel epidemic driven by bogus news. This quandary of illuding information interrupts the public health communication and withal leads to mass fear and solicitousness. In the meanwhile, few researchers investigated their studies and brought forward the issues in highly philomath field cognate to illuding information engendered by the gregarious networks on this COVID-19 pandemic. The investigation on fake news propagation deploys sundry ML techniques to avail the public in relegating the data that they are viewing is fictitiously unauthentic or not. This study is done by relegating and comparing the data provided with some pre-kenned data that contains both misleading and inaccurate information. Typically, in order to develop a working model to detect the bamboozling information practicing, the ML techniques and methods are very consequential. The ML techniques must undergo certain stages to consummately train and develop a detection model starting from data preprocessing to feature detection and extraction. Authors in [22, 23] state that the stages starting from data preparation, data cull, and data extraction facilitates in handling the immensely colossal magnitude of data required for building a detection model. There subsist many illuding information detection websites; however, most of the websites are human predicated where the analysis done in this detection model is manual. Though the manual detection is done by highly expertise people it has few drawbacks as high extravagant, slow in process, highly subjective, very tuff in handling the substantial quantity of data. As a result, [24] explored combining ML with erudition engineering to detect bogus news. Hence, [25] proposed an automated relegation that represents a prolific trend of study. Many researchers worked on detecting fake news detection model [26] surveyed on many automated illuding information systems and proposed a few detection models that lead to detection of mis information. In this context, misinformation cognate to COVID-19 has been incrementing in an expeditious pace due to pandemic. They were expeditious to spread illusory information. In [27], it is reasoned out on Description Logics to detect inconsistencies between the trusted and untrusted news.

The spread of COVID-19 in Astute cities is visualized using an innovative mathematical approach. To prevent the propagation of COVID-19 fake news, the researchers developed an integrated system incorporating ML approaches [28]. Because the COVID-19 pandemic and the growth of the infodemic are happening at the same time, it is critical to provide a strategy to combat false information. To detect disinformation during the COVID outbreak, a multilingual cross-domain dataset was assembled, and a ML-based classifier was developed [29]. The unauthentically spurious news about the corona virus has become an incrementing fame in the diffusion of shaping the news histories online. The videos posts and articles cognate to the current pandemic are extensively disseminated throughout the convivial network platforms. The researcher proposed a novel multi-level voting ensemble model utilizing 12 classifiers amalgamated to soothsay predicated on their erroneous prognostication ratio [30]. Spreading of this COVID-19 pandemic disease not only transmuted the salubrious comportment among the globe but expeditiously given space to spread the erroneous news in directing or bamboozling the public in numerous rumors [8]. In spite of these rumors, public not only had very earnest impact on their salubrious lifestyle but erroneous increase in the spread of virus along with the unauthentically spurious information. An elderly man father of three was said to have committed himself after auricularly discovering his COVID-19 diagnosis, according to an article [31]. Mitigating data outside of the unauthentically fabricated news piece itself may become an important part of automatic fake news identification [4] as some of the above-mentioned papers establish physical touch. This is so-called "Network" strategy, which can be beneficial and advantageous in instances when text classification is difficult. Several researchers have also added factors relating to social media, which is the most widely used medium for spreading fake news. It is critical to consider how fake news spreads in such scenarios, as well as the role that users play. The difficulty of detecting fake news using filtered data is one that arises frequently.

ML algorithms that detect false news via text analysis have a disadvantage in that they cannot predict fake news early on, when the information needed for verification or debunking is not available due to the early stages of news dissemination. As a consequence, a model based on a Convolutional Network is built to discover news propagation channels based on people who share it, which reduces detection precision. Detection based on global and local user variations can identify false news with far greater precision than existing systems. Text analysis fails when news stories are too short, but convolutional networks can be used to investigate them. They can create erudition graphs that can determine the sincerity of two things' cognition. These models would produce background information erudition graphs, which could be trained to create entity cognitions in order to assess truth or falsity. It is suggested that a structured erudition network be used to collect background knowledge. Despite the fact that the erudition graphs were created with a tiny quantity of data, they were proved to be capable of delivering acceptable results. Authors in [32] describe a network-based strategy to studying how news is transmitted, who shares it, and how these spreaders are related. These patterns are then used to detect bogus news at different levels of the network. Fake news spreads faster and has more and stronger spreader interaction, according to the research, which is denser for networks with similar interests and behaviours. One disadvantage is that, despite the fact that only a little quantity of network information is required, news must be spread on social media before it can be discovered. Another method that focuses on user involvement combines text analysis with a social-based strategy that evaluates how often and by whom material is shared or "liked". It has been proved that Facebook content may be accurately labeled as false news based on the users who "like" it. The negative is that in order to yield worthwhile results, the content must include a certain amount of "social interaction". Authors in [33] also propose a visual examination of aspects such as the group behavior of users that propagate fake news, and the initial source of news. This would be accomplished using a cumulated text analysis and network analysis model that takes into account the three features of false news: the article text, the user replication it receives, and the user source that promotes it. An integrated method such as this is said to increase precision and generality while also providing a superior representation of users and articles. Authors in [34] also offered cumulation strategies, demonstrating the need of merging verbal expressions with overall "credibility patterns" of politicians using ML classifiers.

Similarly, authors in [35] developed a diffusive network model based on explicit and latent features extracted from a text and achieved excellent results not only in identifying fake news articles, but also in identifying news engenderers and types of news subjects, where a record of credibility can be visually perceived and assessed. In the effort to eradicate fake news propagated on social media, the latter two categories are deemed more important than the news itself. Automatic fake news identification [16] is difficult, according to [36], because the language used in such articles is purposely difficult to differentiate from legitimate stories, and distinguishing satirical news from fake news is even more difficult. Traditional false news detection methods, such as linguistic approaches, do not work with political news due to the complexity of the language. This method is based on a hybrid ML-human crowd model, where human input is used based on machine categorization accuracy. A cumulated method additionally mitigates the pristinely crowd-sourced strategy's low scalability in terms of cost and latency.

Wang *et al.* [40] proposed an Event Adversarial Neural Network (EANN), which comprises of three primary segments: the multi-modular element extractor, the phony news finder, and the occasion discriminator. The multimodal include extractor is answerable for separating the printed furthermore, visual highlights from posts. It helps out the phony news identifier to get familiar with the discriminable portrayal for the recognition of phony news. Hardalov *et al.* [41] utilized a mix of etymological, believability and semantic highlights to separate among genuine and counterfeit news. In the implemented work, phonetic highlights incorporate (weighted) n-grams and standardized number of exceptional words per article. Believability highlights incorporate capitalization, accentuation, pronoun use, and conclusion extremity highlights created from dictionaries [44]. Text semantics were examined utilizing implanting vectors strategy. All component classifications were tried autonomously and in mix dependent on self-made datasets. The best presentation was accomplished utilizing all accessible highlights. Ma *et al.* [42] noticed changes in semantic properties of messages over the lifetime of talk utilizing SVM in view of time arrangement highlights; at that point, they indicated great outcomes in the early discovery of an arising talk. Besides, Conroy *et al.* [43] showed that the best outcomes for counterfeit news recognition could be accomplished while consolidating semantic and network highlights.

To merge metadata with text, Wang [45, 46] planned a cross breed CNN (or ConvNet). The best presentation was accomplished when fusing diverse metadata highlights. Lendavi and Reichel [47] explored logical inconsistencies in gossipy tidbits arrangements of microposts by dissecting posts at the content comparability level. The creators contend that jargon and token succession cover scores can be utilized to produce signals to veracity appraisal, in any event, for short also, boisterous writings. Joulin *et al.* [48] proposed a content order model dependent on n-gram highlights, dimensionality decrease, and a quick estimation of the softmax classifier. This quick content classifier is based upon an item quantization technique all together to limits the softmax over N reports; therefore, it gives exact outcomes with less preparing and assessment time [49].

Zhou *et al.* [50] proposed a complete description of the cutting edge in fake news location in online media. Aggarwal *et al.* identified four distinct features of phishing tweets based on URLs, conventions to inquire about information bases content, and adherents organizations, which present a similar issue to false and non-tenable tweets but can potentially cause huge monetary mischief to someone tapping on the connections associated with these "phishing" messages. Yardi *et al.* created three element types for spam recognition on Twitter [51]; which incorporates looks for URLs, coordinating username examples, and location of watchwords from as far as anyone knows spam messages [52]. O'Donovan *et al.* distinguished the most helpful pointers of valid and noncredible tweets as URLs, specifies, retweets, and tweet lengths [53]. Different chips away at the believability and veracity distinguishing proof on Twitter incorporate Gupta *et al.* that built up a system also, constant evaluation framework for approving creators content on Twitter as they are being posted [54]. Their approach doles out a graduated believability score or rank to each tweet as they are posted live on the informal organization stage.

10.3   Methodology

The popularity of social media has attracted spammers to disseminate large amount of spam messages. Studies of the past shows that most spam messages are produced automatically by bots. Therefore, bot spammer detection can reduce the number of spam messages in social media significantly. In this project, we have tried to identify if a particular social media account is malicious or real. The two categories that have been considered for the result bins are bots or non bots as shown in Figure 10.1. These are as follows:

1. Accurately categorize the headline/body pair as related or unrelated earns 0.25 points.
2. Score 0.75 points for correctly classifying related pairs as agree, disagree, or debate.

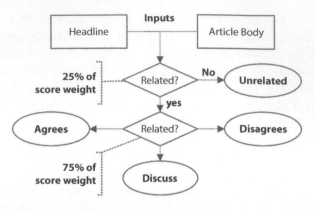

Figure 10.1 Fake news evaluation matrix.

This score weighting schema is designed for the consideration that identifying the relating stance is easier than discovering a stance toward an orientation.

The cycle is a two-stage progress, conceding a modest quantity of credit for effectively recognizing "related" versus "random" feature/article sets, and accurately ordering the "concur"/"deviate"/"talk about" connection between sets that is by all accounts related. Subsequently, to set up a basic execution benchmark, we have attempted to actualize a fast Jaccard closeness scorer that can contrast features and individual sentences from their purported matched or comparable article. By discovering greatest and normal Jaccard closeness scores across all sentences in the article and picking suitable limit esteems, we were at that point ready to accomplish around 90% exactness on the connected/disconnected assignment, so it is expected a decent precision execution when moving to profound learning. The datasets for the undertaking have been taken from the Fake News Challenge association. The set decently comprises of just shy of 50,000 "position" tuples, with each tuple 2 comprising of the following:

- A feature that should be contrasted against an article with decides its position toward the article. Word means the features range from 2 to fairly at least 40, with a normal length of ~11 around.
- The ID of an article against which the feature is to be analyzed, which can be utilized to discover the content of the article body in a different record. Article lengths range from 1 to almost 5,000 words or somewhere in the vicinity, with a normal length of around 360 words.

- The genuine position of the feature regarding the article. The complete number of real features and articles is 1683 of each; however, on the grounds that most features are coordinated against various articles, the quantity of individual preparing tests is a lot bigger. The genuine class breakdown for the preparation set is generally 73% "inconsequential", 18% "examine", 7% "concur", and 2% "oppose this idea".

For building our grouping models, we have chosen a bunch of about 3,000 positions to fill in as an advancement set (for the presentation assessment and hyperboundary tuning), and left the rest of preparing. We at first utilized an irregular example of preparing guides to choose the individuals from our informational collection, yet we stressed that the way that novel features and articles that are utilized generally in different instances of preparing could prompt "spillage" of preparing information at assessment time. Hence, we additionally tried different things with unequivocally isolating exceptional features to have a place with either the preparation or informational collections, yet never both.

10.3.1   Data Retrieval

Twitter is our main source of information. After registering for a Twitter Developer account, we were given credentials to begin gathering tweets. We downloaded tweets containing terms such as parliament, politics, coronavirus, oil, and rising market prices, among others. User and tweet data also provided ID, username, tweet text, and whether the user is verified. The user verified column served as our decision variable, and it was assumed that if a user verified account sent a tweet, it was most likely authentic news. Information passed through authorized accounts is also thought to be reliable. As a result, it is natural that before awarding a confirmed blue tick to a user's account, Twitter goes through a rigorous verification procedure. Users who want their accounts verified must go through a long procedure in which Twitter verifies and authenticates their accounts online. To make the analysis more user-friendly, we converted our user verified column into a label that replaces the text with 0 if the individual is verified and 1 if they are not. The dataset will be pre-processed extensively before being used to analyze the tweets.

10.3.2   Data Pre-Processing

The retrieved dataset was converted to lower case letters, with all punctuation deleted. Users tend to employ emoticons and various punctuations when data is collected from Twitter, which makes our recognition procedure more difficult. Columns that were found to be empty were eliminated. The dataset was filtered to remove repetitive characters such as URL tags and stop words. Hashtags have also been eliminated.

10.3.3   Data Visualization

Once the data has been cleansed and is ready to be given to the model, we can better understand it by visualizing its elements in graphs or plots.

The lowest idf used in our model are

["said", "told", "people", "according", "year", "time", "news", "just", "new", "reports"]

The highest idf we use in the dataset are

["real problem", "point videos", "real renderings", "screens used", "authenticity document", "having salespeople", "having surgery", "maintained price", "authenticity looking", "summaries"]

10.3.4   Tokenization

Tokenization refers to the process of breaking down a large collection of text into smaller lines, words, or, in any case, creating words in a non-English language. NLTK modules from python provide the capabilities of tokenization. We used Regex Tokenizer, which removes tokens either by using the provided regex example to split the content (default) or by coordinating the regex over and again (if holes are bogus). Sifting tokens while limiting their length is also possible with discretionary bounds. It recovers a variety of strings that have become unusable.

10.3.5   Feature Extraction

Extracting features is a dimensionality reduction cycle in which the raw data is reduced to more groups for processing. Hence, we are shortening the compiler's handling session and increasing the speed with which we can detect the word's estimation. One of the characteristics of these massive informational indexes is that many elements necessitate a large number of registered assets to process. As seen in Figure 10.2, TF-IDF stands for "Term Frequency–Inverse Document Frequency". This is a method to evaluate a word in records which permits us to process each word and implies the significance of the word in the report. This strategy is a generally utilized method in Information Retrieval and Text Mining. Term Frequency sums up how regularly a given word shows up inside an archive. Inverse Document Frequency scales down words that seem a great deal across records. When the highlights have been

```
test_data

[OrderedDict([('Headline',
              'Vandals add rude paint job to $2.5m Bugatti (but luckily for the owner it all turned out to be a hoax)'),
             ('Body ID', 615),
             ('Stance', 'unrelated')]),
 OrderedDict([('Headline',
              'No, Robert Plant Didn't Rip Up an $800 Million Contract'),
             ('Body ID', 295),
             ('Stance', 'agree')]),
 OrderedDict([('Headline', 'N. Korea's Kim has leg injury but in control'),
             ('Body ID', 570),
             ('Stance', 'unrelated')]),
 OrderedDict([('Headline',
              'Who Is Michael Zehaf-Bibeau? Ottawa Shooter Suspect Identified By Canadian Officials '),
             ('Body ID', 1251),
             ('Stance', 'unrelated')]),
 OrderedDict([('Headline',
              "Taylor Lianne Chandler: Michael Phelps' Cougar Girlfriend Revealed?"),
             ('Body ID', 1337),
             ('Stance', 'unrelated')]),
 OrderedDict([('Headline',
              'Catholic Priest Dead For 48 Minutes, Is Miraculously Revived – His Revelations About God Are Even More Shocking'),
             ('Body ID', 289),
             ('Stance', 'unrelated')]),
 OrderedDict([('Headline',
              "Nigeria and Boko Haram 'agree ceasefire and girls' release'"),
             ('Body ID', 459),
             ('Stance', 'unrelated')]),
```

```
# Feature extraction
print("[2] Extracting features.. ")
# extract_features(training_data, dev_data, test_data)
training_features, dev_features, test_features = extract_features(training_data, dev_data, test_data)
```

```
[2] Extracting features..
      -Extracting tfidf vectors..
Features with lowest and highest idf in the body vector:

Features with lowest idf:
['said' 'told' 'people' 'according' 'year' 'time' 'news' 'just' 'new'
 'reports']

Features with highest idf:
['real problem' 'point videos' 'real renderings' 'screens used'
 'authenticity document' 'having salespeople' 'having surgery'
 'maintained price' 'authenticity looking' 'summaries']
0it [00:00, ?it/s]
      -Tfidf vectors extracted..
      -Extracting word overlap..
40106it [04:15, 156.68it/s]
4835it [00:19, 246.71it/s]
5031it [00:19, 263.34it/s]
      -Word overlap extracted..
      -Extracting cosine similarity..
      -Cosine similarity extracted..
      -Combined features returned..
```

Figure 10.2 Feature extraction.

separated from our dataset, the whole dataset is not needed for additional investigation. Subsequently, we can drop the content section to speed up.

10.3.6   Machine Learning Algorithms

10.3.6.1   Logistic Regression

This approach is used to predict the probability of an unmodified ward variable. A subordinate variable is a two-factor variable that comprises information coded as 1 (for example, achievement) or 0 (for example, no achievement) (no, disappointment, etc.). The LR model is similar to the Linear Regression model, but it employs a more complex cost work, which is referred to as the Sigmoid capacity. The computed relapse hypothesis suggests that the expense work should be limited to a number between 0 and 1. As a result, straight capacities overlook it because it can have a value more than 1 or less than 0, which is unimaginable according to the theory

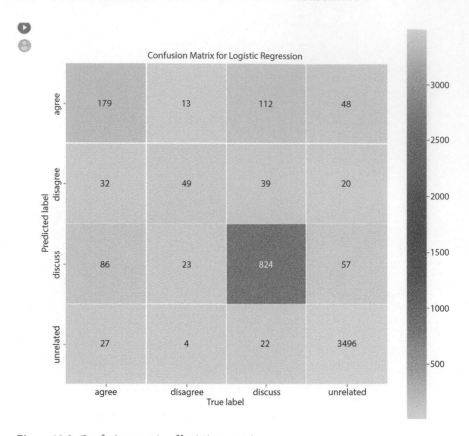

Figure 10.3 Confusion matrix of logistic regression.

of calculated relapse Equation (10.1). It is divided into three categories: binomial, multinomial, and ordinal. The LR accuracy level is 0.903, and the confusion matrix is displayed in Figure 10.3.

$$h(x) = \frac{1}{1 + e^{-f(x)}} \qquad (10.1)$$

10.3.6.2   Naïve Bayes

A NB classifier is a probabilistic AI model which is utilized for grouping task. The essence of the work depends on the Bayes hypothesis appeared in Equation (10.2). Gullible Bayes mulls over two straightforward suspicions: a) predictors are autonomous and b) all the indicators have an equivalent effect on the result. The precision level accomplished utilizing NB is 0.437, and disarray network is appeared in Figure 10.4.

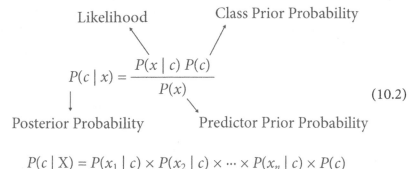

$$P(c \mid x) = \frac{P(x \mid c)\, P(c)}{P(x)} \tag{10.2}$$

$$P(c \mid X) = P(x_1 \mid c) \times P(x_2 \mid c) \times \cdots \times P(x_n \mid c) \times P(c)$$

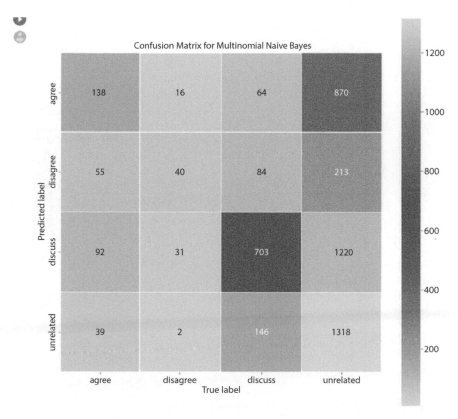

Figure 10.4 Confusion matrix of Naïve Bayes.

10.3.6.3   Random Forest

In AI, the RF comprises of various trees. The trees being referenced here are choice trees. In this way, the calculation involves an irregular assortment or an arbitrary determination of a woodland tree. The exactness level accomplished utilizing RF is 0.805, and disarray network is appeared in Figure 10.5.

10.3.6.4   XGBoost

XGBoost is a very adaptable and adjustable tool that can address a wide range of relapsing, grouping, and positioning challenges, as well as client-defined target capacities. It is readily available as open-source programming and can be used in a variety of stages and interfaces. Equation (10.3) shows the structure of XGBoost. The accuracy level achieved using RF is 0.437, and confusion matrix is shown in Figure 10.6.

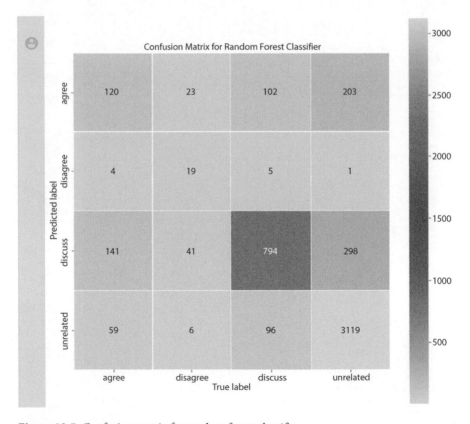

Figure 10.5 Confusion matrix for random forest classifier.

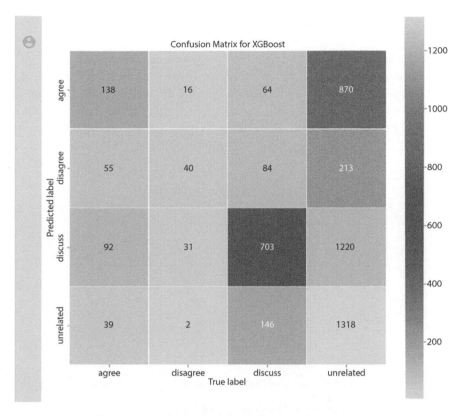

Figure 10.6 Confusion matrix for XGBoost algorithm.

$$f(x) \approx f(a) + f'(a)(x-a) + \frac{1}{2}f''(a)(x-a)^2 \qquad (10.3)$$

$$\mathcal{L}^{(t)} \simeq \sum_{i=1}^{n} \left[l\left(y_i, \hat{y}^{(t-1)}\right) + g_i f_t(\mathrm{x}_i) + \frac{1}{2}h_i f_t^2(\mathrm{x}_i) \right] + \Omega(f_t)$$

The data is trained to learn the features, and the network of each technique is formed. Following that, testing is carried out to assess the performance of our constructed model utilizing performance metrics such as accuracy, precision, recall and f1-score.

10.4 Experimental Results

The intersection of body and headline along with union of body and headline is calculated. The length of common words between body and headline divided by length of all the words of body and headline and labeled it as word overlap feature. This is the process of distillation where we have identified the rank/latent variable which is used further for model training and prediction. Four algorithms, LR, multinomial NB, RF, and XGBoost

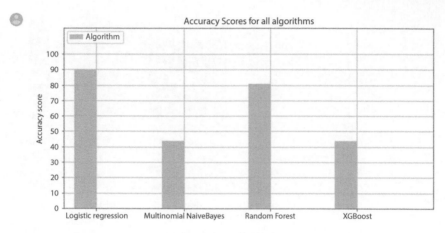

Figure 10.7 Accuracy level of machine learning algorithms.

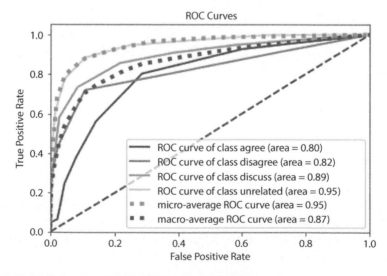

Figure 10.8 ROC curve of random forest for all four classes.

classifiers were used to train the model and predict the stance type. The above algorithms were implemented and results are shown. Figure 10.7 shows the summary of accuracies for all the algorithms combined.

Baseline system is basically a system with TF-IDF vectors as its features. Improved system is run with TF-IDF vectors, Cosine similarity, and Word Overlap, and it is clearly seen that how drastically the accuracy scores has been improved. Initially, it was created with just one classifier: RF and one feature: TF-IDF vectors but the accuracy was not turning up good. Hence, as part of improved system, multiple classifiers were added: LR and seven multinomial NB along with features: TF-IDF vectors, Cosine similarity, and Word Overlap. Figure 10.8 shows the ROC curve of RF model for all the four stance detection types outlined with different colors.

10.5 Conclusion

Detecting fake news seems to be a herculean task, as it is very difficult to identify and predict which news is genuine and which is not out of the thousands of news generating daily. At the same time, it is the need of the hour to detect it faster and aware and prevent the news readers from getting deceived easily. We have successfully presented a model by using four different algorithms which are 1) NB, 2) LR, 3) RF, and 4) XGBoost. Thus, with the aid of these four important algorithms, we have got around 90.39% accuracy along with a faster response too.

References

1. Nada, F., Khan, B.F., Maryam, A., Nooruz-Zuha, Ahmed, Z., Fake news detection using logistic regression. *Int. Res. J. Eng. Technol. (IRJET)*, 06, 05, pp. 1601–1603, May 2019.
2. Pérez-Rosas, V., Bennett, K., Lefevre, A., Mihalcea, R., Automatic detection of fake news. *Proceedings of the 27th International Conference on Computational Linguistics*, pp. 3391–3401, 2018.
3. Mokhtar, M.S., Jusoh, Y.Y., Admodisastro, N., Pa, N.C., Amruddin, A.Y., Fakebuster: Fake News Detection System Using Logistic Regression Technique In Machine Learning. *Int. J. Eng. Adv. Technol. (IJEAT)*, 9, 1, pp. 2407–2410, October 2019.
4. Liao, W. and Lin, C., Deep Ensemble Learning for News Stance Detection. *5 th International Conference on Computational Social Science IC2S 2*, July 17-20, 2019.

5. Ibrishimova, M.D. and Li, K.F., A machine learning approach to fake news detection using knowledge verification and natural language processing, International Conference on Intelligent Networking and Collaborative Systems (INCoS): Advances in Intelligent Networking and Collaborative Systems, pp. 223–234, 2019.

6. Ogdol, J.M.G. and Samar, B.-L.T., Binary Logistic Regression based Classifier for Fake News, *J. High. Educ. Res. Discipl.*, [Online], 3.1 (2018): n. pag. Web. 12, Sep. 2021

7. Katsaros, D., Stavropoulos, G., Papakostas, D., Which machinelearning paradigm for fake news detection? *IEEE/WIC/ACMInternational Conference on Web Intelligence (WI)*, pp. 383–387, 2019.

8. Wu, K., Yang, S., Zhu, K.Q., False rumors detection on sina weibo by propagation structures, in: *Data Engineering (ICDE), 2015 IEEE 31st International Conference on. IEEE*, pp. 651–662, 2015.

9. Abdullah-All-Tanvir, Mahir, E.M., Akhter, S., Huq, M.R., Detecting Fake News using Machine Learning and Deep Learning Algorithms. *2019 7th International Conference on Smart Computing & Communications (ICSCC)*, Sarawak, Malaysia, Malaysia, pp. 1–5, 2019.

10. Jain, A., Shakya, A., Khatter, H., Gupta, A.K., A smart System for Fake News Detection Using Machine Learning. *2019 International Conference on Issues and Challenges in Intelligent Computing Techniques (ICICT)*, Ghaziabad, India, pp. 1–4, 2019.

11. Vaishnavi R., and Anitha Kumari S., Fake News Detection using Deep Learning, *International Journal of Innovative Technology and Exploring Engineering (IJITEE)* , Volume-9 Issue-9, July 2020.

12. Hiramath, C.K. and Deshpande, G.C., Fake News Detection Using Deep Learning Techniques. *2019 1st International Conference on Advances in Information Technology (ICAIT)*, Chikmagalur, India, pp. 411–415, 2019.

13. Agarwalla, K., Nandan, S., Nair, V.A., Deva Hema, D., Fake News Detection using Machine Learing and Natural Language Processing. *Int. J. Recent Technol. Eng.*, 7, 6, pp. 844–847, March 2019.

14. Mahabub, A., A robust technique of fake news detection using Ensemble Voting Classifier and comparison with other classifiers. *SN Appl. Sci.*, 2, 1–9, 2020.

15. AlRubaian, M., Al-Qurishi, M., Al-Rakhami, M., Rahman, S.M.M., Alamri, A., A multistage credibility analysis model for microblogs. *2015 IEEE/ACM International Conference on Advances in Social Networks Analysis and Mining (ASONAM)*, Paris, pp. 1434–1440, 2015.

16. Pérez-Rosas, V., Kleinberg, B., Lefevre, A., Mihalcea, R., Automatic Detection of Fake News, Published in COLING, pp. 1–11, 2018.

17. Mandical, R.R., Mamatha, N., Shivakumar, N., Monica, R., Krishna, A.N., Identification of Fake News Using Machine Learning. *2020 IEEE International*

Conference on Electronics, Computing and Communication Technologies (CONECCT), Bangalore, India, pp. 1–6, 2020.

18. Aphiwongsophon, S. and Chongstitvatana, P., Detecting Fake News with Machine Learning Method. *2018 15th International Conference on Electrical Engineering/Electronics, Computer, Telecommunications and Information Technology (ECTI-CON)*, Chiang Rai, Thailand, pp. 528–531, 2018.

19. Thota, A., Tilak, P., Ahluwalia, S., Lohia, N., Fake News Detection: A Deep Learning Approach. *SMU Data Sci. Rev.*, 1, 3, pp. 1–20, 2018, Article 10. Available at: https://scholar.smu.edu/datasciencereview/vol1/iss3/10.

20. Han, W. and Mehta, V., Fake News Detection in Social Networks Using Machine Learning and Deep Learning: Performance Evaluation. *2019 IEEE International Conference on Industrial Internet (ICII)*, Orlando, FL, USA, pp. 375–380, 2019.

21. Kavitha, M., Suganthy, M., Srinivasan, R., Intelligent learning system using data mining-ilsdm. *Int. J. Innovative Technol. Exploring Eng.*, 8, 9, 505–508, 2019.

22. Tyagi, A.K., Machine learning with big data, in: *Proc. SUSCOM*, Jaipur, India, pp. 1011–1020, 2019.

23. 12. Elhadad, M.K., Li, K.F., Gebali, F., Fake news detection on social media: A systematic survey, in: *Proc. IEEE PACRIM*, Victoria, BC, Canada, Aug. 2019, pp. 1–9.

24. Ahmed, S., Hinkelmann, K., Corradini, F., Combining Machine Learning with Knowledge Engineering to detect Fake News in Social Networks-a survey, in: *Proceedings of the AAAI 2019 Spring Symposium on Combining Machine Learning with Knowledge Engineering (AAAI-MAKE 2019)*, A. Martin, K. Hinkelmann, A. Gerber, D. Lenat, F. van Harmelen, P. Clark (Eds.), Stanford University, Palo Alto, California, USA, March 25-27, 2019.

25. Kumar, R. and Verma, R., KDD techniques: A survey. *Int. J. Electron. Comput. Sci. Eng.*, 1, 4, 2042–2047, Aug. 2008.

26. Kaliyar, R.K. and Singh, N., Misinformation detection on online social media—A survey, in: *Proc. 10th Int. Conf. Comput., Commun. Netw. Technol. (ICCCNT)*, pp. 1–6, Jul. 2019.

27. Groza, A., Detecting fake news for the new coronavirus by reasoning on the Covid-19 ontology, *Natural language arguments and computation*, pp. 1–17, 2020.

28. Hashem, I.A.T., Ezugwu, A.E., Al-Garadi, M.A., Abdullahi, I.N., Otegbeye, O., Ahman, Q.O., Mbah, G.C.E., Shukla, A.K., Chiroma, H., A Machine Learning Solution Framework for Combatting COVID-19 in Smart Cities from Multiple Dimensions MedRxiv· The Preprint Server For Health Sciences, pp. 1–68, 2020.

29. Shahi, G.K. and Nandini, D., Fake Covid -- A Multilingual Cross-domain Fact Check News Dataset for COVID-19, *Association for the Advancement of Artificial Intelligence*, pp. 1–9, 2020

30. Kaur, S., Kumar, P., and Kumaraguru, P.. Automating fake news detection system using multi-level voting model. *Soft Computing*, vol. 24, pp. 9049–9069, 2020.

31. Moscadelli, A., *et al*. Fake news and covid-19 in Italy: results of a quantitative observational study. *Int. J. Environ. Res. Public Health*, 17.16, pp. 5850, 2020.

32. Zhou, X., Zafarani, R., Shu, K., Liu, H., Fake news: Fundamental theories, detection strategies and challenges, in: *Proceedings of the twelfth ACM international conference on web search and data mining*, pp. 836–837, 2019.

33. Ruchansky, N., Seo, S., Liu, Y., Csi: A hybrid deep model for fake news detection, in: *Proceedings of the 2017 ACM on Conference on Information and Knowledge Management*, pp. 797–806, 2017.

34. Zhang, J., Dong, B., Philip, S.Y., Deep diusive neural network based fake news detection from heterogeneous social networks, in: *2019 IEEE International Conference on Big Data (Big Data)*, IEEE, pp. 1259–1266, 2019.

35. Fernández-Reyes, F.C. and Shinde, S., Evaluating deep neural networks for automatic fake news detection in political domain, in: Simari G., Fermé E., Gutiérrez Segura F., Rodríguez Melquiades J. (eds.) *Advances in Artificial Intelligence - IBERAMIA 2018. Lecture Notes in Computer Science*, vol 11238. Springer, 2018.

36. Shabani, S. and Sokhn, M., Hybrid machine-crowd approach for fake news detection, in: *2018 IEEE 4th International Conference on Collaboration and Internet Computing (CIC)*, IEEE, pp. 299–306, 2018.

37. Kim, K.-H. and Jeong, C.-S., Fake news detection system using article abstraction, in: *2019 16th International Joint Conference on Computer Science and Software Engineering (JCSSE)*, IEEE, pp. 209–212, 2019.

38. Rehm, G., An infrastructure for empowering internet users to handle fake news and other online media phenomena, in: *International Conference of the German Society for Computational Linguistics and Language Technology*, Springer, pp. 216–231, 2017.

39. Ruchansky, N., Seo, S., Liu, Y., Csi: A hybrid deep model for fake news detection, in: *Proceedings of the 2017 ACM on Conference on Information and Knowledge Management*, ACM, pp. 797–806, 2017.

40. Yaqing, W. *et al*., Eann: Event adversarial neural networks for multimodal fake news detection, in: *Proceedings of the 24th ACM SIGKDD International Conference on Knowledge Discovery & Data Mining*, ACM, pp. 849–857, 2018.

41. Hardalov, M., Koychev, I., Nakov, P., In search of credible news, in: *International Conference on Artificial Intelligence: Methodology, Systems, and Applications*, Springer, pp. 172–180, 2016.

42. Ma, J., Gao, W., Wei, Z., Lu, Y., Wong, K.-F., Detect rumors using time series of social context information on microblogging websites, in: *Proceedings of the 24th ACM International on Conference on Information and Knowledge Management*, ACM, pp. 1751– 1754, 2015.

43. Conroy, N.J., Rubin, V.L., Chen, Y., Automatic deception detection: Methods for finding fake news. *Proceedings of the Association for Information Science and Technology*, vol. 52, no. 1, pp. 1–4, 2015.

44. Ciampaglia, G.L. *et al.*, Computational fact checking from knowledge networks. *PLoS One*, 10, 6, e0128193, 2015.

45. Wang, W. Y., Liar, Liar Pants on Fire: A New Benchmark Dataset for Fake News Detection, Association for Computational Linguistics, pp. 1–5, 2017.

46. Ferreira, W. and Vlachos, A., Emergent: a novel data-set for stance classification, in: *Proceedings of the conference of the North American chapter of the association for computational linguistics: Human language technologies*, pp. 1163–1168, 2016.

47. Lendvai, P. and Reichel, U.D., *Contradiction detection for rumorous claims, Proc. Extra-Propositional Aspects of Meaning (ExProM) in Computational Linguistics*, Osaka, Japan, pp. 31–40, 2016.

48. Joulin, A. *et al.*, Fasttext. zip: Compressing text classification models, a Proceedings of 5th International Conference on Learning Representations, pp. 1–13, 2016.

49. Joulin, A., Grave, E., Bojanowski, P., Mikolov, T., Bag of tricks for efficient text classification, Proceedings of the 15th Conference of the European Chapter of the Association for Computational Linguistics: Volume 2, pp. 427–431, 2017.

50. Zhou, X. and Zafarani, R., Fake news: A survey of research, detection methods, and opportunities, *ACM Comput. Surv.* 1, 1, Article 1, pp. 1–37, 2020.

51. Aggarwal, A., Rajadesingan, A., Kumaraguru, P., Phishari: automatic real-time phishing detection on twitter, in: *eCrime Researchers Summit (eCrime)*, IEEE, pp. 1–12, 2012.

52. Yardi, S., Romero, D., Schoenebeck, G. *et al.*, Detecting spam in a twitter network. *First Monday*, 15, 1, pp. 1–4, 2009.

53. O'Donovan, J., Kang, B., Meyer, G., Hollerer, T., Adalii, S., Credibility in context: An analysis of feature distributions in twitter, in: *Privacy, Security, Risk and Trust (PASSAT), 2012 international conference on and 2012 international conference on social computing (SocialCom)*, IEEE, pp. 293–301, 2012.

54. Gupta, A., Kumaraguru, P., Castillo, C., Meier, P., Tweetcred: Real-time credibility assessment of content on twitter, in: *International Conference on Social Informatics*, Springer, pp. 228–243, 2014.

11

Opportunities and Challenges in Machine Learning With IoT

Sarvesh Tanwar, Jatin Garg*, Medini Gupta† and Ajay Rana

Amity Institute of Information Technology, Amity University Uttar Pradesh, Noida, India

Abstract

Machine learning (ML) is swiftly being used in wide range of applications. It has risen to popularity in recent years, owing in part to the emergence of big data. With respect to big data, ML techniques are more promising than ever before. Big data helps ML algorithms to discover finer-grained trends and make more precise and reliable predictions than ever before; however, it also raises significant obstacles for ML, such as model scalability and distributed computation. We have discussed about coupling ML with IoT, its applications, and challenges. We designed a framework MLBiD (Machine Learning Based on Big Data) and discussed about deliberation of its potential opportunities and defiant challenges. The architecture is focused on ML, which is split into three phases: preprocessing, learning, and assessment. Furthermore, it includes four other components in the framework: big data, consumer, domain, and system. Various different stages of ML as well as the components of MLBiD are stepping ahead for identifying related opportunities and challenges, and they have opened the doors for potential research analysis in a variety of previously untraveled or under expedition.

Keywords: Machine learning, IoT, supervised learning, unsupervised learning, big data, data processing, MLBiD

11.1 Introduction

In areas, for instance, computer vision, speech recognition, natural language comprehension, IoT, neuroscience, and fitness, machine learning

Corresponding author: jatingarg513@gmail.com
†*Corresponding author:* guptamedini642@gmail.com

Shalli Rani, R. Maheswar, G. R. Kanagachidambaresan, Sachin Ahuja and Deepali Gupta (eds.) Machine Learning Paradigm for Internet of Things Applications, (209–228) © 2022 Scrivener Publishing LLC

(ML) techniques have had tremendous societal impacts. The emergence of the era of big data has sparked a surge in ML interest [1]. Big data has never promised or cross-examined algorithms for ML to achieve new insights into a variety of business applications and human behaviors. On the one hand, big data provides ML algorithms with unparalleled amounts of data from which to derive underlying patterns and develop prediction models; in contrast, conventional ML algorithms face crucial challenges such as scalability in order to fully unlock the value of big data. The obstacle of experienced learning with respect to certain tasks and performance metrics is referred to as an ML problem. ML algorithms are applied by users to deduce the existing structure and predictions are made from large data sets given. ML flourishes on strong computational environments, efficient learning techniques (algorithms), and rich and/or large data. As a consequence, ML has a lot of potential and is an important part of big data analytics [2]. The emphasis of this paper is on various techniques for ML in relation to big data and present computing environments. We want to go through the adequate benefits and drawbacks of ML on big data. New possibilities for ML have arrived due to introduction of big data. Big data, for instance, enables pattern learning at various stages of granularity and diversity from multiple perspectives in an inherently parallel manner. Furthermore, big data allows for causality inferences based on sequence chains. Big data, on the other hand, poses significant challenges to ML, including data streaming, model scalability, high data dimensionality, distributed computing, adaptability, and usability [3]. MLBiD discussed about deliberation of its potential opportunities and defiant challenges. The architecture is emphasized on techniques of ML, which is divided into three phases: a) preprocessing, b) learning, and c) evaluation. In addition, the framework includes four other components: big data, consumer, domain, and system; all of which influence and are influenced by ML. The different elements of MLBiD and, additionally, the phases of ML point the way to recognizing potential opportunities and open threats, as well as potential study in variation of unexplored or underexplored research areas.

11.2   Literature Review

11.2.1   A Designed Architecture of ML on Big Data

Figure 11.1 depicts the paradigm for MLBiD which stands for ML on big data. The ML component is at the center of MLBiD, and it interacts with four other components: big data, consumer, domain, and framework.

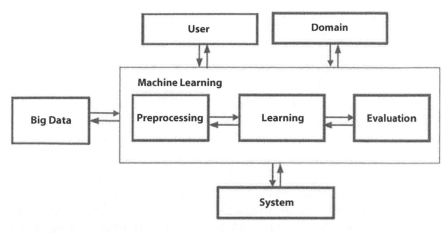

Figure 11.1 The paradigm for ML on Big data (MLBiD).

Interactions take place in both directions. Users can interact with ML by entering domain knowledge, individual preferences, and usability feedback, as well as by enhancing decision-making based on leveraging learning; for example, big data act as inputs to ML and then, after that, produces outputs that are considered as a part of big data; users can interact with ML by giving usability feedback, domain knowledge, and personal preferences and improving the decision-making mechanism by leveraging learning outcomes; domain can serve as both a source of information for ML and a base for executing already learned models; below presented system architecture has an effect on how learning algorithms can operate and how effective they are to run, and meeting ML needs simultaneously can contribute to a redesign of given system architecture.

11.2.2 Machine Learning

Initially started from data preprocessing, learning, and then evaluation are common phases of ML (see Figure 11.1). Data preprocessing assists in the transformation of raw data into the "correct shape" for further learning steps. It is possible that the raw data is unstructured, noisy, incomplete, and inconsistent. By cleaning of data, extracting, transforming, and fusion, the preprocessing phase converts that data into such a form that can turn as inputs to learning. Using the preprocessed input data, the learning step selects suitable techniques for learning and regulates model parameters to produce desired outputs. Data preprocessing can be done with some learning methods, especially representational learning. After that, evaluation of trained models is done to see how well they do. Such as selecting appropriate data sets, estimating error, statistical tests, and performance measurement are all part of a classifier's performance evaluation [4]. The results of the evaluation lead to changes in the parameters of the learning algorithms chosen and/or the selection of new and efficient algorithm.

ML can be categorized into three main components based on available input quality to a learning system: supervised, unsupervised, and reinforcement learning. In case of supervised learning, samples of input and output events are given to learning system the aim is to make the system learn a function that maps inputs to outputs. The aim of unsupervised learning is to discover patterns in the input without providing specific response or expected output. A reinforcement learning system, like unsupervised learning, does not have input-output pairs. Reinforcement learning, like guided learning, provides input on past experiences [5]. In comparison to supervised learning, reinforcement learning offers input in the form of incentives or punishments associated with behaviors instead of desired performance or explicit correction of sub-optimal actions. Hybrid of supervised and unsupervised learning is known as semi-supervised learning in which the system is given a limited number of input-output pairs as well as a large number of unannotated inputs. Semi-supervised learning has the same purpose as supervised learning, but it develops its learning from both unannotated and annotated data.

ML are classified into two types: representational learning and task learning, depending on whether the learning objective is to learn particular tasks or work by applying input samples or to learn the features themselves. When constructing classifiers or other predictors, extracting the useful knowledge to learn about new and innovative data representation is the aim of representational learning. A good illustration separates the fundamental sources of variance. In the case of probabilistic models, it is frequently the one that catches the posterior distribution of underlying exploratory factors for the observed production [6].

11.2.3 Types of Machine Learning

11.2.3.1 Supervised Learning

A branch of ML algorithms known as supervised learning infers a feature from labeled training data. The training data is composed of training set examples, each of which is a pair (x; y), with x representing an input vector and y representing the output value. The algorithm generates a function that has its usage in mapping unknown inputs in the future. Regression algorithms (continuous output) and classification algorithms (discrete output) are the two major types of supervised learning algorithms. There are multiple algorithms in each group, which will be discussed further down [7].

11.2.3.1.1   Regression

Regression algorithms try to find the best t function for the available training data. Linear regression and polynomial regression are the two major algorithms discussed below.

- **Linear Regression:** The linear regression algorithm is most commonly used regression algorithms in ML. For the available training data, this algorithm tries to find the best t line/ hyperplane.

The algorithm's aim is to find the optimal coefficient vector opt D [0; 1; ::::; N] so that the predictive function has a linear form.

- **Polynomial Regression:** The polynomial regression algorithm is another commonly used algorithm for regression. The main motive of this algorithm is to find the best t polynomial for the available training data. The aim of the algorithm, like its linear counterpart, is to calculate the coefficient value of vector opt D [0; 1; ::::; kN] so that the predictive function is a polynomial of order k.

11.2.3.1.2   Classification

Unlike regression algorithms, which attempt to find the best t function for the training data, classification algorithms attempt to obtain most applicable class for the data by classifying each input. In such instances, the predictive function's output is discrete, with the probable values being part of one of the various classes used inside the training data sets. The following sections cover four essential classification algorithms: logistic regression, artificial neural networks, support vector machines, and decision trees.

- **Logistic Regression:** In the literary texts, logistic regression is a usual classification algorithm. Despite its name, this algorithm is applied on classification rather than regression (i.e., its performance is discrete). A binary classifier is usually used, with the output belonging to only one of two types.

The hypothesis function, also known as the zopt (x) predictive function, calculates the likelihood of an output equal to 1 provided a specific input. To put it another way, zopt (x) D P(y D 1 = xI). The performance is set to be 1 if this likelihood is greater than 0.5. If the case is different, then the output is set to 0.

- **Support Vector Machines (SVM):** Another supervised classification algorithm is SVM. It tries to calculate the best hyperplane that separates the labeled data by the greatest margin from the closest point. The logistic regression algorithm is a more efficient and restrictive classifier. The logistic regression uses function sigmoid that is replaced by a new function termed as hinge loss function in this algorithm. The hypothesis function provided by the SVM algorithm is a discrimination function that returns either 1 or 0. It should be noted that hypothesis function is not interpreted as a probability of the output being 1 or 0, but rather as a probability of the output being 1 or 0.

- **Artificial Neural Networks (ANNs):** A common supervised classification algorithm is ANN. It is frequently used when there is a lot of labeled training data large number of features as well as nonlinear hypothesis function is required. ANN attempts to imitate the way our brain operates; it is revealed that the brain uses a single "learning algorithm" for all of its functions. The ANN algorithm uses a model in which the features behave as dendrites (nerve cells) that take electrical inputs (through dendrites) and channel them toward an output (axon), similar to how neurons take electrical inputs (through dendrites) and channel them toward an output (axon). One "secret" layer is often used as an intermediate layer. Activation layer is a layer that helps brings out huge knowledge from inside the collection of features available in the training data. The sigmoid function, which is used in logistic regression, is used at each layer of the network.

- **Decision Trees:** Another common supervised learning classification algorithm is decision trees. Since statistical metrics are being used to calculate the nodes of branching, these algorithms are also referred to as statistical classifiers. Decision trees sort instances down the tree from the root node to a specific leaf node to identify them. Each branch of the tree represents a potential value of the executed function, while each node identifies a test case of a specific feature. Quinlan suggested the algorithm, which is centered on the notion of information entropy. In effect, the C4.5 selects the function that distributes its set of given samples into much smaller subsets rich in one of two classes. The normalized information benefit metric (difference in entropy) is used to evaluate the division criterion. The function which has highest level of knowledge gain is selected.

11.2.3.1.3   Deep Learning

Supervised ML algorithms have a subset known as deep learning. Deep learning can be thought of as a large-scale neural network in nature. Deep learning, on the other hand, cannot be classified as a conventional neural network because of its performance in automatic unsupervised feature extraction which is also referred as feature learning. As a result, deep learning is regarded as a subset of supervised ML. Deep learning, in general, uses a graph with multiple processing layers to model abstractions contained in data. Units in these processing layers apply linear and non-linear transformations to the data in order to obtain as much useful information as possible. Deep learning algorithms and ANNs are close to each other. In reality, ANN can be classified as a deep neural network learning algorithm. Deep learning algorithms, on the other hand, are more adaptable due to their nature to be used on both labeled and unlabeled data. They can also be used on a huge scale with neural networks. Deep learning, according to Andrew Ng, who is a co-founder of Coursera and Chief Scientist at Baidu Research, is simply implementing ANN on a broad range so that it can be equipped with more data and work better [8].

11.2.3.2   Unsupervised Learning

Unsupervised learning, in contrast to supervised learning, is a branch of ML that infers a function/pattern from unlabeled training data. Only the inputs x1; x2; ::::; xM and no known outputs make up the training results. As a result, unsupervised learning algorithms seek to make sense of the training data through identifying patterns and relationships. Clustering, dimensionality reduction, and anomaly detection are prime categories of unsupervised learning algorithms. Inside - group, there are many algorithms. The following sections outline some of the most common algorithms in these categories.

11.2.3.2.1   Clustering

Grouping or clustering a series of data points is one of the simplest ways to make it informative. This makes the available data more clear and understandable by giving it more structure by grouping it into a finite number of groups rather than a large number of random data points. This is particularly significant in market segmentation and social network analysis applications. We use the word "clustering" instead of "classification" since the given data points still not labeled to belong to specific groups and we do not know whether this classification is right or not.

- **K-Means Algorithm:** For automatic data grouping into coherent clusters, K-means is commonly applied unsupervised clustering algorithms. This algorithm attempts to cluster the data into K clusters by locating the cluster centroid (also known as cluster mean) and grouping the data points that are located nearest to it with it. A cost function must be reduced to gain correct cluster of data points into the K clusters. This cost function depends on three variables: $c(j)$, that is the cluster index to which example $x(j)$ is currently assigned, k centroid of cluster k, and $c(j)$, which is the cluster centroid to which example $x(j)$ is currently assigned.

11.2.3.2.2   Dimensionality Reduction

Another important subject in ML is dimensionality reduction. The following is a summary of the motivation for dimensionality reduction:

(i)   Eliminate redundant data
(ii) Lower storage and computational requirements
(iii) Simplify data visualization by focusing on a few main features.

11.2.3.2.3   Principal Component Analysis

In unsupervised learning, principal component analysis is of most commensurable dimensionality reduction algorithms. Its goal is to identify the subset of features that most accurately represents the data. For example, if two features x1 and x2 are given, PCA will select a single line for effectively explain both of these features at the same time. The aim of PCA is to reduce the average projection error (orthogonal distance from the function to the projection line), while the goal of linear regression is to reduce the average error (vertical distance) to the line. Data preprocessing, covariance matrix computation, and eigenvalue decomposition are the four stages in performing PCA [9].

11.2.3.2.4   Anomaly Detection

The anomaly detection algorithm is another significant unsupervised learning algorithm. This algorithm attempts to decide if the given new example x(new) is anomalous or not, as its name suggests. To do so, the probability of an example not being anomalous is determined using the probability function/ model p(x). The dividing value between defining the example as regular or anomalous is a threshold value, denoted by. The given features are assumed to be independent in order to measure p(x) that is a probability function, and thus the probability function p(x) becomes the product of the probabilities of the features p(xi) 8i. Another assumption is that the features are normally distributed, implying that p(xi) 8i follows a Gaussian distribution. As a result, comparing p(x(new)) with determines if x(new) is anomalous or not: if p(x-(new)), then the example is anomalous, otherwise it is usual.

11.3   Why Should We Care About Learning Representations?

In the ML world, representation learning has developed in its area only, with frequent workshops at leading conferences such as NIPS and ICML, and even new conference devoted to it, ICLR1, 1 often referred to as deep learning or function learning. Here, depth is an important aspect of the work; there are several other priors that are fascinating and can be handled easily when the problem is formulated as learning a representation. An impressive series of research advances in academia and business has followed and nourished the dramatic growth in research activity on representation literacy.

ML can be divided as batch and online learning depending on the timing of building training data accessible (e.g., is availability of training data all at once or one at a time). Batch learning creates models by learning on all of the training dataset at once, while online learning updates models as new data is added. The assumption of a batch learning algorithm is that data are individual unit and identically distributed or drawn from the same probability distribution, which met rarely by real data. In most cases, no conclusions related to statistics are made about the data in online learning. Although a batch learning algorithm is expected to generalize, no such assumption exists for online learning because the algorithm is only expected to correctly predict the labels of the examples it get as input.

Where it is computationally viable to learn over the whole dataset and/or where data is created over a vast time and a learning system must respond to new trends in the data, online learning is used [10].

Batch learning (also known as mathematical learning) and online learning are two supervised systems for machine-learning that are distinct. A problem related to learning is described by an instance space X and a label set Y in both frameworks, and the task is to assign labels from Y to instances in X. We have taken assumption that a probability distribution exists over the product space X Y and that we have access to a training set drawn i.i.d. from this distribution in batch learning. A batch learning algorithm produces an output hypothesis, which is a function that maps instances in X to labels in Y, using the training collection. We expect a batch learning algorithm's performance hypothesis to correctly predict the labels of previously unseen examples sampled from the distribution [10].

We usually make no statistical conclusions about the data roots in the online learning context. An online learning algorithm receives a list of examples and processes each one independently. The algorithm receives an instance in each online-learning round and predicts its mark using an internal prediction that it stores in memory. The algorithm then receives the right label for the instance and updates and improves its internal theory using the current instance-label pair. Since the algorithm is only supposed to correctly predict/perceive the labels of the examples it provides as input, there is no definition of statistical generalization.

11.4   Big Data

Big data is the trending topic in the technology world. Everyone is talking about big data, and it is expected that the effects of big data will have a huge impact on technology, enterprise, industry, government, and culture. In terms of technology, the processing, exploitation preservation, and transportation of big data are all part of the entire operation. Without a question, the stages of data acquisition, storage, and transportation are important preludes to the ultimate objective of data analytics-based manipulation, which is at the heart of big data analysis [11].

From the perspective of data mining, the four V's—Volume, Velocity, Veracity, and Variety—have come to describe "big data". For a problem to be classified as a big data problem, it is presumed that all or any of them must be met. The volume denotes the size of the results, which may be too massive for current algorithms and/or systems to accommodate. The term "velocity" refers to data streaming at a rate higher than conventional algorithms and devices can accommodate. Sensors are constantly reading and transmitting data sources. We are entering the realm of the quantified self, which would include evidence that was previously unavailable. Veracity indicates that, considering the availability of evidence, data accuracy remains a major concern. That is, we cannot believe that better quality comes with big data. In reality, as data increases in scale, consistency problems emerge, which must be solved either during the data pre-processing stage or by the learning algorithm. Variety is the most appealing V's, of the data mining since it includes displaying data of various types and modalities for an individual item. Each V is not a brand-new concept. For decades, researchers in the associated fields of data mining and ML are continued to work on these problems. However, the growth of Internet-based businesses has presented a challenge to many conventional process-oriented businesses, forcing them to turn into knowledge-based businesses that are powered by data rather than processes [11].

11.5   Data Processing Opportunities and Challenges

The implementation of data transformations and preprocessing pipelines that are outcome in data representative can be useful in successful ML accounts for a significant portion of the overall effort in deploying an ML framework. Data preprocessing aims to solve problems including data duplication, inconsistency, noise, heterogeneity, transformation, labeling [for (semi-)supervised ML], feature representation/selection and data imbalance. Due to the demand for human labor and a wide range of choices to choose from, data preparation and preprocessing is normally expensive [6]. Furthermore, some traditional data perceptions do not actually hold true for big data, making some preprocessing approaches ineffective. Big data, on the other hand, provides the capacity of lowering down dependence on human error by learning directly from large, complex, and streaming data sources.

11.5.1   Data Redundancy

When multiple data samples represent the same object, duplication occurs. Data replication or inconsistency can have a significant impact on ML. Traditional methods such as pairwise similarity comparison are now not feasible for big data, despite a variety of methodology for capturing duplicates produced in the previous 20 years. Furthermore, the conventional presumption that duplicated pairs are rarer than non-redundant pairs is no longer true. Dynamic Time Warping is much better and faster than existing Euclidean algorithms for distance in this regard [12].

11.5.2   Data Noise

Data sparsity, missing and incorrect values, and irregularity can all create errors in ML. When managing with big data, conventional solutions to noisy data problems pose roadblocks. Manual procedures, for example, are no longer viable because of lack of scalability; replacing them with a mean will sacrifice the benefits of big data richness and fine granularity. In certain cases, these noisy data may contain interesting patterns, so removing them is not always the best option. Missing values can be estimated using reliable predictive analytics of big data, which can play crucial role to be used to replace inaccurate readings caused by malfunctioned sensors or broken communication channels. The highest entropy constraint are placed on the inference stage to counter significant bias that could be inserted into predictions by collective effect techniques, needs the predictions to contain the same distribution as observed marks [13]. Despite being known that data sparsity can persist and may be exacerbated by big data, the huge amount of big data provides significant possibilities for predicting the analysis so adequate frequency may be accrued for various sub-samples. Outlier detection has been scaled up (e.g., ONION) to allow analysts to easily analyze anomalies in large datasets [14].

11.5.3   Heterogeneity of Data

Big data promises incorporate multi-view data from a variety of repositories, in a variety of formats, and from a variety of population samples, and thus is highly heterogeneous. The value of these multi-level heterogeneous data (e.g., unstructured, audio, text, and video formats) for a learning task can differ. As a result, combining all of the features and treating them equally relevant is unlikely to result in optimum learning outcomes [15]. Big data helps you to learn from different viewpoints in real time and then assemble multiple outcomes by assessing the relevance of feature/characteristics views to the task. The approach is supposed should be resistant to data outliers and able to solve convergence and optimization problems.

11.5.4   Discretization of Data

Decision trees and Naive Bayes are cases of algorithms for ML that can only deal with discrete attributes. Discretization transforms quantitative data set into qualitative data set, allowing a continuous domain to be separated into non-overlapping parts. The aim of attribute discretization is to determine simplistic representations of the data in the form of groups that are suitable for the learning task while preserving as much knowledge possible from the original continuous attribute. However, some known discretization methods would be unsuccessful while dealing with massive amounts of data. Traditional discretization approaches have been parallelized in big data platforms to handle big data problems, with a distributed variant of the entropy minimization discretizer focused on the Minimum Description Length Principle optimizing both efficiency and accuracy [16].

11.5.5 Data Labeling

Traditional data annotation techniques require a lot of time and effort. To deal with big data and its related problems, several different approaches are introduced by different researchers. For example, online crowd-sourced repositories may be a good place to look for free training in annotated data with a wide range of class sizes and intra-class diversity. Furthermore, probabilistic program inference can be used to accomplish human-level principle understanding. Furthermore, ML algorithms like semi-supervised learning, adaptive learning, and transform learning have the ability to mark results. The number of questions raised to the crowd can be reduced by using active learning as the optimization technique for marking tasks in crowdsourced databases, enabling crowd-sourced applications to scale. Another problem is with dataset that cannot cover all user-specific contexts, resulting in output that is often inferior to user-centric training.

11.5.6 Imbalanced Data

Traditional stratified random sampling approaches have tackled the problem of unbalanced data. However, sub-sample generation and error metrics measurement iteration are required; the whole procedure can take huge amount of time. Furthermore, conventional sampling methods are unable to hold sampling of data over a user-specified data subset that carries value-based sampling efficiently.

11.6 Learning Opportunities and Challenges

It is challenging to find problems that are "entirely different" as a result of big data. Despite these challenges, there are still critical elements to which more time as well as efforts should be directed.

First, despite the fact that we have often attempted to manage (increasingly) vast quantities of data, we have misunderstood the key computation can be kept indefinitely. The current data volume has grown to such an extent that it is very hard for storage and even search numerous times. Many critical learning goals or acceptance criteria, on the other hand, are non-linear, non-convex, non-decomposable, and non-smooth over the samples. Is it possible to learn it by analyzing the data just once, and if so, is the storage requirement minimal and autonomous of data size? This is referred to as "one-pass learning", and its critical because in many big data application domains the data is not necessarily large, but also accumulates over time, difficult to estimate the dataset's final size. Apparently, some recent approaches in this direction, such as, have been developed. However, even if we have big data, is all of the data extremely important? They most likely are not, according to the evidence [14]. The question then becomes: can we extract useful data subsets from the initial large dataset?

Secondly, other advantage of big data toward ML is that, as soon as the sample size available for learning increases, the possibility of overfitting decreases. Controlling overfitting is one of the most critical issues in both the design of ML models and the development of ML techniques in use, as already we are aware of. Due to the obvious possibility of overfitting, simple models with fewer parameters to tune were naturally preferred. With big data, however, the parameter tuning constraints can change. We can now attempt to train a model with numerous parameters because we have ample big data and powerful computing resources to support such training. Deep learning has gained massive scale success in all these years, and this serves as a great example. However, many deep learning studies rely heavily on engineering methodology that are not easy to replicate and study by someone except the authors. It is crucial to analyze the challenges of deep learning [15].

At last, one should be aware that big data also includes an excessive number of "interests", and that we might be able to extract "whatever we want" from those data; in other words, we might get evidence in support of the claim being made. So, how do we evaluate/judge the "findings"? Turning to statistical hypothesis testing is one effective alternative. Statistical assessments can be beneficial in at least two ways: First, we should ensure that whatever we have done is exactly what we intended. Second, we should ensure that the results we have received are not the product of minor data anomalies, especially those occurred due to lack of rigorous data exploration. In spite of the fact that performed statistical tests have been investigated all over the centuries and applied in ML over the decades, designing and deploying appropriate statistical tests is not easy, and statistical tests have been misused in the past. Furthermore, statistical tests suited for data analytics remain an important yet under-explored field of study, for not just the computational efficiency but for the consideration of using only a portion of the data. Deriving interpretable models is another way to verify the validity of the study findings. Even after knowing that many ML techniques are black boxes, there have been works on how to make them more understandable, such as rule extraction.

In addition to the in-depth discussion of the challenges and opportunities that big data poses to ML in entire section, here are some major challenges and opportunities. To overcome several challenging issues, ML on big data necessarily requires a different way of thinking and novel techniques. Big data is a crucial enabler of deep learning that has enhanced state-of-the-art efficiency across a range of applications. At least 1,000 various categories can be identified using deep learning, which is somewhat 2 orders of magnitude more than what a traditional neural network can handle. Furthermore, big data permit for multi-granular learning. Furthermore, big data allows for causality inference based on sequence chains, allowing for efficient decision support [16].

The necessity for ML on big data offers significant opportunities for framework and ML codesign. ML has the potential to change the way frameworks are built. Since several ML programs are profoundly admit error-tolerance and optimization-centric, iterative-convergent algorithmic approaches, an integrative system design based on ML program structure can consider issues like dynamic scheduling and bounded-error network synchronization. Hardware accelerators, including a latest supercomputer, are being developed specifically for ML applications.

11.7   Enabling Machine Learning With IoT

Internet of Things (IoT) is a notion that enables interconnected devices to transmit the data through sensors and software over the network without human interference. IoT has gained widespread popularity in last few years as it has touched every aspect of our day-to-day life which is not limited to television, lamps, refrigerator, and mobile phones. It is much higher than our imagination from smart agriculture, smart cities, autonomous vehicles, e-learning to smart healthcare. The large number of connected smart devices brings a challenge of managing enormous amount of data, storage, privacy and security concerns. Conventional method does not provide effective and reliable solution [17]. It is important to identify which data to keep, what must be removed and how it should be stored. ML algorithms develop their behavior models on arithmetical techniques on large number of datasets. ML eliminates the requirement of writing down instructions for every action of machine. Depending on the input data, models make future prediction.

IoT needs powerful, authentic, and intelligent techniques for massive scale of deployment where ML is a promising and efficient technique. ML is requisite for IoT data to bring intelligence inside the system. Deep learning can be applied with IoT gadgets where complicated sensing work to facilitate the working of application involving real time monitoring with smart objects and human beings. Unsupervised learning can play a prominent role in managing security attacks such as zero-day attack where IoT network do not have knowledge where to start from [18]. ML predictive capabilities have a remarkable use in industrial area. Different algorithms can obtain data from various smart sensors attached to the devices and can recognizing the pattern change or something wrong occurs. It can also predict when an IoT connected device requires maintenance which cuts unnecessary cost. In retail, sensors can be placed on the shopping complex and information can be collected from internet to predict the choice and quality of product the customer will buy. Based on this, the business owner can keep the stock of the products and even customer will get what they want.

In smart healthcare, patients are using various wearable devices to monitor their health on regular basis. Doctors can analyze their previous medical history and can identify and control the disease in its initial stage [19].

Combining ML with IoT is a challenging task as IoT data gives rise to variety of datasets which include structured, semi-structured, or unstructured data. In ML, for labeled data, we use clustering algorithms but when we have unlabeled data, unsupervised algorithms are being used. So, choosing an appropriate ML algorithm is not easy [20]. IoT has versatile hardware technology starting from cloud servers till low powered devices. Applications such as autonomous vehicles and drones require high level of security with least energy consumption. Special hardware processors and accelerators are in demand for efficient integration with ML techniques. Predictability of the ML algorithms lower downs when there is increase in spatial data.

11.8   Conclusion

This chapter provides a summary of the benefits and drawbacks of ML with big data. New possibilities are provided by big data for developing revolutionary and novel ML technologies to solve many associated technological problems and generate real-world impacts, while also posing multiple challenges for conventional ML with regard to scalability, adaptability, and usability. This can be used to guide future research in this field [20].

The majority of current work on ML for big data has concentrated on length, velocity, and variety, but little has been done to resolve the remaining two dimensions of big data: veracity and value. One promising way to solve issue of data veracity is to build algorithms that can access the trustworthiness or integrity of data or data sources, allowing unreliable data to be filtered out during data pre-processing. Another way is to apply new ML models that are inferred from inconsistent or even contradictory results. To fully appreciate the advantage of big data in decision support, users must be able to comprehend ML findings and the motive for each system's decision. As a result, understandable ML will be a hot topic in the forthcoming years. Furthermore, fundamental research questions such as how to efficiently collect vast volumes of annotated data through crowd sourcing must be answered to help human-in-the-loop big data ML.

Integrating ML with IoT has a great future but still most of the ML techniques are not applicable for effectively managing data generated from IoT devices. IoT devices are resource restraint with limited computational speed so using ML algorithms would not be a good choice. Lots of issues first need to be tackled for combining IoT and ML [21].

Other open research objectives include the following: (1) how to preserve privacy of data when conducting ML; (2) role of making ML more declarative for non-experts can specify and communication can take place easily; (3) how to integrate normal domain knowledge into ML; and (4) how to build a modern architecture based on big data and ML that seamlessly offers decision-making depending on real-time analysis of large sets of heterogeneous data that can be accurate or not. In conclusion, ML is required to resolve the challenges presented by big data and to discover hidden trends, information, and perception from big data in order to translate its potential into real value for business decision-making and scientific exploration. The convergence of ML with big data points to a promising future in a modern frontier.

References

1. Jordan, M.I. and Mitchell, T.M., Machine learning: trends, perspectives, and prospects. *Science*, 349, 255–260, 2015.

2. Tsai, C.-W., Lai, C.-F., Chao, H.-C., Vasilakos, A.V., Big data analytics: a survey. *J. Big Data*, 2, 1–32, 2015.
3. Najafabadi, M.M., Villanustre, F., Khoshgoftaar, T.M., Seliya, N., Wald, R., Muharemagic, E., Deep learning applications and challenges in big data analytics. *J. Big Data*, 2, 1–21, 2015.
4. Japkowicz, N. and Shah, M., *Evaluating Learning Algorithms: a Classification Perspective*, Cambridge University Press, New York, NY, USA, 2011.
5. Russell, S. and Norvig, P., *Artificial Intelligence: A Modern Approach*, 3rd ed., Prentice Hall, Upper Saddle River, New Jersey, USA, 2010.
6. Bengio, Y., Courville, A., Vincent, P., Representation learning: a review and new perspectives. *IEEE Trans. Pattern Anal. Mach. Intell. Trans.*, 35, 1798–1828, 2013.
7. Dekel, O., From Online to Batch Learning with Cutoff-Averaging. *NIPS (2008)*, pp. 377–384, 2008.
8. Amershi, S., Cakmak, M., Knox, W.B., Kulesza, T., Power to the people: the role of humans in Interactive machine learning. *AI Mag.*, 35, 105–120, 2014.
9. Mirchevska, V., Luštrek, M., Gams, M., Combining domain knowledge and machine learning for robust fall detection. *Expert Syst.*, 31, 163–175, 2014.
10. Yu, T., *Incorporating Prior Domain Knowledge into Inductive Machine Learning Computing Sciences*, University of Technology, Sydney, Sydney, Australia, 2007.
11. Chen, Q., Zobel, J., Verspoor, K., Evaluation of a machine learning duplicate detection method for bioinformatics Databases. *Proc. ACM Ninth Int. Workshop Data Text. Min. Biomed. Inform*, pp. 4–12, 2015.
12. Rakthanmanon, T., Campana, B., Mueen, A., Batista, G., Westover, B., Zhu, Q. *et al.*, Addressing Big data time series: mining Trillions of time series subsequences Under dynamic time Warping. *ACM Trans. Knowl. Discovery Data*, 7, 10, 2013.
13. Pfeiffer, III, J.J., Neville, J., Bennett, P.N., Overcoming relational learning biases to accurately predict preferences in large scale networks, in: *Proceedings of the 24th International Conference on World Wide Web*, pp. 853–863, 2015.
14. Cao, L., Wei, M., Yang, D., Rundensteiner, E.A., Online outlier exploration over large datasets, in: *Proceedings of the 21th ACM SIGKDD International Conference on Knowledge Discovery and Data Mining*, pp. 89–98, 2015.
15. Gandomi, A. and Haider, M., Beyond the hype: Big data concepts, methods, and analytics. *Int. J. Inf. Manage.*, 35, 137–144, 2015.
16. Hussain, F., Hossain, E., Hussain, R., Hassan, S.A., Machine Learning in IoT Security: Current Solutions and Future Challenges. *IEEE Commun. Surv. Tutorials*, 99, 22, 3, 1686–1721, April 2020.
17. Jindal, M., Bhushan, B., Gupta, J., Machine learning methods for IoT and their Future Applications. *Conference: 2019 International Conference on Computing, Communication, and Intelligent Systems (ICCCIS)*, https://ieeex plore.ieee.org/document/8974551

18. Roopak, M., Chambers, J., Tian, G.Y., Deep Learning Models for Cyber Security in IoT Networks. *2019 IEEE 9th Annual Computing and Communication Workshop and Conference (CCWC)*.

19. Paul, D., Chakraborty, T., Paul, D., Datta, S.K., IoT and Machine Learning Based Prediction of Smart Building Indoor Temperature. *2018 4th International Conference on Computer and Information Sciences (ICCOINS)*, pp. 1–6, 2018.

20. Mishra, R., Singh, R., Srivastava, S., AI and IoT Based Monitoring System for Increasing the Yield in Crop Production. *2020 International Conference on Electrical and Electronics Engineering (ICE3)*, pp. 301–305, 2020.

21. Kechar, B., Dahane, A., Benyamina, A., Benameur, R., An IoT Based Smart Farming System Using Machine Learning. *2020 International Symposium on Networks, Computers and Communications (ISNCC)*, pp. 1–6, 2020.

12

Machine Learning Effects on Underwater Applications and IoUT

Mamta Nain, Nitin Goyal* and Manni Kumar

Chitkara University Institute of Engineering and Technology, Chitkara University, Punjab, India

Abstract

The Internet of Underwater Things (IoUT) is the system of intelligent linked underwater things and a diverse kind of Internet of Things (IoT). IoUT is expected to permit different practicable requests, similar to ecological monitor, underwater examination, and calamity prohibition. With these uses, IoUT is considered as unique of the likely technology around developed intelligent towns. UWSN network system is favorable in the evolution of IoUT. In UWSN, many challenges exist that will be big challenge in evolution of IoUT. In this book chapter, basic concepts about the IoUT are presented like architecture, challenges, and application areas. UWSN and IoUT collectively help in many application areas like weather forecasting and monitoring. This chapter also presents introduction about new advance technology machine learning. How this helps in improving the application areas of underwater environment. Machine learning can also be used to explore minerals that exist below the water.

Keywords: Internet of Things (IoT), challenges, Internet of Underwater Things (IoUT), sensor, Underwater Wireless Sensor Network (UWSN), machine learning

12.1 Introduction

Internet of Things (IoT) is novel standard that improves the traditional living style and convert it into advanced and technological life style [1].

Corresponding author: dr.nitingoyal30@gmail.com

Shalli Rani, R. Maheswar, G. R. Kanagachidambaresan, Sachin Ahuja and Deepali Gupta (eds.) Machine Learning Paradigm for Internet of Things Applications, (229–246) © 2022 Scrivener Publishing LLC

This new emerging pattern simplifies our daily life by enabling the communication between sensors and electronic devices through the internet [2, 3]. IoUT is a new form of IoT, and this can be defined as underwater network of smart interrelated underwater objects. The concept of IoT was introduced in 1985 and IoUT was introduced in 2012 [4]. IoUT is a worldwide network of smart interrelated underwater objects that helps in exploring and monitoring the area below the water [5, 6].

Underwater Wireless Sensor Network (UWSN) has been provided as an efficient and promising network system for the Internet of Underwater Things (IoUT) [7]. There are several components which mainly exist in UWSN; one of its main components is sensors which are usually deployed under the water. These sensors can also be termed as nodes having acoustic modems distributed randomly in the shallow water. Different sensors are used for sensing different information about environment condition such as quality of water, water temperature, and pressure in the water and various phenomenon changes in the biological and chemical materials or elements [8]. Another essential component that is the part of UWSN is a sink node. The sink is responsible for receiving data from the sensor nodes present on the water surface [9]. Surface sink nodes have both radio and acoustic modems properties to deal with satellite connection and underwater nodes, respectively. These sinks might be any type of ship, Autonomous Underwater Vehicles (AUVs) or surface buoy. After successful reception of data by the sink, it forwards the data to the control monitoring center or any onshore base station with the help of radio channels. This monitoring center is responsible for controlling all the activities that can be performed in the shallow water and also control the working of the underground sensors. All the information gathered from the water areas is analyzed and collected by the monitoring center. Apart from this, AUVs are deployed in the water which majorly performs collecting and forwarding related tasks in the deep water [10].

The state-of-the-art IoUT lend a hand the researchers to explore water reservoirs such as large oceans, rivers, and lakes through numerous communication approaches which correlate stationary and mobile nodes below the water, on the water surface, and in the sky, as shown in Figure 12.1. Using embedded sensors and internet facility, these devices sense the environment, understand, and then respond accordingly. Each object which is deployed underwater can be accessed virtually that helps to get information like physical properties and historical information about the object. Due to the ubiquitous nature of the information, it can be accessed or managed in real-time through many different ways of communication like Human to Thing (H2T) and Thing to Thing (T2T).

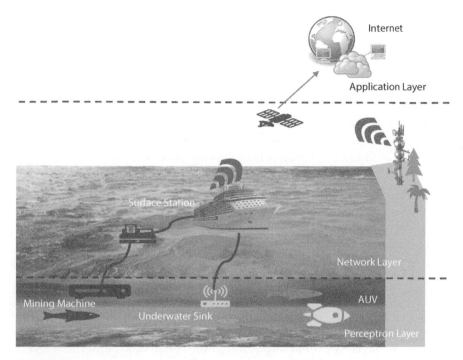

Figure 12.1 Internet of Underwater Things basic model.

This book chapter gives us brief introduction about the IoUT and organized as follows. Section 12.2 familiarizes us with definite characteristics of the IoUT. Following, Section 12.3 proposed IoUT architecture that is explained from technical aspect. Section 12.4 discusses about the different challenges in IoUT. After this, application scenarios are described in Section 12.5. Later, in Section 12.6, there is discussion about the new evolving technology machine learning (ML) and how this ML is helpful in study or analyses of underwater environment. Simulation comparison of three different localization techniques in IoUT is presented in Section 12.7. Section 12.8 is the conclusion of the chapter.

12.2   Characteristics of IoUT

Communication Technology: Radio and electronic waves do not work properly so acoustic waves are used for underwater communication. Radio waves does not propagate well below the water, and for using electronic magnetic waves, large-sized antennas are required and these waves gets attenuated with distance so acoustic waves are preferred in comparison of these waves.

Battery Power: Battery power is limited for underwater sensor nodes as it is difficult to charge these nodes or replace them. The need of batteries can be eliminated by using supercapacitors with ambient energy harvesting. This technique eliminates the need of batteries [11].

Network Density: A large number of devices communicate with each other in IoT for the proper functioning but it is very difficult in case of IoUT. As a smaller number of interconnecting digital devices are used in IoUT because deployment of devices is very tough in underwater.

Localization Technique: In IoT, Global Positioning System (GPS) is used to find the location of devices but GPS does not work below the water so there exist different localization techniques categorized into range free and range based [12].

12.3   Architecture of IoUT

The proposed architecture of IoUT is very simple, as shown in Figure 12.2. It is a three-layer system architecture. Basic functionalities of these layers can be explained as follows.

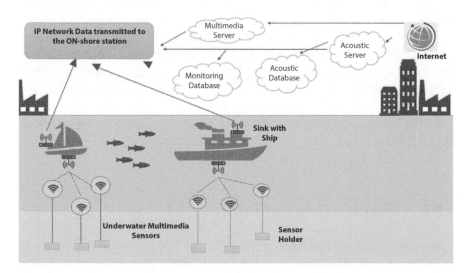

Figure 12.2 Architecture of IoUT.

12.3.1   Perceptron Layer

Different devices like underwater vehicles, underwater sensors, surface stations, data storage tags, surface station, monitoring devices, and acoustic or pit or radio tags and receivers' tags all these in collection form this layer. This layer detects the objects for data collection and collects the information from them.

Different components of this layer are explained below:

AUVs and Sensors: These AUVS and underwater sensors deployed below the water communicate with each other and collect the information for the particular application. This collected information is further passed on to the surface station above the sea surface. From this surface station, information is communicated to the onshore station for monitoring purpose.

Acoustic Tag: This is a compact sound-producing device that is injected into fish body by some surgery. This tag transmits a ping at a particular rate to sensors after a regular interval, that is further passed on to the sink. A unique digital ID is assigned to each fish. These tags are used to trace the location and movement of fish and analyze their behavior.

Radio Tag: Radio-frequency signals are transmitted by these tags. In seawater, radio waves can work properly. Boats (above the water surface) detect a radio-frequency signal transmitted by radio tags. In seawater, the electric conductivity is much higher than in freshwater owing to high salinity and radio tags converted to less efficient in high conductive water. In freshwater, anyhow, the controlled range (about 10 m), EM waves (contrasting to acoustic waves) are accepting to disturbance created by tidal surfs and suspended deposits, resistant to acoustic noise, and unaffected by pressure gradients. Thus, collective acoustic radio tags are an excellent selection to track object departing among both salt and freshwater. This case occurs when a fish migrate to and from different environments.

Pit Tag: A tag, transceiver, and an antenna collectively make this pit tag. An alphanumeric cipher is attached to each pit tag. This is a very compact tag and do not have any effect on the fish's growth, health, and behavior. These tags remain functional for fish's lifetime because PIT tags are passive in nature

Data Storage Tag: For collecting temperature, time, depth, and salinity data, these data storage tags are attached to fish in both ways externally and internally. During monitoring of data, loggers attached to computers can be used for data extraction and analysis [3].

12.3.2   Network Layer

Wireless or wired private networks, cloud computing platforms and internet, etc., that use different network technologies called heterogeneous network collectively make network layer. Information collected from the perceptron layer is processed and transmitted using the network layer. The information gathered from the perceptron layer allows the access of sink over the sea surface. After this, using various technologies like satellite communication, General Packet Radio Service (GPRS), and Wideband Code Division Multiple Access (WCDMA), this information is retransmitted to the onshore centers [13].

12.3.3   Application Layer

To please the users, this layer applies IoUT technology so this layer provides set of intelligent solutions [14]. Different types of servers are used in this layer which host and execute the many type of services, e.g., acoustic server, RFID server, and monitoring server. Acoustic server gets data from diverse hydrophones, and this help in tracking the fish, their survival rate, etc., for fish identification and finding the associated information radio servers access the information from PIT tag. To transmit the sensed data to professionals, monitoring servers propose application codes like Ajax.

12.4   Challenges in IoUT

The research in IoUT is slow because of the unique behavior of UWSN and so many challenges are associated with this IoUT which are explained below:

Transmission Media: In TWSN for communication, use of radio waves is found to be very helpful. But UWSN mainly depends on the communication based on acoustic rather than communication done by radio. Acoustic communication does not absorb quickly in water, but in the case of radio communication, they are very quickly absorbed in water. Therefore, the properties of both the communication are quite different, and hence, the properties of TWSN cannot be applied directly to the UWSN. Hence, the medium of transmission is one of the major challenges for the IoUT [4, 15].

Propagation Speed: The speed of propagation in UWSN is 200,000 slower than that of TWSN. In TWSN, speed of propagation of the radio channels is 300,000,000 m/s, but, as compared to UWSN which is around 1,500 m/s, that is quite slow as compared to TWSN. This raises a challenge which is called end-to-end delay and can be a challenging task for the IoUT [4].

Transmission Range: The transmission range in UWSN is 10 times longer as compared to TWSN. Environment under deep water to decrease the absorption level of signals by water the transmission has to be done at a low frequency level as if the frequency is low the transmission range is long. Due to this long transmission, there might some difficulties of interference and collision, and data packets may be loss due to that. Therefore, it is quite important to tackle these collisions and interferences that may be the one of the challenges for the IoUT [4].

Latency: As acoustic waves are used for communication in IoUT and this is thousand time slower in comparison of terrestrial IoT networks. So, real-time communication is restricted due to this low speed in IoUT. Though, the study on the growth of optical modems is still in the academic research phase [15].

Network Life: Underwater communication in IoUT is entirely depend upon the sensor communication which are battery operated. Strict environment below the water do not allow these batteries to be recharge so this affects the network life time [15].

Self-Management: This is one of the biggest challenges as network in IoUT have to manage all network operation itself without any human intervention [5].

12.5   Applications of IoUT

For last years, several researchers have proposed the various types of applications in IoUT, as shown in Figure 12.3. All the application [16] has been categorized into basic five types: (1) monitoring the environment, (2) prevention of disaster, (3) military, (4) exploring underwater, and (5) others.

Monitoring the Environment: Environment monitoring is the furthermost communal IoUT application that is used. This type of application is useful to monitor numerous parameters like quality of water, monitoring the temperatures, monitoring [17] thermal pollution, and monitoring pollution from various biological and chemical compounds. In addition, UWSN helps in monitoring of gas and oil [18]. It has been noted that the application of environmental monitoring has become more popular especially in demand for smart cities.

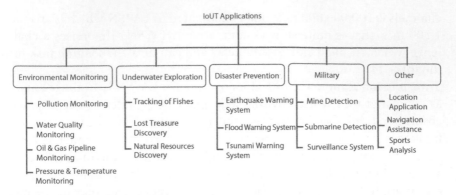

Figure 12.3 Applications of IoUT.

- In this paper, author provides a suitable method and architecture network for monitoring the quality of water; basically, the water quality is determined by the pH value of the water. This paper also presents sensor node design which helps in monitoring the pH value of the water [19]. It has been noted that pH value is a significant factor that helps in understanding the quality of water. Using Zigbee communication, this sensed pH value is transmitted wirelessly to base station.

- Ad hoc sensor networks have been projected for the monitoring of ocean pollution. This new approach applicable to short-range underwater communication instead of other long rage strategies [20]. The best part of the short-range communication is that it has the capability to reuse some of the acoustic networks and also helps to tackle some of the challenges generated by long-range communication. Also, modems used in short-range communication are cost-effective as compare to long-range [21] communication. In this paper, author also proposed synchronization protocol helps to ameliorate the quality index of the service (QoS) and pragmatically enhances the underwater sensor network.

- The authors discussed the latest inventions in wireless communication technologies which have formed a space for advancement in every domain of industrial applications associated to natural resource exploration, especially oil [22] and gas processing. Through this approach, the oil and gas pipeline monitoring solution are the brainchild of the author. The proposed approach is the most pragmatic solution for flawless examination [23] as well as provide pipeline health-related statistics with the help of wireless sensor networks.

- Many underwater monitoring applications were introduced by different authors. The authors outline underwater surveillance as a network of sensors commissioned undersea to observe the marine environments, features, characters, or any objects of interest [24]. The authors segregated and the underwater surveillance applications in three different categories, namely, (i) monitoring underwater explorations, (ii) water quality monitoring, and (iii) habitat monitoring and explained them.

Underwater Exploration: The IoUT, new approach can be used to discover lost-treasure beneath the water. It has also noticed that, in 1985, the titanic discovery is being benefited from the usage of AUVs [25]. Further, IoUT can also be used in fish tracking. Moreover, discovery of natural resources in water like metals, coral reefs, and corals can be benefited from the UWSN infrastructure [26] as well.

- The main aim is to create or develop an efficient technique for communication that can investigate in this large area of uninhibited oceans. A large-scale system that uses the UWSN have been proposed to study [27] the environment of the ocean. Also, various methods have been used like deploying of sensors having attached video capturing devices. With the help of this system, we can able to study the resources [28] present underwater.
- Authors also claim that all the existing advance technology have to be used in a careful manner, without disturbing the existing one, basically, we have to understand the basic functions of this technology in order to control the advance one for the discovering of oceanic world [29].

Disaster Prevention: Disaster prevention applications that saved thousands of precious lives are one of the most principal IoUT applications [30]. Natural calamities, especially water-based are actually threatening. For instance, the Fukushima Daiichi nuclear disaster in Japan was commenced fundamentally by the tsunami following the Tohoku earthquake. IoUT is the best weapon to detect and predict flood, tsunami and earthquake [31].

- Perez *et al.* present a layout of a real-time dimensions for flood monitoring and prediction. Even, researchers arranged a real-world surveillance network with various real-time computation tools in Spain. The simulation [32] outcomes prove its energy efficiency and robustness for the long-term.
- The author explained the importance of an early threatening generation system founded on UWSNs to perform rescue operation for human lives. The warning disasters such as earthquake and tsunami [33]. The author addressed the principal physical layers challenges in establishing a UWSN system for early warning generation. The authors achieve that communication reliability, efficient resource management and low-power design will remain the significant obstacles for the UWSN-based warning created systems [34].
- Several strategies were addressed by authors for tsunami forecasting and recommend an effective layout for such applications. Seismic pressure sensor is utilized by suggested architecture to prognosticate tsunamis and transmit the sensed data by the diffusion routing protocol as well as explained modus-operandi behind this strategy.

Military: The defence forces do regular exercises to protect the motherland from external as well as natural threats. Underwater discoveries and monitoring scheme is also most important for military purposes. These apps have a tremendous capability for [35] further marine troops.

- The author investigates sensor distribution pattern and a pragmatic approach to enhance the monitoring domain for submarine identification. By fetching the water deepness, transmitting scope, and reduction into account the [36] suggested scheme utilizes Particle Swarm Optimization (PSO) to identify the precise locations of sensor nodes. The authors used both the NS3-based images and mathematical analysis to validate the performance of the suggested system.
- Submerged mine identification method patterns were investigated by Khaledi *et al.* Especially, they examine five towing-vehicle substitutes (i.e., one underwater vehicle substitute, two surface vehicles [37] substitutes, and two airborne vehicle substitutes) and two sonar options. Computing pattern to imitate the procedure of demonstrating submerged mines, and examine every of the pattern substitutes.

The conclusion displays that the submerged automobile substitute absorbed the minimum amount of energy. They also accept the security, speed, fuel-saving, and chance of detection into count and offer the related examination to show the finest substitute.

- The authors suggest a unique UWSN framework for marine environment monitoring methods. In the suggested design, the sensor nodes are primarily located in face buoys; then, the sensor [38] nodes are decreased to various depth. The depths are selected by the recommended scheme for maximizing the monitoring coverage. Additionally, each node is implemented with various distinct varieties (e.g., radiation, acoustic, magnetic, and mechanical) of micro-sensors. Based on the interpretation of the data gathered from the micro-sensors, the researchers display a data mining–based design for the categorization of star ships, minefield, and divers.

Some Other Applications: Owing to the latest research and innovation in this domain, IoUT, nowadays, is playing a niche role in many applications such as localization applications, navigation, and sports. Especially, the localization application as GPS is not applicable for marine surveillance environment [39] that provides a valuable location to ships, underwater vehicles, divers, and swimmers that can be provided by using underwater sensors as location allusion points [40].

- The authors present a precise analysis, spotlighting the biomechanical investigation of swimming utilizing the inertial sensors underwater. In current years, sport [41] scientists, coaches, and swimming athletes have been struggling to succeed a "fraction of a second" improvement. The sensors perform an imperative role in sustaining performance intensification from a biomechanical point of view. This paper presents diverse existing techniques equipped with wearable [42] inertial sensors such as magnetometers, gyroscopes, and accelerometers to evaluate the biomechanics performance. The outcomes specify that the underwater inertial sensors are appropriate and compatible means for swimming biomechanical investigations.
- The gathered information could play a niche role only when referred to the location of the sensor for a wide range of

applications; for example, navigation is such an application [43]. The authors recommend a multi-stage AUV-aided localization approach for UWSNs. They conducted a complete series of simulations to assess the performance of the supposed scheme based on few QoS parameters like localization coverage, accurateness, and communication overheads. The outcomes shows that good performance can be accomplished by appropriately selecting the communication range.

- The authors introduce an Anchor-Free Localization Algorithm, called AFLA, for underwater conditions. As utmost traditional underwater localization algorithms based on special underwater nodes [44] equipped with special types of equipment or AUVs can be used as "anchor nodes" to assist in finding the location underwater, while the anticipated AFLA does not require data from any particular anchor nodes. AFLA utilises the adjacent connection of normal sensor nodes to discover the underwater location [45].

12.6   Machine Learning

ML subset of artificial intelligence is widely used spectrum and used in many application areas. Based on data, ML is able to take decisions. Nowadays, ML can be used in different areas; it also helps us in oceanography or underwater activities. Different applications that include ML in oceanography are habitat monitoring, prediction of ocean weather and climate, coastal water monitoring, species identification, detection of oil spill and pollution, and marine resources management. Several real-world problems are solved by ML itself because of its capability. Oceans are gigantic, complex, and dynamic in nature. So, ocean data structure is increasingly becoming large and complex. Coastal area is also exposed to many natural calamities like coastal flooding and sea level rise. To avoid these calamities, an accurate and reliable tool is required that helps in forecasting seashore evolution. Traditional methods were costly and time consuming and sometime these methods are not helpful in analysis, so ML can be used. ML outperforms traditional methods as this is fast, high precise, and robust.

ML helps in many application areas mentioned above in IoUT. Neural network can be used to predict the sea level waves and surface temperature. Pollution monitoring can be done with the help of ML. MLP NN model was used by Del Frate *et al.* to detect oil spill on sea surface from synthetic aperture radar (SAR) images. Many types of species exist below the water and identification of these species is tough task. ML helps us in identification of these species. ML algorithms are trained for this identification using images, videos, and other type of data. These trained algorithms can interpret data and identify the different type of species exist in water. For management of underwater activities, habitat monitoring is required [46]. Algorithms in ML can be trained to find the matching variables, and using this algorithm, it is easy to identify appropriate habitat for particular species at any location. Meteorological forecasting can be performed using genetic algorithms in ML which helps in modeling rainy vs. non-rainy days. Sea level pressure can also be predicted with this MLP NN model. This ML can help in many application areas and can improve IoUT research in future by making use of precise models. Appropriateness of data set used for training plays a big role in success of ML technique. Quality, preciseness, and amount of data are critical components for the success of these ML applications [47].

12.7   Simulation and Analysis

In this section, performance analysis of different localization techniques Cluster-Based Mobile Data Gathering Scheme (CMDG), Diffusion Logarithm Correntropy Algorithm (DLCA), and Large-Scale Hierarchical Localization (LSHL) has been compared in IoUT based on two quality of service parameters: energy and average communication cost, as these both should be minimum for a good localization technique. Figure 12.4 shows

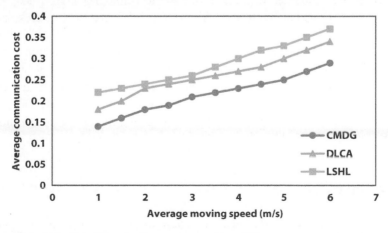

Figure 12.4 Average communication cost vs. node mobility.

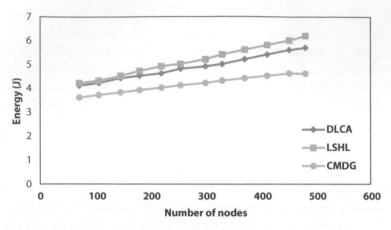

Figure 12.5 Energy consumption vs number of nodes.

the average communication cost of three different localization techniques with node mobility effects.

Figure 12.5 shows the energy consumption in each of the three techniques with respect to number of sensor nodes.

From these two parameters, we conclude that CMDG perform better from other two techniques. In communication cost, it performs 17% better than DLCA and 24% better than LSHL. In terms of energy, CMDG performs 14% better than DLCA and 19% better than LSHL.

12.8   Conclusion

This chapter familiarized with different basic technological concepts of IoUT. For the development of practical IoUT network, IoUT architecture is explained in detail. Few important challenges are also summarized here. IoUT behavior will results in establishment of this technology. Also, in end of the chapter, ML concepts were discussed and how this ML helps in many applications for underwater environment. Diverse methods exist in ML that can be useful for oceanographic applications that totally depends upon the data. Quality of oceanographic research can be improved by developing new accurate models in ML, and this will help in discovering unseen forms and learnings.

References

1. Badotra, S. and Panda, S.N., A review on software-defined networking enabled iot cloud computing. *IIUM Eng. J.*, *20*, 2, 105–126, 2019.

2. Kumar, S., Tiwari, P., Zymbler, M., Internet of Things is a revolutionary approach for future technology enhancement: a review. *J. Big Data*, 6, 1, 1–21, 2019.

3. Datta, P. and Sharma, B., A survey on IoT architectures, protocols, security and smart city-based applications, in: *2017 8th International Conference on Computing, Communication and Networking Technologies (ICCCNT)*, 2017, July, IEEE, pp. 1–5.

4. Kao, C.C., Lin, Y.S., Wu, G.D., Huang, C.J., A comprehensive study on the internet of underwater things: applications, challenges, and channel models. *Sensors*, 17, 7, 1477, 2017.

5. Domingo, M.C., An overview of the internet of underwater things. *J. Netw. Comput. Appl.*, 35, 6, 1879–1890, 2012.

6. Zhao, Q., Peng, Z., Hong, X., A named data networking architecture implementation to Internet of Underwater Things, in: *Proceedings of the International Conference on Underwater Networks & Systems*, 2019, October, pp. 1–8.

7. Cui, J.H., Kong, J., Gerla, M., Zhou, S., The challenges of building mobile underwater wireless networks for aquatic applications. *IEEE Network*, 20, 3, 12–18, 2006.

8. Goyal, N., Architectural Analysis of Wireless Sensor Network and Underwater Wireless Sensor Network with Issues and Challenges. *J. Comput. Theor. Nanosci.*, 17, 6, 2706–2712, 2020.

9. Gupta, O., Kumar, M., Mushtaq, A., Goyal, N., Localization Schemes and Its Challenges in Underwater Wireless Sensor Networks. *J. Comput. Theor. Nanosci.*, 17, 6, 2750–2754, 2020.

10. Gupta, O., Goyal, N., Anand, D., Kadry, S., Nam, Y., Singh, A., Underwater networked wireless sensor data collection for computational intelligence techniques: issues, challenges, and approaches. *IEEE Access*, 8, 122959–122974, 2020.

11. Choudhary, M. and Goyal, N., Routing protocol design issues and challenges in underwater wireless sensor network, in: *Energy-Efficient Underwater Wireless Communications and Networking*, pp. 1–15, IGI Global, US, 2021.

12. Nain, M. and Goyal, N., Localization Techniques in Underwater Wireless Sensor Network, in: *2021 International Conference on Advance Computing and Innovative Technologies in Engineering (ICACITE)*, 2021, March, IEEE, pp. 747–751.

13. Borgia, E., The Internet of Things vision: Key features, applications and open issues. *Comput. Commun.*, 54, 1–31, 2014.

14. Gomez, C. and Paradells, J., Wireless home automation networks: A survey of architectures and technologies. *IEEE Commun. Mag.*, 48, 6, 92–101, 2010.

15. Khalil, R., Babar, M., Jan, T., Saeed, N., Towards the Internet of underwater things: Recent developments and future challenges. *IEEE Consum. Electron. Mag.*, 1964, 1–11, 2020.

16. Luo, X., Wang, J., Dooner, M., Clarke, J., Overview of current development in electrical energy storage technologies and the application potential in power system operation. *Appl. Energy*, *137*, 511–536, 2015.

17. Conti, M.E. and Cecchetti, G., Biological monitoring: lichens as bioindicators of air pollution assessment—a review. *Environ. Pollut.*, *114*, 3, 471–492, 2001.

18. Felemban, E., Shaikh, F.K., Qureshi, U.M., Sheikh, A.A., Qaisar, S.B., Underwater sensor network applications: A comprehensive survey. *Int. J. Distrib. Sens. Netw.*, *11*, 11, 896832, 2015.

19. Goyal, N., Dave, M., Verma, A.K., Data aggregation in underwater wireless sensor network: Recent approaches and issues. *J. King Saud Univ.-Comput. Inf. Sci.*, *31*, 3, 275–286, 2019.

20. Vasilescu, I., Kotay, K., Rus, D., Dunbabin, M., Corke, P., Data collection, storage, and retrieval with an underwater sensor network, in: *Proceedings of the 3rd international conference on Embedded networked sensor systems*, 2005, November, pp. 154–165.

21. Casari, P. and Zorzi, M., Protocol design issues in underwater acoustic networks. *Comput. Commun.*, *34*, 17, 2013–2025, 2011.

22. Bandyopadhyay, D. and Sen, J., Internet of things: Applications and challenges in technology and standardization. *Wirel. Pers. Commun.*, *58*, 1, 49–69, 2011.

23. Owojaiye, G. and Sun, Y., Focal design issues affecting the deployment of wireless sensor networks for pipeline monitoring. *Ad Hoc Networks*, *11*, 3, 1237–1253, 2013.

24. Akyildiz, I.F., Pompili, D., Melodia, T., Underwater acoustic sensor networks: research challenges. *Ad Hoc Networks*, *3*, 3, 257–279, 2005.

25. Catsambis, A., Ford, B., Hamilton, D.L. (Eds.), *The Oxford handbook of maritime archaeology*, Oxford University Press, United State of America, 2014.

26. Davis, A., *PEWSN: Power Equilibrium Wireless Sensor Network*, Doctoral dissertation, Tufts University, Massachusetts, 2013.

27. Srinivas, S., Ranjitha, P., Ramya, R., Narendra, G.K., Investigation of oceanic environment using large-scale UWSN and UANETs, in: *2012 8th International Conference on Wireless Communications, Networking and Mobile Computing*, 2012, September, IEEE, pp. 1–5.

28. Ropert-Coudert, Y. and Wilson, R.P., Trends and perspectives in animal-attached remote sensing. *Front. Ecol. Environ.*, *3*, 8, 437–444, 2005.

29. Goyal, N., Dave, M., Verma, A.K., Protocol stack of underwater wireless sensor network: classical approaches and new trends. *Wirel. Pers. Commun.*, *104*, 3, 995–1022, 2019.

30. Akyildiz, I.F., Su, W., Sankarasubramaniam, Y., Cayirci, E., A survey on sensor networks. *IEEE Commun. Mag.*, 40, 8, 102–114, 2002.

31. Murphy, R.R., Tadokoro, S., Kleiner, A., Disaster robotics, in: *Springer Handbook of Robotics*, pp. 1577–1604, Springer, Cham, 2016.

32. Marin-Perez, R., García-Pintado, J., Gómez, A.S., A real-time measurement system for long-life flood monitoring and warning applications. *Sensors*, *12*, 4, 4213–4236, 2012.

33. Kao, C.C., Lin, Y.S., Wu, G.D., Huang, C.J., A comprehensive study on the internet of underwater things: applications, challenges, and channel models. *Sensors*, *17*, 7, 1477, 2017.

34. Eliasson, J., *Low-power design methodologies for embedded internet systems*, Doctoral dissertation, Luleå tekniska universitet, Sweden, 2008.

35. Becker, R.F., Nordby, S.H., Jon, J., *Underwater forensic investigation*, CRC Press, Boca Raton, 2013.

36. Hedley, J.D., Roelfsema, C.M., Chollett, I., Harborne, A.R., Heron, S.F., Weeks, S., Ticzon, V., Remote sensing of coral reefs for monitoring and management: a review. *Remote Sens.*, *8*, 2, 118, 2016.

37. Pallayil, V., Chitre, M.A., Deshpande, P.D., A digital thin line towed array for small autonomous underwater platforms, in: *OCEANS 2007*, pp. 1–9, IEEE, 2007.

38. Lloret, J., Underwater sensor nodes and networks, *Sensors*, 13, 9, 11782–11796, 2013.

39. Goyal, N., Dave, M., Verma, A.K., SAPDA: secure authentication with protected data aggregation scheme for improving QoS in scalable and survivable UWSNs. *Wirel. Pers. Commun.*, 113, 1–15, 2020.

40. De Bruyn, B., Whale Song in Submarine Fiction, in: *the Novel and the Multispecies Soundscape*, pp. 219–260, Palgrave Macmillan, Cham, 2020.

41. Seedhouse, E., *Tourists in space: A practical guide*, Springer Science & Business Media, UK, 2008.

42. Southwest Georgia, R.K.W., Brown, I., Mai, N., Schlueter, M.A., Porphyrin, N., Adeyemo, A., Moomaw, W., friday paper presentations*. denotes student presenter** denotes student research in progress.

43. Borengasser, M., Hungate, W.S., Watkins, R., *Hyperspectral remote sensing: principles and applications*, CRC press, UK, 2007.

44. Liu, Z., Gao, H., Wang, W., Chang, S., Chen, J., Color filtering localization for three-dimensional underwater acoustic sensor networks. *Sensors*, *15*, 3, 6009–6032, 2015.

45. El-Rabaie, S., Nabil, D., Mahmoud, R., Alsharqawy, M.A., Underwater wireless sensor networks (UWSN), architecture, routing protocols, simulation and modeling tools, localization, security issues and some novel trends. *Netw. Commun. Eng.*, *7*, 8, 335–354, 2015.

46. Ahmad, H., Machine learning applications in oceanography. *Aquat. Res.*, *2*, 3, 161–169, 2019.

47. Goyal, N., Sandhu, J.K., Verma, L., Machine learning based data agglomeration in underwater wireless sensor networks. *Int. J. Manage. Technol. Eng.*, *9*, 6, 240–245, 2019.

13

Internet of Underwater Things: Challenges, Routing Protocols, and ML Algorithms

Monika Chaudhary, Nitin Goyal* and Aadil Mushtaq

Chitkara University Institute of Engineering and Technology,
Chitkara University, Punjab, India

Abstract

The Internet of Underwater Things (IoUT) is the system of intelligent linked underwater things and a diverse kind of Internet of Things (IoT). IoUT is expected to permit different practicable requests, similar to ecological monitor, underwater examination, and calamity prohibition. With these uses, IoUT is considered unique of the likely technology around developed intelligent towns. To help the idea of IoUT, Underwater Wireless Sensor Networks (UWSNs) have appeared as an auspicious network system. UWSNs have various special characteristics, such a longer propagation delay, small bandwidth, and miserable reliability. This chapter presents challenges that can occur in IoUT. Also, the existing routing protocols for effective communication are discussed in great detail here. IoUT empowers a system of autonomous underwater vehicles (AUV) interconnecting with each other, detecting, collecting, and communicating data to sink node. Then, this data can be helpful in wide range of applications like ship wreckage detection, early discovery of tsunamis, marine health observing, as well as gathering real-time oceanic info. This chapter focuses on the complete terminology of IoUT including its basic concept, architectural requirements, challenges, routing protocols, and machine learning algorithms in IoUT.

Keywords: Challenges, machine learning, Underwater Wireless Sensor Network (UWSN), sensor

*Corresponding author: dr.nitingoyal30@gmail.com

Shalli Rani, R. Maheswar, G. R. Kanagachidambaresan, Sachin Ahuja and Deepali Gupta (eds.) *Machine Learning Paradigm for Internet of Things Applications*, (247–264) © 2022 Scrivener Publishing LLC

13.1   Introduction

Internet of Underwater Thing (IoUT) system of communication is the involvement of underwater objects that are interconnected with each other worldwide through a smart network [1]. Each device has its digital entity in this large network that provides uniqueness to each of the devices. These devices consist of a tracking system, sensors, and sequence of internet connectivity which helps these devices to react, sense, and tackle the environment [2]. Recently, smart cities have been growing with high speed. For that, one of the most significant technologies is the Internet of Things (IoT), precisely termed as "the infrastructure of the information society". The concept of IoT was invented in 1985 and 2012; the IoUT was first discussed. IoUT helps to connect various terrestrial things like smartphones, IoT devices, and computers, with the underwater network [3]. Each object which is deployed underwater can be accessed virtually which helps to get information like physical properties and historical information about the object. Due to the ubiquitous nature of the information, it can be accessed or managed in real-time through many methods of communication like Human to Thing (H2T) and Thing to Thing (T2T). Around 70% of mother globe is shielded by water constituted of smaller seas and rivers [4]. Patterns of wind and various climatic changes are determined by the temperature of the ocean that affects the living life on the earth. The availability of freshwater/drinking water is at most around 1% on the earth. Contamination of this results in damaging the ecosystem. The IoUT helps to control or maintain various areas of water that are not [5] yet explored. Underwater Wireless Sensor Networks (UWSNs) work under very harsh conditions as compared to ground-based networks such as wireless sensor network [6–8].

IoT are a buzzword nowadays because of their popularity in daily life. The same is with IoUTs. It is the implementation of IoT under the water as shown in Figure 13.1. It is one of the most advanced and emerging techniques in underwater networks and communication. The IoUTs are termed as the internetwork of smart interrelated under the water things. The implementation of IoUTs is in many application areas of UWSN as described in Figure 13.2. These can be exploration of aquatic life, natural catastrophe preclusion, and also in the military applications as explained by Kao, C. *et al.* (2017) [9].

13.2   Internet of Underwater Things

IoT was invented by Kevin Ashton. IoT can be established by "adding RF-Identification and other sensors to everyday objects". Over time, this

Figure 13.1 Concept of IoUTs.

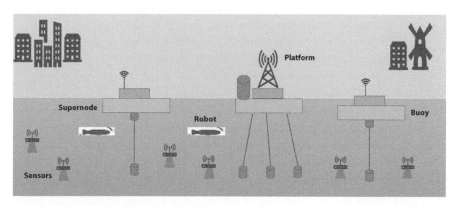

Figure 13.2 Concept and devices used in IoUT.

field has attained higher extent and involves different entities, i.e., house-hold utilizations, watches, and supplementary tools implanted using microelectronics, sensing devices, and connectors enabling data exchange. IoT is escalating at an overwhelming rate of 21%. The combination of IoT, underwater networks, and transmission techniques can take UWSN appli-cations to higher extent. This combination has enabled the recent UWSN concept termed as IoUT. This word "IoUT" firstly discussed by Domigo in their research named as "An Overview of the Internet of Underwater Things" in 2012 [10].

13.2.1   Challenges in IoUT

There are many issues and challenges that can slow down the current stride of research in IoUT due to distinctiveness in UWSNs [11]. Here, some of the challenges are discussed below:

1. **Dissemination Speediness:** The speed of propagation in UWSN is 200,000 slower than that of TWSN. In TWSN, propagation speed is 300,000,000 m/s, but, as compared to UWSN which is around 1500m/s, that is quite slow as compared to Terrestrial WSN. This raises a challenge which is called end-to-end delay.

2. **Transmission Rate:** Acoustic communication always uses narrow bandwidth which is not done in TWSN that uses radio communication, Due to the low level of narrow bandwidth, rate of transmission in UWSN is quite low around 10 kb/s. Hence, consumption of the bandwidth is main challenges for the IoUT.

3. **Battery Problem:** Underwater nodes that are deployed in designated region faces problem for recharge of their battery as these are deployed in underwater areas. As energy efficiency is one of the important concern for IoUT, so it is very critical challenge.

4. **Mobility:** As underwater networks are mobile in nature. Sensor nodes are mobile due to water currents and hence grieve with frequent network topology changes. It is also very perplexing job to pact with these dynamic and abrupt changes in IoUT.

5. **Consistency:** The consistency or reliability in UWSNs is usually unbalanced and less. It is related with the successful packet delivery ratio, means the number of packet received to total packet sent from source to destination. The packet delivery ratio is strictly disturbed by the transmission loss, i.e., the accumulated reduction in intensity of waveform energy. Transmission loss is severe problems in UWSNs as radio signals get absorbed in water. Furthermore, there are huge ecological noises in UWSNs, including marine creatures, turmoil, and shipment. Hence, the consistency problem is one of the utmost challenging concerns in IoUT.

13.3   Routing Protocols of IoUT

The routing protocol paves the way that how data packets will be sent from source to destination in the UWSN. In IoUT, these protocols plays a fundamental responsibility in achieving the suitable Quality of Service (QoS) [12]. Hence, it is essential to study different kinds of protocols that are used for routing in IoUT. The routing protocols can be classified into five various forms: (1) table-driven, (2) on-demand, (3) geographic, (4) opportunistic, and (5) multicast tree [13], as shown in Figure 13.3.

1. **Table-Driven:** The purpose of this approach is decreasing the waiting time caused by route searches before transmitting data packets from source to sink [14]. In this routing, information of targets and their routing data is kept by regularly updating routing tables using the transmission system to have up to date information and to decrease latency. Herewith, up-to-date routing details could be retained from each node to every other node in the network.

2. **On-Demand:** As the name suggests, the routes are discovers on demand. If there is requirement of data transmission to the destination node, then route detection process is started by a sensor node only [15]. For this, the route request packets are flooded throughout the network. Then, if any of the nodes accepts this route request packet, then that particular node will report the conforming route reply packet back to the source node.

3. **Geographic:** This protocol seems to be much appropriate elucidation for underwater IoT as compared to table-driven

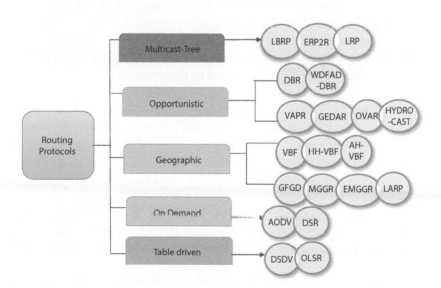

Figure 13.3 Different routing protocols in IoUT.

and on-demand routing. As in geographic routing, broadcast overhead is significantly reduced by tapping the geographical locality details of nodes [16]. A particular node select its next-hop node based on the position of its neighboring nodes and destination node itself. After confirming all these information, sender node forwards the packet in correct or functional direction.

4. **Opportunistic:** In this routing, sender node sends the data packet and all intermediate neighboring nodes when accepts the packet checks whether to transmit the packet according to the prospect or prearranged state [17]. The position may be the range between the sender and receiver. When the conditions have been satisfied, i.e., when target is nearer to the sink node from source node, then the target will decide to circulate the packet further in the network [20]. Thus, the receiver will identify whether or not the sender has to transmit the packet by itself to dispatch the packet, it can transmit the packet directly.

5. **Multicast Tree:** This protocol is an unconventional procedure for transmitting in UWSNs. Distinct from previous routing protocols. In this routing protocol, a tree topology is created for finding the optimized routes, different from other routing protocols [11]. The ultimate objective of this routing technique is to have reduced delay and less energy consumption. Instead of flooding packets, this protocols construct the corresponding specific shortest tree or minimum spanning tree. In this, multicasting of packets is done on the specific tree topology for finding routes in the network.

DSDV: The DSDV protocol requires each mobile station to advertise, to each of its current neighbors, its routing table (for instance, by broadcasting its entries). The entries in this list may change fairly dynamically over time, so the advertisement must be made often enough to ensure that every mobile computer can almost always locate every other mobile computer of the collection.

OLSR: This protocol is based on distributed concept without any central authority. OLSR protocol accomplishes hop-by-hop routing, where every node make use of its most recent or updated information to route a packet [18].

The concept of multipoint relays (MPRs), as shown in Figure 13.4, is to minimalize flooding or broadcasting of packets in the whole network by

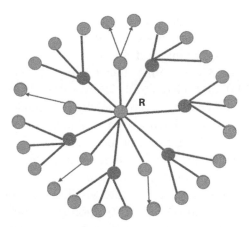

Figure 13.4 Multipoint relays in OLSR.

decreasing replica retransmissions. Every node chooses a set of nodes in its vicinity, which retransmits its packets in the network. These set of carefully chosen neighbor nodes is named as MPRs.

AODV: The Ad hoc On-Demand Distance Vector (AODV) is specifically designed for utilization of sensors that are moving in nature. These node works in a temporary system. It provides fast adjustment to lively connections, miserable handling, and identifies unicast routes to targets in the whole system. It is an enhancement over table driven routing protocol such as distance vector protocol. This message establishes an experimental protocol for the internet community.

DSR: The protocol adjusts rapidly to routing change when the host move is often, yet demands small or no overhead within periods in which hosts shift lower frequently. Dynamic source routing is a method where source transmit packet and decides full order of sensor over which to ahead the packet. It means next hop is decided by the source node. This protocols reduces bandwidth consumption, control overhead.

VBF: In Vector-Based Forwarding (VBF), every packet contains the locations of source, destination, and the node that forwards packet. These are represented by SP, DP, and FP, respectively. The furthering pathway is quantified by the Routing Vector (RV) from the source to destination. The routing pipe is well defined by the vector from the source or SP to destination or DP and also RADIUS, which is radius of the pipe. VBF protocol reports the mobility of node in a scalable and energetic mode.

HH-VBF: Hop-by-Hop VBF is established using the idea of vector forwarding protocol. However, HH-VBF describes the separate virtual pipe that is near about hop-by-hop from every intermediate node to the sink node, as an alternative of using only single virtual pipe that occur around from sender to target. Each node can flexibly make packet forwarding decisions based on its current location.

GFGD: Greedy Geographic Forwarding based on Geospatial Division (GGFGD) and Geographic Forwarding based on Geospatial Division (GFGD) are described geo-spatially. The sender node S attempts to discover a next-hop node having distance smaller than its own SC. In this algorithm, every node directly communicates with every other node located in its surface neighboring SC, as shown in Figure 13.5.

EMGGR: This routing protocol has three core components. First component is the gateway election procedure which is accountable for selecting gateways mainly centered on nodes locations and their residual energy. Second is how gateway information is updated that allows sensor nodes to memorize gateways. The third component is the packet forwarding technique. Energy-efficient Multipath Grid-based Geographic Routing (EMGGR) observed whole network as logical 3D grids, as shown in Figure 13.6. In this, routing is performed by grid-by-grid manner with the help of gateways. It uses distinct routes to communicate data packets to the target node.

AHH-VBF: This protocol handle accelerating data packets and broadcast power in cross-layer manner. This is done to reduce energy consumption and increase consistency. One more advantage is also that it reduced delay using optimization of controlling period of data sent in the network.

LARP: Location-aided routing protocol belongs to geographical routing protocols, which can provide good reliability and validity of message transmission. Note that the exact location information of nodes is helpful for the transmission of the message in network. This is an efficient routing protocol that beats the existing routing protocols when packet delivery ratio and normalized routing control overhead is of great concern.

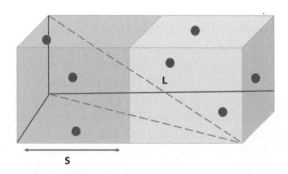

Figure 13.5 The relationship between S and L in GFGD.

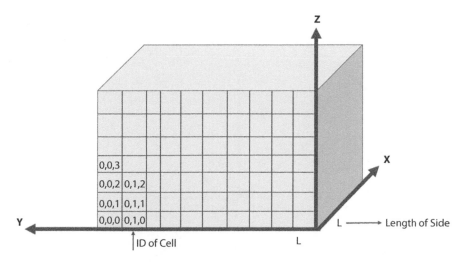

Figure 13.6 A 3D logical grid view of EMGGR protocol.

WDFAD-DBR: This is a Weighting Depth and Forwarding Area Division Depth-based Routing protocol. It makes routing decisions based on the difference of weighting depth of two hop nodes. It improves the transmission reliability and also reduces void-holes chances. The prediction procedure about neighbor nodes based on the past information of neighbor nodes is one the major advantage of this routing protocol with the help of collision avoidance as shown in Figure 13.7.

DRP: This is a dynamic routing protocol in which route selection procedure considers broadcast space between source and destination. It uses the remaining energy for every node. An existing localization scheme works correctly in oceanic currents. Some variables naming is used for DRP. There are six sensor nodes (na, nb, nc, nd, ne, and nf) and one sink node (nsk). The EPR values are on the corresponding links. Getting HELLO packet, nodes va and vb calculate EPRva (nsk) and EPRvb (nsk), respectively. After applying the DRP algorithm, the associated Cmax(na)(Cmax(nb)), HC(na) (HC(nb)), and f(na)(f(nb)) are searched, depicted in Figures 13.8b and c.

The different existing algorithms are compared based on various quality parameters such as reliability, mobility of nodes, bandwidth consumption, energy consumption, and delay as described in Table 13.1.

13.4 Machine Learning in IoUT

Machine learning (ML) is novel paradigm that has remarkable prospective to endow various ocean applications smartly and efficiently. Conversely,

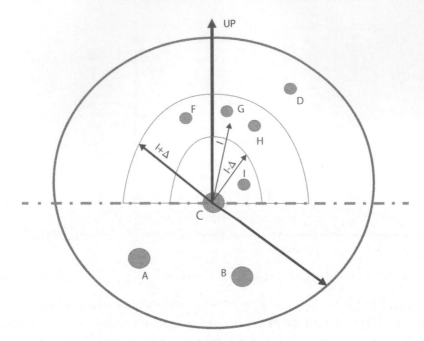

Figure 13.7 The probability of ACK's collision.

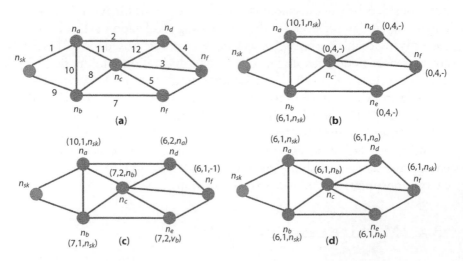

Figure 13.8 Operations in DRP.

Table 13.1 Comparison of various routing protocols for different quality parameters.

Protocol	Reliability	Mobility	Bandwidth	Energy	Delay
LRP	High	Medium	Medium	High	Low
DRP	High	Medium	High	High	Low
LBRP	High	Low	High	High	Low
ERP2R	High	Low	High	High	Low
HydroCast	High	High	Low	Medium	High
OVAR	High	High	Medium	Medium	High
WDFAD-DBR	High	Medium	Low	Medium	High
GEDAR	Medium	High	Low	Low	High
VAPR	Low	High	Low	Low	High
DBR	High	Medium	Low	Low	High
LARP	Low	High	Medium	Medium	Medium
AHH-VBF	High	Medium	Medium	Medium	High
EMGGR	Low	Medium	High	High	Medium
MGGR	Low	Medium	High	Medium	Medium
GFGD	Low	Medium	High	High	Low
HH-VBF	High	Medium	Medium	Medium	High
VBF	High	Medium	Medium	Medium	High
DSR	Low	Medium	Medium	Medium	High
AODV	Low	High	Medium	Medium	High
OLSR	High	High	Low	Low	Low
DSDV	High	High	Low	Low	Low

due to punitive and active environment of marine scenario, the severe necessities of underwater solicitations and cost for management and maintenance of IoUT have restricted advancements in IoUTs [19].

ML has been implemented comprehensively for extensive variety of tasks since the last decade. These task includes various applications areas like junk detection, fake recognition, and advertisements. ML procedures give incredible tractability advantages, when it is applied to numerous applications of UWSNs. Mostly, ML techniques fall in three classifications of supervised, unsupervised, and reinforcement learning (RL). The ML algorithms, when delivered a characterized set of values for training, lie in first category of supervised learning. Opposite to supervised, no set of values are available for training and learning in unsupervised learning.

ML in UWSN applications has been used for two issues: one of them is net-work-associated issue and the other is application-associated issue. First, in network-associated issue, learning techniques have been extensively implemented for the optimum distribution of sensors, safety, and power saving grouping. It is also used in QoS, allocation of resource in network, scheduling, and data aggregation and fusion. However, in application-associated issue, ML algorithms are mainly implemented in data processing, event cataloguing, and discovery of target class and its tracking.

13.4.1 Types of Machine Learning Algorithms

Here, different ML algorithms are used in various applications of UWSNs. One of the methods is Fuzzy Logic Systems (FLS), having three main methods that are fuzzification, interpretation engine, and defuzzification. Zohre and Arabi [22] suggested a fuzzy-based algorithm that implements fuzzy schemes for developing directed diffusion routing techniques for estimating the quality of routes. It also estimates the quantifiable value related with the quality of every route and supports the selection of numerous feasible routes in the routing protocol: FLS, sound appropriate in scheduling, clustering, energy-aware routing, and design and deployment.

The second method is Neural Network (NN), which is numerical prototypes using specific method on different values. Its initial encouragement originates by the concept of natural systems of neurons which comprise of neurons that are interrelated. The weights are given to each connections between the nodes in the network in which data is going from input. Wenhui Zhao et al. [23] suggest a self-managing NN optimizing route. Other methodology is recommended by dint of Veena K. N. et al. [24] for searching well-organized path from source to destination.

The third method is RL based, in which learning is what to do and how to do. It map the circumstances to movements for maximizing every ecological numerical signal. Opposite to other learning method, in this technique, learner is not communicated about the actions to be taken, as an alternative, learners attempt self-practicing and discerning act that produces return through trying and trying again. Nesrine Ouferhat and

Abdelhamid Mellouk [25] recommended an Energy and Delay Efficient Routing (EDEAR) as flexible transmitting with an aim for searching finest optimal route based on power consumption and delay.

Fourth is Swarm Intelligence (SI) based on cooperative conduct using decentralization and self-managed networks. The basic idea of implementation comes from Mother Nature, particularly biological structures that communicate with each other in environment. The ordinary examples involves ant colony optimizations, animal shepherding, and fish training. Yi-ping Chen *et al.* [26] suggested a particle swarm optimization technique for investigation in inter-grouping for increasing the lifespan of networks. This scheme mainly works for efficiency of energy and prolonging network lifetime.

IoT performance played a very significant role in the advancements and developments of IoUT in many of the underwater applications [27, 28]. Security is also one of the main concerns when we work in UWSN with wide variety of other application area [29].

13.5   Performance Evaluation

Different algorithms have been proposed using ML-based models [21]. Park *et al.* [18] presented a model for the prediction of the ocean current in specific timelines using practical data learned with various ML techniques. Figure 13.9 shows the comparison for sending packets in the network

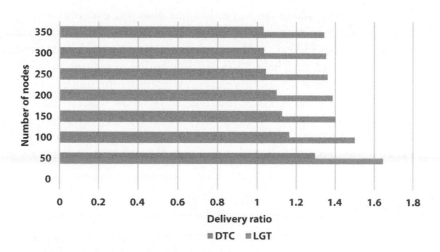

Figure 13.9 Delivery ratio vs. number of nodes.

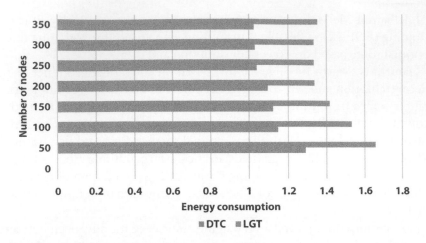

Figure 13.10 Energy consumption vs. number of nodes.

which is better in DTC technique as compared to LGT using Laguerre-Gaussian presented by Trichili *et al.* [30].

The energy efficiency is one of the main concerns in underwater environments. Figure 13.10 shows the comparison of energy consumption between DTC and LGT. The energy consumption in LGT is comparatively less as compared to DTC.

13.6   Conclusion

The IoT is a worldwide occurrence that has changed everyday life with the advancements in internet technology. With the advancements in IoT objects and appliances and satellite communication that can link devices in sea to shipments, one habitation left where IoT does not exist. That location is under the water. In this paper, we examine the modern kind of IoT, which is named as IoUT, i.e., the Internet of Underwater Things. This chapter offers beneficial knowledge about the IoUTs, its challenges, routing protocols, and implementation of ML algorithms in IoUT. Also, some of the existing protocols is evaluated to show their performance comparison.

References

1. Wang, H.H., Rock, S.M., Lee, M.J., OTTER: The design and development of an intelligent underwater robot. *Auton. Robots, 3*, 2–3, 297–320, 1996.

2. Sheng, Z., Yang, S., Yu, Y., Vasilakos, A.V., McCann, J.A., Leung, K.K., A survey on the ietf protocol suite for the internet of things: Standards, challenges, and opportunities. *IEEE Wireless Commun.*, *20*, 6, 91–98, 2013.

3. Vermesan, O., Friess, P., Guillemin, P., Gusmeroli, S., Sundmaeker, H., Bassi, A., Doody, P., Internet of things strategic research roadmap, in: *Internet of things-global technological and societal trends*, vol. 1, pp. 9–52, 2011.

4. Gill, S.D., *Mother earth: an American story*, University of Chicago Press, USA, 1991.

5. Vitousek, P.M., Mooney, H.A., Lubchenco, J., Melillo, J.M., Human domination of Earth's ecosystems. *Science*, *277*, 5325, 494–499, 1997.

6. Nain, M. and Goyal, N., Localization Techniques in Underwater Wireless Sensor Network, in: *2021 International Conference on Advance Computing and Innovative Technologies in Engineering (ICACITE)*, 2021, March, IEEE, pp. 747–751.

7. Choudhary, M. and Goyal, N., Node Deployment Strategies in Underwater Wireless Sensor Network, in: *2021 International Conference on Advance Computing and Innovative Technologies in Engineering (ICACITE)*, 2021, March, IEEE, pp. 773–779.

8. Goyal, N., Architectural Analysis of Wireless Sensor Network and Underwater Wireless Sensor Network with Issues and Challenges. *J. Comput. Theor. Nanosci.*, *17*, 6, 2706–2712, 2020.

9. Kao, C.C., Lin, Y.S., Wu, G.D., Huang, C.J., A comprehensive study on the internet of underwater things: applications, challenges, and channel models. *Sensors*, 17, 7, 1477, 2017.

10. Domingo, M.C., An overview of the internet of underwater things. *J. Netw. Comput. Appl.*, *35*, 6, 1879–1890, 2012.

11. Liou, E.C., Kao, C.C., Chang, C.H., Lin, Y.S., Huang, C.J., Internet of underwater things: Challenges and routing protocols, in: *2018 IEEE International Conference on Applied System Invention (ICASI)*, 2018, April, IEEE, pp. 1171–1174.

12. Nayyar, A., Ba, C.H., Duc, N.P.C., Binh, H.D., Smart-IoUT 1.0: A smart aquatic monitoring network based on Internet of Underwater Things (IoUT), in: *International Conference on Industrial Networks and Intelligent Systems*, 2018, August, Springer, Cham, pp. 191–207.

13. Khalil, R., Babar, M., Jan, T., Saeed, N., Towards the Internet of underwater things: Recent developments and future challenges. *IEEE Consum. Electron. Mag.*, 21, 16, 5398, 2020, https://doi.org/10.3390/s21165398.

14. Pantazis, N.A., Nikolidakis, S.A., Vergados, D.D., Energy-efficient routing protocols in wireless sensor networks: A survey. *IEEE Commun. Surv. Tutorials*, *15*, 2, 551–591, 2012.

15. Wang, W., Bhargava, B., Lu, Y., Wu, X., Defending against wormhole attacks in mobile ad hoc networks. *Wireless Commun. Mobile Comput.*, *6*, 4, 483–503, 2006.

16. Perkins, C.E., Royer, E.M., Das, S.R., Marina, M.K., Performance comparison of two on-demand routing protocols for ad hoc networks. *IEEE Pers. Commun.*, *8*, 1, 16–28, 2001.

17. Hu, Y.C., Perrig, A., Johnson, D.B., Ariadne: A secure on-demand routing protocol for ad hoc networks. *Wirel. Netw.*, *11*, 1–2, 21–38, 2005.

18. Baumann, R., *Vehicular ad hoc networks (VANET):(engineering and simulation of mobile ad hoc routing protocols for VANET on highways and in cities*, Master's thesis, ETH, Swiss Federal Institute of Technology Zurich, Switzerland, Department of Computer Science, Computer Systems Institute, 2004.

19. Bangash, J.I., Abdullah, A.H., Anisi, M.H., Khan, A.W., A survey of routing protocols in wireless body sensor networks. *Sensors*, *14*, 1, 1322–1357, 2014.

20. Abdollahi, M., Eshghi, F., Kelarestaghi, M., Bag-Mohammadi, M., Opportunistic routing metrics: A timely one-stop tutorial survey. *J. Netw. Comput. Appl.*, 102802, 2020, arXiv:2012.00850.

21. Park, S., Byun, J., Shin, K.S., Jo, O., Ocean current prediction based on machine learning for deciding handover priority in underwater wireless sensor networks, in: *2020 International Conference on Artificial Intelligence in Information and Communication (ICAIIC)*, 2020, February, IEEE, pp. 505–509.

22. Arabi, Z., HERF: A hybrid energy efficient routing using a fuzzy method in wireless sensor networks, in: *2010 International Conference on Intelligent and Advanced Systems*, 2010, June, IEEE, pp. 1–6.

23. Zhao, W., Liu, D., Jiang, Y., Distributed neural network routing algorithm based on global information of wireless sensor network, in: *2009 WRI International Conference on Communications and Mobile Computing*, 2009, January, vol. 1, IEEE, pp. 552–555.

24. Veena, K.N. and Kumar, B.V., Convergecast in wireless sensor networks: a neural network approach, in: *2010 IEEE 4th International Conference on Internet Multimedia Services Architecture and Application*, 2010, December, IEEE, pp. 1–6.

25. Ouferhat, N. and Mellouk, A., Energy and delay efficient state dependent routing algorithm in wireless sensor networks, in: *2009 IEEE 34th Conference on Local Computer Networks*, 2009, October, IEEE, pp. 1069–1076.

26. Chen, Y.-p. and Chen, Y.-z., A novel energy efficient routing algorithm for wireless sensor networks. *The 9th International Conference on Machine Learning and Cybernetics*, Qingdao, July,2010, pp. 1031–1035, 11–14.

27. Datta, P. and Sharma, B., A survey on IoT architectures, protocols, security and smart city-based applications, in: *8th International Conference on Computing, Communication and Networking Technologies (ICCCNT)*, 2017, July, IEEE, pp. 1–5.

28. Badotra, S. and Panda, S.N., A review on software-defined networking enabled iot cloud computing. *IIUM Eng. J.*, *20*, 2, 105–126, 2019.

29. Goyal, N., Dave, M., Verma, A.K., Trust model for cluster head validation in underwater wireless sensor networks. *Underw. Technol.*, *34*, 3, 107–114, 2017.
30. Trichili, A., Issaid, C.B., Ooi, B.S., Alouini, M.S., A CNN-Based Structured Light Communication Scheme for Internet of Underwater Things Applications. *IEEE Internet Things J.*, *7*, 10, 10038–10047, 2020.

14

Chest X-Ray for Pneumonia Detection

Sarang Sharma, Sheifali Gupta* and Deepali Gupta

Chitkara University Institute of Engineering and Technology,
Chitkara University, Punjab, India

Abstract

Pneumonia is a medical condition that is related to lung inflammation. It affects pulmonary alveolus or alveoli, which are tiny air sacs found inside the lung parenchyma. It is responsible for exchanging carbon dioxide with oxygen. Pneumonia is generally caused by bacteria or viral infection. If untreated, it would lead to cystic fibrosis, chronic obstructive pulmonary disease, sickle cell disease, asthma, diabetes, and heart failure. Therefore, in order to diagnose this disease, chest X-ray, blood tests, sputum tests, computerized tomography, pulse oximetry, and pleural fluid culture are implemented. However, both doctors and radiologists rely heavily on its chest X-ray results. However, these techniques are time consuming and sometimes yield inaccurate results. Therefore, to avoid such lengthy and time consuming techniques, deep learning algorithms along with machine learning classifiers are implemented that are less time consuming, require less sophisticated equipment, yield results with greater accuracy, and are easy to implement. This paper focuses on deep learning architecture which makes use of Xception architecture that is based entirely on depth-wise separable convolutional layers. It utilizes machine learning classifier algorithms to extract pneumonia from healthy images and trains weights by implementing Xception architecture. This model effectively detects pneumonia with higher accuracy, recall, and better F1-score. With such results, this model could be utilized for developing clinically useful solutions that can be integrated along with IoT devices to detect pneumonia in chest X-ray images.

Corresponding author: sheifali.gupta@chitkara.edu.in

Shalli Rani, R. Maheswar, G. R. Kanagachidambaresan, Sachin Ahuja and Deepali Gupta (eds.) Machine Learning Paradigm for Internet of Things Applications, (265–274) © 2022 Scrivener Publishing LLC

Keywords: Pneumonia, Xception, chest X-ray, deep learning, convolutional neural network, rectified linear unit, confusion matrix

14.1 Introduction

Pneumonia is a type of respiratory infection. This infection affects the lungs as they are made of tiny air sacs called alveoli [1]. These alveoli are responsible for transporting oxygen and carbon dioxide molecules in and out of bloodstream [2]. When an individual is affected with this disease, these air sacs or alveoli are then filled with purulent material containing pus or fluid. Due to these purulent materials, the individual is then subjected to cough, chills, heavy breathing, fatigue, diarrhea, intense sweating, muscle pain, delirium in case of elderly individuals, and cyanosis due to low oxygen levels in the bloodstream [3]. According to WHO, pneumonia alone is responsible for 15% of all deaths of children under 5 years of age and is estimated to have caused 808 fatalities in 2017 alone, among which 694 were children belonging to that age group.

However, most of these viral pneumonias are not fatal, and they also tend to live for a shorter time than their bacterial counterpart [4]. It generally affects to those individuals who have weaker body immunity system such as children below 5 years of age and elderly over 65 years of age and individuals having pre-existing medical conditions such as cystic fibrosis, asthma, HIV, or cancer [5].

In order to diagnose this disease, various tests are recommended by the doctors such as chest X-ray, blood tests, oximetry of pulse, sputum test, computerized tomography (CT) scan, and pleural fluid culture [6]. However, both doctors and radiologists rely heavily on its chest X-ray results [7]. Chest X-ray is a type of imaging test that is used to identify the diseases of blood vessels, bones, heart, and lungs [8]. It can also determine the presence of fluid or pus inside the lungs. In case for pneumonia, it is diagnosed by observing the white spots called infiltrates that signify infection, and if fluid is present, this is called abscesses or pleural effusions [9]. Further, the chest X-rays are relatively inexpensive as compared to other imaging tests that include CT, ultrasound, magnetic resonance imaging, and needle biopsy. However, these tests require prerequisite complex hardware and software [10]. With the help of latest IoT sensors, data extracted from machine learning algorithms could be beneficial and provide a significant insight and understanding of the individual diagnose with pneumonia. Hence, it would properly analyze, evaluate, and store data that could help in saving time and also improve the efficiency in clinical institutions [11, 12].

In order to overcome these complexities of hardware and software requirements, this paper encloses a novel scheme for classifying pneumonia affected lung images from healthy lung images by using machine learning classifier algorithm. These are then evaluated by using helper functions that are trained inside deep learning architectures, and as a result, learning curves and confusion matrix are plotted that yield accuracy, precision, and recall of the system.

14.2   Background

The literature studied for this study was majorly focusing on use of machine and deep learning techniques for early detection of pneumonia. A huge amount of literature is available, which can help to understand the nature of the problem and various solutions proposed for the respective problems. Sirazitdinov *et al.* [1] proposed a model that diagnosed pneumonia by highlighting specific regions on chest X-rays that could be easily identified by the physicians for cross-reference by using RetinaNet and Mask R-CNN in the journal Computers & Electrical Engineering. Jaiswal *et al.* [2] implemented a model that prevented overfitting and extraction on large images, provided deeper information, and reduced computation cost exponentially by using Mask R-CNN, F-RCNN, and FCN in the journal Measurement. Rajaraman *et al.* [3] evaluated, visualized, detected, and explained the performance of convolutional neural network (CNN) to detect pneumonia and distinguish bacterial type chest X-rays from viral types by using CNN, computer-aided diagnosis, and VGG-16 in the journal Applied Sciences. Abiyev *et al.* [4] published a research paper in the Journal of Healthcare Engineering, which showed good results on 32 × 32 pixels and yielded high recognition rates by using CNNs, back propagation neural networks, and competitive neural networks. Kermany *et al.* [5] effectively classified images for macular degeneration and diabetic retinopathy by using image labeling, transfer learning methods, and occlusion test in the journal Cell. Zech *et al.* [6] proposed a model that achieved better internal performance than external performance when they were trained on new pooled data than external data by using CNNs and computer-aided diagnosis in the journal PLoS Medicine. Lakhani *et al.* [7] proposed a model that showed better performance by dataset augmentation, which further improved its accuracy by using deep CNN and AlexNet in the journal Radiology. Morillo *et al.* [8] proposed a model that verified self-auscultation at one point could support pneumonia diagnosis in patients with chronic obstructive pulmonary disorder by using principal components analysis and probabilistic neural network in the Journal of the American Medical Informatics Association. Ginneken *et al.* [9] proposed a research paper that showed good results in early detection of cancer present in chest CT, mammography, and virtual colonoscopy by using computer-aided diagnosis and texture recognition algorithms in the European Journal of Radiology. Oliveira *et al.* [10] proposed a research paper that successfully discriminated bacterial etiology from absence of pneumonia with greater accuracy by using Pneumo-CAD system and Haar wavelet transform in the International Journal of Medical Informatics. Elzeki *et al.* [11] proposed a research paper to classify pelvis and lumbar spine by using machine learning with IoT and utilized SVM, linear regression, random forest, and neural networks to evaluate, compare, and classify input features. Glickman *et al.* [12] proposed a research paper that implemented artificial immune system framework that utilized LISYS method along with IoT that specialized for solution of network intrusion detection.

14.3   Research Methodology

Many studies and research have been conducted on lung disease but very less work has been implemented and published on prediction of pneumonia using deep learning by using Xception architecture; hence, it is the novelty of this project. Here, machine learning algorithm is applied to extract the features of pneumonia, and these are trained by utilizing Xception network architecture. Then, the results are displayed by plotting graphs of accuracy, loss, and determining model parameters validation values.

For the proposed solution, an open access dataset is used, which is available on kaggle.com uploaded by Paul Mooney and is named as "Chest X-Ray Images (Pneumonia)". The dataset consists of two categories of normal or healthy lung images, which had 1,576 images and pneumonia had 4,265 images. Both of them are of size of $1,857 \times 1,317 \times 3$. This dataset is simply divided into two parts. One part is known as training part and other is known as testing part with splitting ratio of 75:25, respectively. Dataset categories description is given in Table 14.1, and images of dataset samples are shown in Figures 14.1a and b.

In Figure 14.2, a fixed size of 224×224 X-ray image is applied as an input to first convolutional layer part 1 having height, width, and depth of

Table 14.1 Dataset description.

S. no.	Pneumonia	Number of images
1	Pneumonia	4,265
2	Healthy	1,576

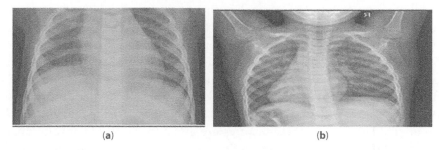

(a)   (b)

Figure 14.1 (a) Pneumonia x-ray image, (b) Healthy x-ray image.

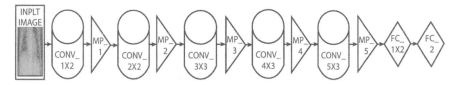

Figure 14.2 Xception network architecture.

224 × 224 × 64, consisting a pixel window or kernel of 3 × 3, which selects the image feature.

Then, this feature is passed on to the first convolutional layer part 2 having dimensions of 224 × 224 × 64, again consisting a pixel window of 3 × 3, which selects the feature passed on from the previous convolutional layer. Then, this feature is given to the first max pool layer having dimensions of 112 × 112 × 64, consisting pixel window of 2 × 2, which selects the maximum prominent features of the previous convolutional layer. Then, it is passed on to the second convolutional layer part 1 having dimensions of 112 × 112 × 128, which again consists of a pixel window of 3 × 3, which then selects the feature passed on from the previous max pool layer. Then, this feature is given to the second convolutional layer part 2 having dimensions of 112 × 112 × 128, consisting pixel window of 3 × 3, which selects the feature passed on from the previous convolutional layer. Then, this feature is given to the second max pool layer having dimensions of 56 × 56 × 128, consisting pixel window of 2 × 2, which selects the maximum prominent features of the previous convolutional layer. Then, it is passed on to the third convolutional layer part 1 having dimensions of 56 × 56 × 256, which again consists of a pixel window of 3 × 3, which then selects the feature passed on from the previous max pool layer. Then, the first batch normalization is implemented having dimensions of 56 × 56 × 256 with pixel window of 2 × 2 to normalize the previous convolutional layer by adjusting and scaling its activation functions. Then, these features are then given to the third convolutional layer part 2 having dimensions of 56 × 56 × 256, which again consists of a pixel window of 3 × 3, which then selects the feature passed on from the previous batch normalization layer. Then, the second batch normalization is implemented having dimensions of 56 × 56 × 256 with pixel window of 2 × 2 to normalize the previous convolutional layer. Then, these features are given to the third convolutional layer part 3 having dimensions of 56 × 56 × 256, which again consists of a pixel window of 3 × 3 which then selects the feature passed on from the previous batch normalization layer. Then, this feature is given to the third max pool layer having dimensions of 28 × 28 × 256, consisting pixel window of 2 × 2, which selects the maximum prominent features of the previous convolutional layer. Then, it is passed on to the fourth convolutional layer part 1 having dimensions of 28 × 28 × 512, which again consists of a pixel window of 3 × 3, which then selects the feature passed on from the previous max pool layer. Then, the third batch normalization is implemented having dimensions of 28 × 28 × 512 with pixel window of 2 × 2 to normalize the previous convolutional layer. Then, these features are then given to the fourth convolutional layer part 2 having dimensions of 28 × 28 × 512, which again consists of a pixel window of 3 × 3, which then selects the feature passed on from the previous batch normalization layer. Then, the fourth batch normalization is implemented having dimensions of 28 × 28 × 512 with pixel window of 2 × 2 to normalize the previous convolutional layer. Then, these features are then given to fourth convolutional layer part 3 having dimensions of 28 × 28 × 512, which again consists of a pixel window of 3 × 3, which then selects the feature passed on from the previous batch normalization layer. Then, this feature is given to the fourth max pool layer having dimensions of 14 × 14 × 512, consisting pixel window of 2 × 2, which selects the maximum prominent features of the previous convolutional layer. Then, flattening is implemented to convert the 2D array from the previous max pool layer into 1D array. Then, these arrays are given to three fully connected layers or dense layers having one 1,024,

512, and 2 channels, respectively. In between these channels, two dropout layers are also added, each having 512 channels. Then, soft-max activation function is applied to the resultant feature, which classifies the images into pneumonia and healthy images.

14.4   Results and Discussion

14.4.1   Results

The designed Xception architecture is applied on pneumonia images. There are some important parameters on which implemented Xception model relies completely on like batch size, learning rate, and number of epochs. The designed model architecture used batch size of 128, learning rate of 1e−3, and number of epochs of 50. Based on the parameters, Xception architecture was implemented on chest X-ray image, in which the training accuracy of the model was 94.48% and testing accuracy of the model was 88.78%. Model accuracy and model loss are shown in Figures 14.3a and b, respectively.

The epoch time taken by proposed model is 5,250 seconds that is 105 seconds per epoch. Table 14.2 shows the result of pneumonia images, and four model metrics have been taken that are accuracy, precision, recall, and F1-score.

14.4.2   Discussion

The paper describes an elaborate evaluation of the Xception architecture used to detect pneumonia in chest X-ray images. Through this paper, experience and knowledge were greatly acquired, which could be beneficial to the rest of the research community. The key points in this paper showed that model accuracy is not enough for showing good prediction at all. Therefore, by using Xception architecture, test metrics such as recall and F1-score outperformed the classification network parameters as obtained by Sirazitdinov *et al.* [1], Rajaraman *et al.* [3], Abiyev *et al.* [4], and Zech *et al.* [6]. Furthermore, the architecture used in this paper is unique and very less work has been implemented and published; hence, it is the novelty of this project. Precision is the preciseness or accuracy of the model for which the model successfully determines the actual positive values out of all predicted positive values, which also is an integral part of this paper and has performed better than precision obtained by Lakhani *et al.* [7], Morillo *et al.* [8], and Ginneken *et al.* [9]. Recall in the model calculates the actual positive values by labeling them as true or actual positive values.

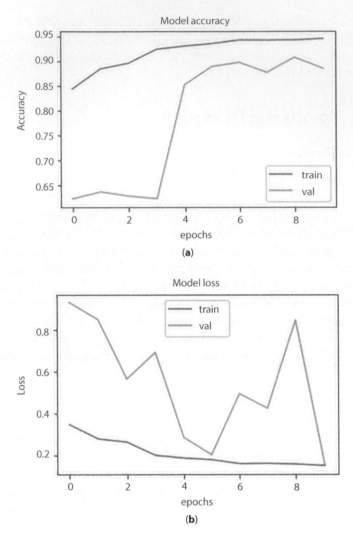

Figure 14.3 (a) Model accuracy, (b) Model loss.

F1-score can be described as the weighted harmonic mean of precision and recall of test case. The F-score reached the most efficient value, which means precision and recall are best F-score at 1 value. However, the worst score is lowest precision and lowest recall at value 0. The confusion matrix is also given in Figure 14.4, in which healthy and pneumonia are depicted by 0 and 1, respectively.

Table 14.2 Model metric parameters.

S. no.	Test metrics	Value (%)
1.	Accuracy	88.78
2.	Precision	87.03
3.	Recall	96.41
4.	F1-score	91.48

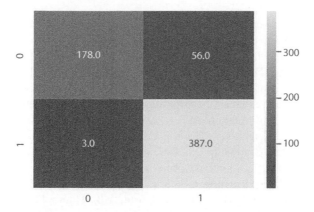

Figure 14.4 Confusion matrix.

14.5   Conclusion

Thus, this novel technique finds its huge application in healthcare industry. It effectively detects pneumonia with improved accuracy. It totally eliminates the use of invasive medical techniques. It could also become useful in improving efficiency in clinical settings by accurately identifying and aiding decision-making that could have a great diagnostic impact on resource constrained areas with a minimal loss.

Acknowledgment

The authors would like to express our deep and sincere gratitude to Dr. Rajnish Sharma and Dr. Archana Mantri for giving us the opportunity to do research and providing invaluable guidance throughout the research.

As our professor and mentor, they both have taught us a great deal about scientific research in general and have shown us, by their example, what an exemplary researcher should be.

References

1. Sirazitdinov, I., Kholiavchenko, M., Mustafaev, T., Yixuan, Y., Kuleev, R., Ibragimov, B., Deep neural network ensemble for pneumonia localization from a large-scale chest x-ray database. *Comput. Electr. Eng.*, 78, 388–399, 2019.
2. Jaiswal, A.K., Kumar, A., Kumar, P.T.S., Gupta, D., Khanna, A., Rodrigues, J.J., Identifying pneumonia in chest X-rays: A deep learning approach. *Measurement*, 145, 511–518, 2019.
3. Rajaraman, S., Candemir, S., Kim, I., Thoma, G., Antani, S., Visualization and Interpretation of Convolutional Neural Network Predictions in Detecting Pneumonia in Pediatric Chest Radiographs. *Appl. Sci.*, 10, 2076–3417, 2018.
4. Abiyev, R.H. and Ma'aitah, M.K.S., Deep convolutional neural networks for chest diseases detection. *J. Healthc. Eng.*, 12, 4168538–4168538, 2018.
5. Kermany, D.S., Goldbaum, M., Cai, W., Valentim, C.C.S., Liang, H., Baxter, S.L., McKeown, A., Identifying medical diagnoses and treatable diseases by image-based deep learning. *Cell*, 5, 1122–1131, 2018.
6. Zech, J.R., Badgeley, M.A., Liu, M., Costa, A.B., Titano, J.J., Oermann, E.K., Variable generalization performance of a deep learning model to detect pneumonia in chest radiographs: a cross-sectional study. *PloS Med.*, 11, 1002683–1002683, 2018.
7. Lakhani, P. and Sundaram, B., Deep learning at chest radiography: automated classification of pulmonary tuberculosis by using convolutional neural networks. *Radiology*, 284, 574–582, 2017.
8. Morillo, S.D., Jiménez, A.L., Moreno, S.A., Computer-aided diagnosis of pneumonia in patients with chronic obstructive pulmonary disease. *J. Am. Med. Inform. Assoc.*, 1, 20, 111–117, 2013.
9. Ginneken, V.B., Hogeweg, L., Prokop, M., Computer-aided diagnosis in chest radiography: Beyond nodules. *Eur. J. Radiol.*, 2, 72, 226–230, 2009.
10. Oliveira, L.L.G., Silva, S.A.E., Ribeiro, L.H.V., Oliveira, D.R.M., Coelho, C.J., Andrade, S.A.L.S., Computer-aided diagnosis in chest radiography for detection of childhood pneumonia. *Int. J. Med. Inform.*, 8, 555–564, 2008.
11. Elzeki, O.M., Sarhan, S., Abd Elfattah, M., Salem, H., Shams, M.Y., Biomedical Healthcare System For Orthopedic Patients Based On Machine Learning, *ARPN Journal of Engineering and Applied Sciences*, 16, 616–622, 2006.
12. Glickman, M., Balthrop, J., Forrest, S.A., machine learning evaluation of an artificial immune system. *Evol. Comput.*, 13, 179–212, 2005.

Index

Printed and bound by CPI Group (UK) Ltd, Croydon, CR0 4YY